D0193061

THIS BUSINESS OF

Music

Marketing

and Promotion

Tad Lathrop and
Jim Pettigrew Jr.

BILLBOARD BOOKS

AN IMPRINT OF WATSON-GUPTILL PUBLICATIONS

NEW YORK

For Kevin and Kyoko
— TL

To the loving memory of Mary Ellen Coleman Pettigrew
— JP

Copyright © 1999 by Grayson F. Lathrop

All rights reserved. No part of this publication may
be reproduced or used in any form or by any means—
graphic, electronic, or mechanical, including photocopying,
recording, taping, or information storage and retrieval
systems—without written permission of the publisher.

Excerpts from "Keeping the Dream Alive" by Bud Scoppa
reprinted by permission of ASCAP and *Next* magazine.

"Think Different" excerpt courtesy of Apple Computer, Inc.
Used with permission.

This edition first published in 1999 in the United States by
Billboard Books, an imprint of Watson-Guptill Publications,
a division of BPI Communications, Inc., 1515 Broadway,
New York, NY 10036-8986

Library of Congress Cataloging-in-Publication Data
Lathrop, Tad.
     This business of music marketing and promotion / Tad Lathrop and
Jim Pettigrew, Jr.
       p.   cm.
     Includes bibliographical references and index.
     ISBN 0-8230-7711-X
     1. Music trade—Vocational guidance.   2. Popular music—Writing
and publishing.   3. Sound recordings—Marketing.   I. Pettigrew,
Jim.   II. Title.
ML3790.L37   1999
780' .68'8—dc21   98-39920
                                                    CIP
                                                      MN

ISBM: 0-8230-7711-X

Manufactured in the United States of America

Senior Editor: Bob Nirkind
Text Design, Line Art, and Composition: Nancy Carroll
Production Manager: Ellen Greene

2 3 4 5 6 7 8/05 04 03 02 01 00 99

Contents

PART **MUSIC MARKETING AND**
3 **PROMOTION ON THE INTERNET**

Acknowledgments

This book benefited from the advice and assistance of a number of knowledgeable people. My thanks go out to all of them, and especially to Bruce Iglauer, for his thoughtful review of the manuscript; Roy Gattinella, for his valuable input and feedback; Eva Dickenson-Post and Luann Sullivan Myers for their generous contribution of marketing materials and information; Stephanie LeBeau, for her clarification of the radio promotion process; Nancy Carroll, for her design and production skill (and for being the ideal book-making partner); and Bob Nirkind and Glenn Heffernan at Billboard Books, for their support of this project.

Thanks are also due to the helpful professionals at ASCAP, BMI, the Harry Fox Agency, and the American Federation of Musicians; to the media staff at CRS Advertising; and to Jeff Young, Bob DePugh, Keith Hatschek, Steve Savage, and Jim Bruno.

Finally, a special thanks to Jim Pettigrew, whose energy, determination, and enthusiasm made him the best writing collaborator one could ever hope to find.

TAD LATHROP
San Francisco, California
July 1998

I'd like to thank my daughter, Danellen, for her patience, her protective sense, and her courage.

My gratitude also goes to Vonda Ragsdale, my assistant and a very special person; to Bob Nirkind, our senior editor, for his understanding and support; to Tad Lathrop, my friend and co-author, for his unceasing enthusiasm and hard work on this project; to Bob Fillie for the cover art; and to Nancy Carroll for the page design.

I am grateful to three close friends who contributed to the manuscript. Russell Shaw and Katie Garcia furnished valuable Internet data and Frankie Ansley transcribed the interviews.

My sincere appreciation also goes to Mark Pucci of Mark Pucci Media for his contacts and advice and to the music business professionals who lent their experience and expertise to this book. Without their invaluable input, the scope of this manuscript would have been seriously diminished.

Several friends and family members were more than generous with their support. They include Mary Dan and Bob Miller, Samantha and Ed Rose, Rick Dandes, Frances and Urquhart Ansley, Don Pettigrew, Claudia and Clint Schlottman, Debbie and Charlie Raiford, James T. Bass, Dr. Linda Coleman, Kadie Coleman, Rhonda and Mark Harkness, Anne and Roger Ditmer, Russ Holloway, Kay and Tommy Jenkins, Dr. Ted Blau, Paul Salter, David Mohlerm, and Tom Dennard. Thanks also to two supportive groups: the Golden Isles Lions Club and the Coastal Georgia Writers Group.

Home Away from Home Department: My thanks to two St. Simons Island restaurants, Pizza Inn/Kim Chi's Chinese (ever-dependable takeout), and El Potro's Fine Mexican Dining (the salsa's always hot and the Carta Blanca's always ice-cold).

Special mention has to be made of Click and Clack—the Tappet Brothers. These hosts of NPR's "Car Talk" never fail to cheer me up and make me laugh on Sunday evenings. By the way guys, sometime, please play a passage from ZZ Top's "Daguello." The words go like this: "I was riding downtown in some cold blue steel....I'm bad, I'm nationwide."

JIM PETTIGREW JR.

St. Simons Island, Georgia

March 1998

Preface

This *Business of Music Marketing and Promotion* is intended as a source of practical information for anyone currently involved in, or thinking about getting involved in, selling music to the listening public.

If you're a musician with some finished recordings, and you need guidance on how to get the music out to the world, you'll find it here.

If you're an entrepreneur aiming to launch your own music company, and you're looking for ways to set the business wheels in motion, you'll find a wealth of ideas here.

If you're a manager wondering how to spin gold from the threads of a musical client's creativity, you'll find pertinent information in these pages.

If you're a record company marketer seeking ideas for expanding your marketing program, you'll find them here.

If you're investigating what's involved in selling music on the World Wide Web, you'll find a section here devoted to that subject.

If you're none of the above, but you're researching possible careers and want to know what goes on in the commercial end of the music field, you've come to the right place.

Overview of the Contents

This Business of Music Marketing and Promotion is set up in four main sections.

Part 1 begins with an overview of the current music marketplace and the forces that are shaping it (and providing new opportunities for resourceful entrepreneurs). Subsequent chapters offer a behind-the-scene look at a national marketing campaign as conducted by a large record company and a music publisher. This "big picture" summary lays the groundwork for the detailed guidelines to follow.

Part 2 deals with the specifics of music marketing and promotion. It explains all the steps involved in planning and carrying out a complete marketing program, with separate chapters devoted to packaging, pricing, store-based distribution, direct marketing, promotion (including exposure in print media and on radio and television), live performing, and managing the entire process.

Part 3 is devoted to the Internet and how it can be used to distribute and promote music—and to make money.

Part 4 contains discussions with professionals active in the business of selling music. They offer a range of perspectives on marketing, from a major-label executive's views to those of a midsize-label owner, a record retailer, an independent marketer, and several Internet entrepreneurs.

The Appendix will guide you to other sources of information and professional assistance.

How to Use the Book

This Business of Music Marketing and Promotion is designed to be used however you prefer. It can be read from cover to cover for a complete "crash course." Or it can be dipped into as needed and then kept on hand for future reference. For a quick overview of the entire field, read Part 1. For in-depth information on separate aspects of the marketing and promotion process, consult Parts 2 and 3. For "real world" applications of marketing concepts, read the interviews in Part 4.

However you choose to use the book, we sincerely hope it proves helpful in your search for marketing ideas and guidance.

Note: This publication has been written with the aim of providing accurate and up-to-date information about the music industry. However, business customs, technology, and monetary values change over time. Furthermore, every business situation is unique; readers' circumstances will invariably have differences from those that the authors describe, even if the circumstances may appear similar. For these reasons, the authors and the publisher bear no responsibility for actions taken by readers based on information provided in this book. Readers are urged to seek the current advice of appropriate professionals.

The Music Marketing Environment

CHAPTER

1

Selling Music in the New Entertainment Marketplace

Welcome to the world of selling sound—a demanding, complex, and at times mercurial (not to mention exciting) area of the entertainment industry.

It's not an area for the timid or laid-back. Instead, music marketing is a pressure-cooking enterprise—like a game played for really high stakes—that requires decision-making skills, aggressive action, ingenuity, and access to information.

It's not easy, but it can be done. It's being done all around us, worldwide, every day, to the tune of millions of dollars.

WHAT IS MUSIC MARKETING AND PROMOTION?

The selling of music, for profit, is the bottom line of music marketing and promotion. Simply put, this is the money trail of commercially recorded music.

The marketing process includes shaping a "product" (as recorded work is termed in the music industry) and then getting it into the shelves of record stores and other outlets that service music customers.

Like a human twin, music promotion is very closely related. It involves the positioning or "pushing" of music in the mass media so that fans will become aware of the product and then be inclined to purchase it. Key components here are radio airplay, television airtime, and Internet exposure. The publicity side of the promotion field involves magazine articles and news-media stories about the artist and/or new release, guest appearances on talk shows, and album reviews in the press.

Live performance is another kind of promotion. But it's also a kind of "shelf space." In music, the performer him- or herself is often considered a part of the product, and the concert stage is a physical outlet for getting that product to customers.

That's the marketing and promotion arena in a nutshell. In the coming chapters, we'll look at each component in much more detail.

THE CURRENT MARKETPLACE

"The only constant in the music business is that it's always changing. Always."
—RECORD PROMOTER

Anyone currently entering the arena is doing so at an opportune time. Today's music marketplace is remarkably different from what it was just a short time ago. The old music industry structure is rattling under the forces of technological change, increased competition, and rapidly shifting public tastes. The rules of commerce—once dictated by a handful of corporations and the executives who ran them—have become infinitely more flexible. Thanks are due largely to a new generation of independent musicians, alternative record labels, maverick promoters, and Internet-based music sellers inventing their own creative ways to reach increasingly diverse audiences.

At one time, individual music makers were reliant on a bureaucracy of talent-hunting middlemen and music-business insiders to get their music to a broad audience. Now, with the Internet permitting a direct link between music maker and music customer, that is no longer necessarily so.

In a corner of the industry, independent record labels and entrepreneurs have long provided alternative marketing channels. These ran parallel to the superhighways dominated by the major labels. But the "indies" were the exception, not the rule.

Now, more than ever, individuals outside the mainline music industry are gaining a real presence as leaders in marketing innovation.

How We Got Here

In a sense, the music business has always been an industry of innovators—of individuals pushing their wares to the listening public using all existing methods and, when necessary, creating some new ones.

This was true as far back as 1900, when the music business in the United States was a much simpler industry than that of today. It was a make-do environment back then, devoid of many of the communication channels, institutions, systems, and regulations that structure today's commercial landscape. In many ways, it was a market free-for-all.

Sheet music was the key music product at the time, and music publishers sold it largely through retail outlets (the F.W. Woolworth chain, for one). To promote the products, they employed music salesmen called song pluggers. Singers and performers themselves, the pluggers would belt out the songs right on the premises of the retailers, hoping to attract attention to the sheet music being sold. They energetically plugged the tunes in other settings as well, from music halls and bars to city streets—wherever they could be certain of finding a crowd of people.

But over time, developing technologies opened the door to new and more sophisticated possibilities for music distribution and promotion.

The phonograph record, pioneered in the early part of the 20th century by the Victor Talking Machine Company and another company called Columbia, was a breakthrough in the mass distribution of music, allowing consumers to purchase recorded performances. Its invention was accompanied by the development, by Rudolph Wurlitzer, of a coin-operated playback machine that could be used commercially in hotels, restaurants, and other public settings. It caught on, and by the early 1930s, so-called jukeboxes were being used across the United States.

Radio developed alongside the phonograph industry. As with most new technologies, it was initially perceived as a threat by established industries. At first, record label brass feared that listeners would simply tune in their sets and stop buying records. But the opposite proved to be true: radio airplay greatly stimulated sales of the 78-rpm discs of the period.

With the growing number of ways consumers could purchase and listen to music came an increase in the number of ways creators could earn money for their work. Tracking and collecting the income from those uses became a vital concern of artists. In 1914 a group of song-writers formed the American Society of Composers, Authors, and Publishers (ASCAP) to ensure that music creators would be compensated for public performances of their work. Today, ASCAP and its chief competitor, Broadcast Music, Inc. (BMI), serve as central clearing-houses for the channeling of money from music users (such as radio and TV stations) to music creators.

By the fifth decade of the 1900s, the basic infrastructure of today's marketing and promotion system was in place: a set of formats for the commercial sale of music (phonograph records and sheet music) accompanied by communication methods (radio, movies, jukeboxes, and live performances) that exposed people to a range of performers and sounds and helped convince those people to purchase the records and sheet music.

The 1950s saw the beginnings of dramatic news ways that music was brought to—and could be enjoyed by—the public.

The introduction of television, which occurred in the late 1940s, changed forever the arena of mass media by bringing visual performances into the homes of mass audiences. Television had the additional effect of boosting radio's use of recorded music. This happened because prior to TV, radio concentrated largely on broadcasting live performances; TV's early variety shows siphoned off radio's audience for this kind of programming, forcing radio to focus more on playing records. Ultimately, stations began to specialize, narrowcasting their broadcasts to suit local listeners' tastes (such as for country music, rhythm and blues, show tunes, and, later, rock and roll). Today, radio programming is highly segmented, with different stations specializing in different music "formats."

The 1950s also brought the appearance of the 45-rpm "single" record and the $33\frac{1}{3}$-rpm long-playing disc (popular in stereo by the early 1960s). The radio arena saw the introduction of stereo FM broadcasting (with its improved signal quality) in the mid-1960s.

All of these innovations led to improvements in the music listening experience, to more choices in how audiences could consume music, and to the overall growth of the music industry.

The dawn of the 1980s heralded even more dramatic changes. Music Television (MTV) ushered in the era of the music video—yet another means of getting music to audiences. Digital recording technology began to eclipse traditional analog production methods, leading to the rapid and overwhelming acceptance of a new playback format, the compact disc (CD), that could store more music than an LP record and (arguably) offer higher-quality sound.

As we move into the new century, the forward momentum of technology shows no sign of abating, with personal computers and the Internet currently capturing the interest of consumers and sparking the creativity of musicians and music sellers. Each new innovation affects the way that music is created, packaged, and brought to the public.

Challenges and Opportunities

Individuals and companies entering the music marketing arena need to be aware of the following current trends that are presenting new challenges and opportunities:

Development of New Forms of Entertainment. The music industry is increasingly challenged by new forms of entertainment competing for the attention and dollars of consumers. Video games, computer software, and more cable TV channels are just a few of the current sources of competition for music sellers.

Consolidation of Ownership of the Supply Chain. Increasingly, large media conglomerates are gaining ownership of the traditional businesses that control the flow of products from the makers to the consumers. Such domination of the marketplace by a few giant companies makes it more difficult for smaller companies to break in to the business. (See "Vertical and Horizontal Integration" on page 109.)

Expansion of the Internet. The World Wide Web is providing an alternative marketing solution for individuals and small businesses threatened by the media conglomerates mentioned in the previous paragraph. The Web offers smaller businesses the possibility of bypassing standard marketing channels and selling their music to customers directly.

Development of New Technologies. New technologies are continuing to change the face of music commerce. As just one example, CD recording hardware is becoming more affordable, opening up the possibility of the mass public being able to download music off the Internet and "burn" custom CDs at home. This poses a direct challenge to non-Internet retailers and to CD manufacturers. The ultimate effect of this and other technologies on the current music manfacturing and distribution system remains to be seen, but change of some kind is a certainty.

Sources of Income

Today's marketplace—with its many available product formats and music outlets—offers numerous possible sources of income for the music seller. Here are some of them:

- Retail sales of CDs, tapes, and other formats
- Ticket sales for live performances
- Royalties and fees earned from performances of recordings on radio and television, in movies, and in commercial venues such as restaurants and nightclubs
- Royalties earned from cover versions (that is, other performers' versions) of music, created for use on record, in live performances, on television and radio, and in movies
- Fees for re-recording and play by Muzak and other background music companies, and for reproduction of music in music boxes and musical toys
- Retail sales income and royalties earned from sheet music
- Sales of T-shirts, jackets, tour books, and other promotional merchandise

Approaches to Doing Business

How does one go about tapping these sources of income? As the music business has expanded, and as new channels of activity have emerged, several different approaches to doing business have become common.

The Traditional Approach. Until recently, artists and their representatives have had—with very few exceptions—only one workable way to get their music to the public. Here's what they've had to do:

- Sign a contract with a major record company (who takes care of the record marketing and promotion process).
- Align the act with an established music publisher. Basically, the publisher takes charge of all administrative and promotional matters related to songwriting (as opposed to record creation).
- With the music publisher, affiliate with one of the performing rights organizations (the largest are ASCAP and BMI), who track radio and TV airplay and handle the royalties for such use.
- Hook up with an established management agency. Management oversees all the career decisions of the performer-songwriter.
- Sign with a large talent and booking agency, which handles the business of touring and live performance.
- Hire an independent publicity firm. Some publicity is done by the record label, but the indie publicist adds fuel to the act's media exposure plan (involving coverage in magazines and newspapers and on TV and the Internet).

The Alternative Route: Doing It Yourself. In recent years, the music business has witnessed an array of adventurous souls bypassing the traditional avenues of commerce—in essence, taking care of business themselves. Here is a brief summary of an alternative or "guerrilla" method of getting music to an audience:

- Record the CD in a small studio.
- Order mass duplication and storage of the CDs.
- Form a small publishing company and deal directly with the performing rights agencies.
- Use the Internet to promote the CD and the act.
- Sell the CD via the Internet, direct mail, and toll-free phone orders.
- Convince smaller record stores to stock the CD.
- Personally book live club dates.
- Make personal contact with area media to publicize the act.

THE MARKET-AWARE MUSIC SELLER

So today, with some of the basics remaining the same—but with many other factors changing—the business of music marketing is more complex, volatile, and challenging than ever. All of this sharpens the demands on the modern marketing person, who has to decide which route is best for his or her music product and then make the right decisions about how to travel that route.

Regardless of which path you choose for your music, your success as a marketer will depend on your knowledge, skills, and attitude. Today, smart marketing requires the following:

- Knowledge of how to target and reach an audience

- Awareness of all the current sources of music income

- The creativity to envision and develop new sources of income

- Knowledge of the established procedures of music commerce

- The ability to develop new business procedures—to innovate and find a new way

- Knowledge of how technology can be used to advantage

- Willingness to take the initiative—to work proactively rather than passively wait to be "discovered"

In the current wide-open, rapidly changing business environment, you, the marketer, have to assume the roles of lifelong learner, market expert, media maven, pioneer, innovator, and—very importantly—self-starter. If you're a musician, no one is going to work as hard or apply as much dedication as you in getting your music across to an audience. You are always the best advocate for your creative work. The same is true of any producer of a commercial product.

THE MUSIC MARKETER'S ADVANTAGE

As we mentioned earlier, marketing music is not an easy task—but it can be done. In some ways, music has a distinct advantage over other types of products. Its powerful built-in attraction has long been recognized. Through history, music has been used by societies all over the world to heighten the experience of social occasions, religious ceremonies, and other events and simply to provide entertainment. Whether the instrument is the human voice, an animal bone and hollow gourd, a harpsichord, or the latest electronic device, the phenomenon is essentially the same: music reaches deep within human consciousness, arousing a range of emotions, lifting the spirit, and sparking the imagination. That kind of value is priceless—and a boon to anyone involved in music marketing.

Music can also reach across language and cultural barriers. American pop music, for example, is embraced all over the world. Nowadays, music from any country can easily seep into the music repertoires— and the markets—of any other country.

Armed with those unique selling points, and with music that you believe in and a desire to move ahead in the music industry, you're poised for action.

In the next two chapters you'll get a behind-the-scenes look at how music companies conduct a campaign to market a new recording. Then later, in Parts 2 and 3, you'll be able to explore what's involved in bringing your own product to market.

CHAPTER

2

The Traditional Record Company Marketing Process

These days, it's a familiar scenario: A few nights ago, while watching a music news show on television, you caught a featurette on an interesting new band. Earlier today, while reading your local newspaper during lunch, you noticed a very positive review of the band's new CD.

Suddenly, it is Friday evening. Payday. You ease by your favorite music store. Just inside the doors, there's a new display, with cardboard cutouts, mobiles, and posters near the front listening booths. You check out the new CD—and sure enough, you like what you hear. It's going home with you. In the checkout line, you begin reading the story of the new release on the jacket.

Driving home, you hear a song from the new release on your favorite FM radio station.

You, in all likelihood, are a serious fan of music. And it's equally likely that your purchase of that CD happened in part because of a recent marketing and promotion campaign by a major record label.

BEHIND THE RECORD COMPANY WALLS

A record company relies on the effective interaction of several departments. Together—from marketing to advertising, sales, promotion, and publicity (as shown on page 11)—they work as a team to reach a common goal: the "selling through" or maximizing sales of a musical product.

Here's how the process works, in a fictional example.

THE CLOCK TICKS

For weeks now, word has been buzzing around the industry about a hot new blues-rock band, Four Gone Conclusions (4GC), that has exploded out of Tampa, Florida.

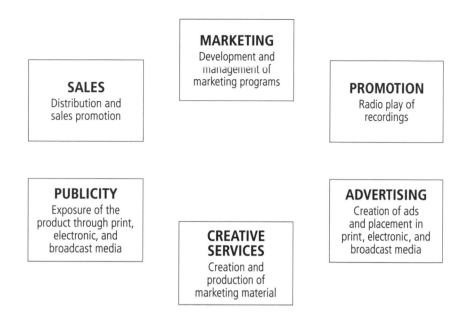

Departments involved in marketing activities of a large record company. (Organization varies from company to company.)

At a recent music business convention in Las Vegas, the band brought the house down, playing live after the keynote address and the awards ceremony. Negotiations began that night between the act's management and the label vice president of A&R (artists and repertoire, or talent acquisition) of Rhythm Oil Records, a national label.

When the contracts were ready, the band was signed at an exclusive party in Hollywood. Packed with pop-music press and label brass, the partygoers enjoyed Cuban food and local beer from Tampa as the sound system resonated with the group's first (self-produced) CD.

PRESSURE RISES

The next morning, the various gears of the label machinery are already starting to move. There's plenty to do in every department.

At 10 a.m. there is a companywide planning meeting, to lay the groundwork for the band's first label release. First, there is a general discussion of the act. Opinions and ideas are bounced back and forth.

Next, the marketing director begins to map out specifics of the marketing plan. She makes the following points:

- The band should appeal to educated males and females, ages 21 to 50-plus, because of its sophisticated mix of modern blues, classic blues interpretations, and love songs.

- Emphasis will be placed on the members' literacy, musicianship, and songwriting talent.
- The act's image—somewhat dark and mysterious—will be kept and fine-tuned. The band will, however, continue to do significant charity work. (It's been learned that this appeals to fans in the targeted age and education bracket.)
- The band will be shaped as a mainstream contemporary blues act, cross-marketed to blues, jazz, and modern music fans.
- Because of the band's artistic depth and fan appeal, the plan will involve a high-budget promotional push, including a lavish contest on the Internet.

The label people then listen to a couple of rough studio tracks of the band's new CD. Just before the meeting ends, it's announced that famed producer John X. Smith has agreed to come out of retirement to finish 4GC's new CD. (This fact alone has press potential.)

TEAMWORK IN ACTION

Now the label dynamics really begin to heat up. Timing, communication, and teamwork are vital now—and each department knows it. There can be no weak link in the chain; the label just may have a hit act here and the executives can smell it. Here's a peek behind the scenes, as each department moves into action.

Marketing

Now is a very busy time in the marketing department. Several key decisions have been made, but more loom in the immediate future.

There is intense debate over the CD title and jacket art—two critical decisions for a new act.

The band's management—not part of the label—is pushing hard for the CD to be titled *Ybo Arising.*

One of the tracks is an eerie, haunting 12-bar ballad based on the following true story:

> In 1855, the Wanderer, the last slave ship to come to North America, anchored in coastal Georgia. The captive cargo were Ybo, members of a fiercely proud West African tribe. Soon after docking, though, the captives committed suicide, rather than face servitude. Chained together and clad in rags, the men and women descended into the water, singing and chanting, "The water brought us here, and the water will take us away."

> In the Georgia lowlands, there is now a legend that on moonless nights near Ybo Landing, on St. Simons Island, you can hear the distant clanking of the slaves' chains.

Everyone in marketing likes the song and its story. It fits the act's multiracial image and should appeal to the target audience.

One problem arises, however: how to illustrate the title song on the CD jacket.

During an ice-breaker meeting with band members and label brass, a tip comes from the lead guitarist. There is a painting in coastal Georgia that would be perfect for the jacket art.

Armed with this tip, the marketing director contacts Ana Bel Lee, a noted Low Country Georgia artist. She has a painting that depicts the Ybo tragedy. Her artwork, however, has dual scenarios:

Left: In chains and rags, the captives descend into the water, to their doom.

Right: Back in West Africa, the tribe members are rising out of the surf—naked and free.

The artist, though, refuses at first. The painting is not for sale. After more discussion, she becomes intrigued with the band and its interest in charity work. Finally she agrees to release worldwide rights, with one stipulation: the painting will then be auctioned off—with a $50,000 minimum—and the proceeds given to Lions Clubs International, earmarked for childrens' eye care.

The label agrees, and a courier is sent to Jacksonville, Florida, to pick up the artwork and deliver it to the label's Hollywood office. An independent artist is hired to design the CD cover and "flow in" the cover type: the band's name, its logo, and the album title.

Marketing is now in high gear, and an all-department meeting is held to report on progress.

Sales

At the same time, the sales department is busy with equally important preparations. The label has a standing agreement with WEA (Warner-Elektra-Atlantic), one of the largest distributors in North America. The sales vice president makes personal contact with the distributor's VP to alert them to a hot new release.

The sales team members then check over their master calendar of retail stores around the country, showing rack space and extra (preferred) display areas, along with their cost and availability.

To his astonishment, the sales VP discovers that Crazy Joe's El Cheapo, a nationwide chain of music stores, has listening booth, front-of-store, and end-cap (prominent rack) space available for the period coinciding with 4GC's release. Hastily, the VP phones the company and reserves the display areas nationwide. The VP knows that these stores are frequented by members of the band's target audience.

Members of the sales department also make personal contact with key independent music stores around the country, in markets projected to be favorable to the band: Boston, Denver, Chicago, New York, Atlanta, and Tampa are among them. The master calendar of rack space is updated daily.

Also, the sales department requests that marketing create a set of promotional materials for the release, including cardboard cutouts, mobiles, and posters.

Following a meeting of the label president and the band's management, the suggested retail price for the CD is set at $17.99, and the stereo tape is set at $10.99, consistent with other new releases.

The sales vice president checks in with mass-duplicating plants in Seattle, Washington, and Birmingham, Alabama, to make sure they will be ready when the master disc is delivered. There will be an initial run of 75,000 CDs and 25,000 cassettes. With very tight security, the order is placed for 2,500 CDs as advance copies for promotion and publicity.

Next, the sales VP meets with the advertising department. It's decided that a full-page ad will be placed in *Billboard* for three weeks to coincide with the CD release. Also, an "image" ad will be ordered in a carefully timed issue of *Rolling Stone*. Additional support ads will be placed in *Spin, down beat,* and *Living Blues* magazines. Across the country, smaller support ads will be placed in lifestyle and entertainment publications.

One advance copy of the semi-final mix is delivered from the recording studio, with tight security. In the president's office there is a listening session for all departments.

Now the key components of the release are starting to come together.

Promotion (Radio and Music Television)

Simultaneously, the promotion department is hard at work on 4GC's radio and music television campaign. The CD's title track, "Ybo Arising," will be the first single release.

The focus of promotion will be on two specific areas: (1) AAA (Adult Album Alternative) radio nationwide and (2) blues and jazz formats (many localized) nationwide.

The vice president of national promotion makes personal contact with several key radio programmers around the country. They include the program directors of national radio networks. Personal calls also go out to the hosts of nationally syndicated shows such as National Public Radio's "Jazz After Hours" and "House of Blues."

There is a great deal of coordination and timing to be considered as the VP of national promotion briefs the regional promotion people dotting the country in urban areas from San Francisco to Miami. There are daily conferences by phone and e-mail, as each professional lays the groundwork for the CD's delivery to stations. This has to be done with pinpoint accuracy, so that no station or network feels slighted.

The label promotion people stay in constant contact with the field reps. One by one, the reps plan special listening parties, tailored to their individual markets. These are geared for local deejays, veejays, and press people.

The VP of national promotion orders one dozen leather jackets, imprinted with the band's logo. These expensive items will be given as promotional merchandise to the most vital radio programmers around the nation. Also, an order is placed for 200 boxed sets of Cross pens imprinted with the band's logo. These may eventually become collectors' items, drawing more attention to the act.

Publicity

At the same time, the publicity department has been extremely busy preparing for the act's media exposure campaign.

Even before any materials are ready, and while the band is still in the studio, the vice president of national publicity is glued to the phone and the e-mail keyboard.

There are roughly two dozen "priority" contacts around the country, who receive personal calls tipping them in advance about the impending huge campaign. These contacts are influential music editors and album reviewers at key national magazines, news syndicates, and major-market daily newspapers.

Much the same is true inside the tour publicity office. These specialists work closely with the group's talent agency (not part of the record label) to support the live concert schedule. Weeks in advance of a nightclub or large-hall date, they send press materials and concert tickets to local media in the surrounding area.

Ditto for the college press publicity team—professionals who work closely with hundreds of college newspapers, large and small, all over the nation.

The Material Scheme. A couple of days after the band was signed, the VP of national publicity ordered a complete set of PR materials, or "press kits," to be created for the office. The following steps are now carried out:

- A professional entertainment writer is hired to interview the band and draft the artists' biography, or "bio." This tells the story of 4GC, how they got together, and where they stand, artistically.

- A noted music business photographer is hired to plan and shoot the group's publicity photos. There will be three each of studio portraits and live onstage shots, with some in black and white and some in color.

- A sleeved cardboard jacket is ordered, with the label's and the band's logo. This jacket keeps the other materials neatly organized.

- A publicity assistant draws up a one-page fact sheet. This is a thumbnail of information about the band. It's useful for TV appearances and interviews on live radio.

- Another assistant studies the band's existing press (mostly nightclub reviews). Three stories are chosen, then laid out neatly on $8\frac{1}{2}$-by-11-inch paper. The clippings, as they're called, are then photocopied.

As the materials are being mass-duplicated, the publicists work as a team, studying the master media list on a computer database. A mass-mailing list is then tailored for the CD release. The list includes national magazine music editors, daily newspaper entertainment editors, college newspaper music editors, lifestyle/entertainment weekly editors, and key freelance music writers nationwide.

The Web Site. The VP of national publicity hires a freelance designer to create a new Web site for the band and link it to the label's main site. The publicity staff writes the copy and then the words, graphics, and sound are made ready for installation and uploading.

Each office member helps design a rather elaborate contest to debut on the Web site; the top prize will be an all-expenses-paid weekend for two at the Chicago Hilton and a limousine tour of famed Chicago blues clubs.

The Video. Working with an independent filmmaker, the VP of national publicity maps out the band's music video. Some location footage from coastal Georgia will be used, along with some computer-generated imagery.

International

Four weeks before the CD release in North America, the label's vice president of international affairs confers with overseas reps in countries where it's believed the band may have a potential fan base. These include Belgium, France, England, Brazil, Japan, and Malaysia. As soon as they're ready, advance copies of the CD and press kits will be sent to each rep for preview.

Now the components of the band's debut campaign are fully in place. Each department at the label checks and double-checks its work, and there are numerous briefings so that every employee is up to speed.

MORE TEAMWORK: THE NON-LABEL PARTNERS

At the same time, the band's non-label representatives are busy with more preparations.

4GC's management firm signs the band with SevenStars/Crown, a top talent agency specializing in modern blues and blues-rock. To support the new CD, the agency books the act in key clubs around the country. Also, the agency adds the act to a 22-city package tour, which will play in medium-size halls. The tour includes the Robert Cray Band, Tinsley Ellis, Blues Traveler, and the Radiators.

The management also cuts a deal with Ol' Rattler, a popular Tampa local beer, to co-sponsor 4GC's part in the package tour. The beverage company will provide stage backdrops, posters, and tasting parties across the country as part of the brewer's own expansion program.

The management company also makes an agreement with Four Dogs Music, an established publishing house based in Austin, Texas. Four Dogs then signs an agreement with ASCAP to handle the band's performing rights worldwide.

Now, after weeks of teamwork, planning, and preparation, things are ready to happen. And they will happen with dizzying speed.

THE BREAKOUT: RELEASE DAY ARRIVES

The recording is completed in the studio. Here's what happens then:

- The master discs are couriered to the mass duplicators. Advance discs are also rushed to the label president and the various department heads.
- After duplication, the CDs are boxed with jacket art and then shipped to the distributor's warehouses around the country. There, the promotional materials are paired with the CDs.

- The units are then delivered to stores, and the displays and listening booths are stocked in the dead of night.

- At the same time, promotion people across the country hand-deliver CDs to programmers, along with the various promotional items. Then a flurry of sneak previews begin in various markets across the country.

- The publicity people take delivery of their materials. Along with the CD copies and promotional items, the press kits are hand-delivered or overnighted to key editors and reviewers. Using temps and college interns to assist, publicity begins a nation-wide mass mailing.

- The finished video, review copies of the CD, press kits, and promotional items are delivered to MTV, VH-1, and other music television channels.

- Mentions of the new release begin popping up on CNN Entertainment News, syndicated radio shows, the Web's SonicNet, and elsewhere.

- In its pitches to editors, publicity heavily emphasizes the story of the title tune and the charitable destiny of the original jacket art. NPR's "All Things Considered" does a two-minute featurette on the new release and the upcoming charity auction.

- The ads appear in the selected media. CD reviews and feature stories crop up in national magazines, daily newspapers, and lifestyle weeklies.

- The title song begins to appear in the various radio formats. The band members are interviewed live on certain major-market radio stations.

- The band's Web site, linked to the label's main site, receives a growing number of hits.

- Increasingly, the band plays to sold-out clubs and medium-size performance venues.

- In one major-market promotional push by the tour sponsor, the Tampa beer company peppers the Tampa-St. Petersburg-Clearwater area with "co-op" TV, radio, and print ads, tagging the band, the new CD, and the beer brand.

- At the college level, the listening parties for local press—also co-sponsored by the beer company—prove extremely popular. These generate a great deal of "street buzz" within the target audience.

THE END RESULT

Here's what has happened: A psychological barrage of data about the band and the new CD has been hurled at the target audience. Leaving no stone unturned, the label and related partners have made it increasingly unlikely that members of the target market will never have heard of the band and the new CD.

And that, briefly, is how the CD ended up in your hands.

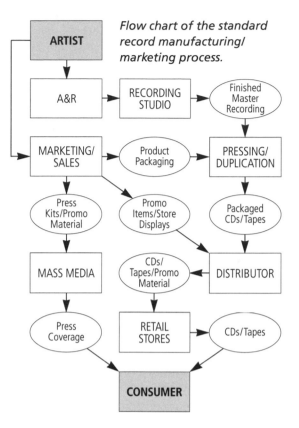

Flow chart of the standard record manufacturing/marketing process.

EPILOGUE

At a $100-a-plate banquet in Tampa's Convention Center, the original artwork is auctioned off (carried live on VH-1). The auction is held "Asian-style"—each bidder must pay each bid amount; no refunds.

Shortly after bidding is opened by Lions Clubs of North America vice president Ron Jones, a fierce bidding war ensues. Quickly, the money stacks up, far surpassing the painter's $50,000 mandate.

As the room falls silent, the label president waves her hand to top the others: $16,900. The painting will hang in the label's Hollywood office.

The Lions Clubs representative is given a check for $167,600 for kids' eye care all over the world—thus generating an avalanche of press coverage and good feeling about the band and the label.

4GC closes the evening with a short live set.

Soon, "feelers" come in from "The Tonight Show" and other national TV programs. The band receives invitations to open for ZZ Top in Honolulu and the Rolling Stones in Paris. The album's title song appears on *Billboard* magazine's Modern Rock Tracks chart. Back at the label, reports of brisk sales come in, along with reorders.

Soon, the entire process will start all over again.

3

The Traditional Music Publisher Marketing Process

Just as it's important to know how a record company works (as described in the previous chapter), it is equally imperative to understand how a music publisher fits into the total picture of music marketing.

Put simply, the traditional music publisher acts as both a watchdog for the songwriter and a partner in exploiting songs for profit. (In the music business, the term *exploit* doesn't have its usual negative connotation; here it simply means "to put to productive use.") The publisher takes care of all the legal and financial matters that relate to the commercial uses of a music composition. As a partner, the publisher seeks opportunities to promote the music whenever and wherever possible.

BEHIND THE MUSIC PUBLISHER'S WALLS

The goal of a music publisher is to obtain the publishing rights to as many workable music compositions as possible and then market those tunes in as many ways as possible—over a long period of time. The large music library in the publisher's vaults ensures a steady stream of revenue from year to year. Helping to make this happen are the following personnel:

- **Chief executive.** He or she guides the entire company and shares in all the major decisions, including signing new songwriters and composers, pairing songs with artists, and solving strategic problems.

- **Professional manager.** The person in this vital position is constantly on the lookout for music compositions that may have potential in all manner of markets and styles of arrangement, from elevator music to heavy metal, country, and jazz.

This person must have a very keen ear, because a song's true potential may be buried deep within a rough demo tape, or in hand-written lyrics. The professional manager signs songwriters, matches songs with recording artists, and may often help the songwriter-artist-producer team in carefully shaping lyrics and arrangements to bring out a song's real hit power. Professional managers are usually aided by personnel who review new songs and make recommendations for acquisitions.

- **Business and legal affairs.** This department handles the publisher's contractual matters and advises on business decisions large and small.

- **Copyright department.** Personnel in this area handle registration of the company's songs with the U.S. Copyright Office, file for copyright renewals, and register songs with performing rights organizations.

- **Royalties and accounting.** This is an exacting area that involves keeping track of advances to songwriters, company expenses, and taxes; reviewing royalty statements from music licensees; and calculating and making payments to songwriters.

- **Independent personnel: producers, PR representatives, arrangers, and session musicians.** Often, there's an array of independents closely associated with the publisher. They may include a record producer, who's in charge of the studio process, from the first test recordings to the final post-production touches. An indie public relations (PR) person may be brought in if a song is doing well in the charts. Often he or she will help with secondary publicity targets—such as publications dealing with lifestyle and non-music topics—to maximize the artist's or song's exposure. An indie arranger may be asked to help "fix" a song with suggestions on solos or arrangement "sweetening" and to score the song in written notation for legal and sheet-music needs.

TRACING THE PATH OF A PUBLISHED SONG

You, like many other music fans, undoubtedly read the jacket information on the back of a CD when you purchase one. In the case of pop music, the songs are usually written by members of the band. But have you ever been reading a jacket and suddenly noticed there's a tune written by someone you have never heard of?

How did that song end up on the CD? It's very likely that a music publisher was involved.

Let's follow the path of a song, through the eyes of a music publisher, from the first rough draft to the top of the pop charts and beyond.

4GC Rides Again

In the last chapter we followed a fictional band, Four Gone Conclusions (4GC), through the process of working with a record company to release and market an album.

Using 4GC again, let's look at what happens on the publishing side of a marketing campaign.

We now flash back to the beginning of the process:

The record label deal is finalized and the record company gears up for retail sales and radio promotion. Immediately, the band's management attends to a different but equally important part of the band's career: their potential for earning money from an array of commercial uses of their music.

(Keep in mind, here, that every time—worldwide—a musical work is performed or broadcast on radio, TV, the stage, a jukebox, or any other medium, the songwriters earn royalties. See page 220 for more on this topic.)

Right away, 4GC's general manager signs each member (all are songwriters) with Four Dogs Music, an established publisher based in Austin, Texas. Working with 4GC on a 50-50 basis, the publisher will now represent the band's music in several important ways not handled by the record label.

Copyright

First, the publisher registers all the band's music with the U.S. Copyright Office. This provides legal protection from theft or plagiarism of both music and lyrics. It's a critically important step for any original music. (Although a composition is considered copyrighted at the time it is written, registering it with the Copyright Office adds legal weight to the claim of ownership.)

Performance Rights

Next, the publisher registers each band member and clears the members' respective songs with the American Society of Composers, Authors, and Publishers (ASCAP), a performing rights organization based in New York. (The other large music rights house is Broadcast Music, Inc. [BMI].)

ASCAP will now oversee the calculation, collection, and payment of all performance monies due the band member-publisher team. For a popular song, the royalty fees can end up accruing from a dizzying array of sources, including radio and TV airplay, "cover" versions by other performers, jukeboxes, nightclubs, bars, restaurants, stores, and even parking lots that play recorded background music. Large or tiny, they all have to pay—and ASCAP is almost impossible to argue with.

Contrary to what you might think, the royalty calculation process is anything but a guessing game. Both ASCAP and BMI use sophisticated computer-based data-processing systems. These systems can calculate, very precisely, the number of times a given record is broadcast in a range of media.

Based on such findings, ASCAP and BMI tabulate their individual members' performance "credits." Then, periodically, the organizations furnish members with statements and payments. (For more information on ASCAP and BMI, see page 221.)

Mechanical and Synchronization Rights

The publisher has also affiliated with the Harry Fox Agency in New York. This large company will now take care of all mechanical rights to 4GC's music—which includes the collection and payment of licensing fees for new versions of the music used on other artists' CDs and tapes. It also handles synchronization rights, which cover the use of the music in audiovisual media such as movies, television, and home video. This important side of music publishing can add a very lucrative dimension to a song's total earning picture. (See page 217.)

A Song Is Born

Let's go back a little further in time. About a year before 4GC's label deal, a Tampa high school student wrote a song (her longtime hobby). Titled "Cubano Skiffle," it's a lively dance tune about unwinding on a Saturday night. After doing some research on the Internet (including visiting Four Dogs Music's Web site) the school's music director helps her with the demo recording process. Using a borrowed machine, they record a crude demo tape in mono—just an acoustic guitar and a singer from the school's jazz band. They compose a cover letter, introducing the student and the song. The lyrics are neatly printed out. Certified and insured, the package is sent to Four Dogs Music.

A week later, to the astonishment of the school, the young lady receives a letter from Four Dogs. They're interested in the song. If she and a parent or guardian sign with Four Dogs, the tune will be cataloged, copyrighted, and registered with ASCAP. The letter includes the necessary forms to fill out.

The Right Song for the Job

Months pass, during which 4GC is signed to Rhythm Oil Records and Four Dogs Music. Soon, in a recording studio planning meeting, it's discovered that the band is one song short for their new CD. Hastily, a search is launched for just the right number. Song after song is ruled out. This is a key decision because the nonoriginal song has to fit the image of the group and the context of the rest of the CD.

Back at the publisher, the professional manager hears about this and quickly begins searching the vaults. "It's a long shot," he decides, "but 'Cubano Skiffle' just might be the right song." The same evening, a more professional demo is recorded locally and then overnighted to the band's producer and the label president.

A heated debate soon ensues. Is the tune too cutesy? Maybe. Is it too "pop" for the band's image? Would it have any single-release potential? Finally, a consensus emerges: everyone likes the lyrics; they're fun, upbeat. The problem is the arrangement.

Then, with Four Dogs' professional manager and arranger on a phone conference call, the band and the producer iron out a suggestion: slow down the number slightly and turn it into a sexy, bump-and-grind shuffle (much like the Rolling Stones' version of the Buddy Holly classic "Not Fade Away"). Far into the night, the band experiments with tempos and such color-adding instruments as maracas, timpani, gourds, and steel triangle.

At the next day's listening session, everyone is enthusiastic about the latest "take," including the label president and the departments of promotion, sales, and publicity. "Cubano Skiffle" will round out the new CD. Quickly, the news travels to the publisher and then to Tampa, where the high-schooler and her music teacher are flabbergasted. The publisher helps them set up a college trust fund for the song's revenues.

The Second Single Release

Flash forward to the present: Now that 4GC's first single release, "Ybo Arising," has peaked and is waning on the charts, it's time to discuss the all-important second release. From Austin, the publisher lobbies hard for it to be "Cubano Skiffle."

Both the publisher and the label brass begin the polling process, contacting key pop music programmers, club deejays, and reviewers across the country. The responses are positive.

As the responses come in, a couple of key pointers are discovered, sending the label into a tizzy: various major-market pop radio stations have started getting listener requests for the song; also, label reps in large cities have noticed the tune in dance clubs, both teen and adult. Phone calls and e-mail messages flash back and forth between the label and the publisher.

It's a Hit

The song is rushed into release, and soon it becomes obvious that the band has a major runaway hit on its hands. As one radio network after another adds the record to its playlist, the song spreads like wildfire in dance clubs across the country—even spawning a new dance craze.

The Publisher: A Powerful Ally

Quickly, the record company goes into a fever of activity to cover its bases in retail, radio and TV, and PR (as described in the previous chapter). Here's how the music publisher steps in, as an ally, to help ensure sell-through of both the single and the CD.

The publisher hires several independent promotion people around the country. They'll call on smaller radio stations and clubs—even lounges—not usually serviced by the record label. (Both publisher and label work very carefully so as not to step on each other's toes, with constant updates by phone and e-mail.) This publisher-fueled effort greatly speeds up expansion of the single's base.

The publisher also brings in an independent publicist. Again, he'll concentrate on media not normally covered by the label. In a very selective range of outlets, emphasis will be placed on the story of the teen songwriter. Coverage will include a story in *Highlights for Kids* magazine and an interview on a Nickelodeon Channel broadcast. The publicist also assists the label with tour publicity.

The publisher works swiftly in other areas. Arrangements are made to publish the lyrics in *Song Hits* and similar magazines. Notification comes in that pieces of the song will be heard in an upcoming episode of NBC's "Law and Order."

With the publisher and label working together, the song's hit potential is maximized, and it slips into *Billboard* magazine's top 10.

From the publisher's standpoint, the song's a surefire winner, and soon revenues will begin coming in from several different sources. ASCAP notifies the publisher that "Cubano Skiffle" has become extremely popular with copy bands across North America. The Harry Fox Agency calls to say a feeler has come in from Tadasu Toys, Ltd., in

Tokyo. An agreement is then worked out allowing the company to produce a line of teddy bears with the band's logo; when squeezed, the toys will play the hit song's melody. Finally, word comes in that Raven Della, an Argentine soap-opera star and pop singer with a huge pre-teen and teen audience all over South America, Central America, and Mexico, will cover the song on her new CD. The two acts' management companies discuss the idea of double-bill concerts in Mexico City, Rio de Janeiro, and Buenos Aires.

Soon, the music publisher will start this process all over again, with songs old and new.

Hands-On Music Marketing and Promotion

CHAPTER

4

Previewing the Total Marketing Program

Before diving into the process of handling your own marketing and promotion, it's worth taking a look at what the competitive climate is like in the current marketplace.

Most encouragingly, the climate is improving for independent sellers of music. In 1996, according to an article in the *San Francisco Examiner,* independent record sales accounted for more than 21 percent of the entire music market. In 1997, one estimate placed the independent-label share of the music market at close to 30 percent. That is a very substantial bite out of a pie once claimed almost entirely by major labels like Warner, Sony, MCA, Geffen, and Arista.

Cited in the *Examiner* article was a small San Francisco-based label called Ubiquity Records. The co-founders, Jody and Michael McFadin, launched the label with only $1,000 in seed money. They initially concentrated on reissuing rare soul tracks for the deejay market. At first, sales were modest. But after several years, and after changing the product focus to broaden appeal, the label achieved annual sales of over $1 million.

The McFadins were by no means alone. Thousands of other enterprising music makers and marketers added impetus to the late-nineties surge of grassroots business activity and growth in market share.

This indicates that while the music industry has always had its share of independents, opportunity seems to be ever growing for entrepreneurs who are inclined to take the marketing of music into their own hands.

At the same time, there are plenty of roadblocks on the path to profitability in the music business. Not least among them is the trend toward consolidation of ownership—via mergers and buyouts—of distribution outlets, including retail chains. Fewer decision makers in the distribution pipeline may mean fewer sales outlets for small labels.

POPULAR PERCEPTION

The large, corporate record labels are difficult-to-impossible to compete against.

With the kinds of budgets and distribution systems commanded by the major labels, the small label has little chance of making an impact.

ALTERNATE REALITY

Small, independent labels, with their low overhead and ability to focus marketing efforts on fewer releases, can be quite competitive in the marketplace. In 1997, the market share held by the independents was around 30 percent, according to one estimate.

The hardest part of music as a profession may no longer be the creation of the record; technology has advanced to the point where professional-quality sound can be achieved at amazingly low cost with relative ease. But with this production ease and economy comes more competition. Nowadays, the most daunting challenge may be ensuring that the independent record gets into the hands of distributors, retail outlets, and customers who are already swamped with large quantities of new product.

Meanwhile, while all this action is occurring on the independent-label front, the challenge for major-label marketing staff has never been greater. There's nothing quite like flattening sales and shrinking market share—as faced many in the industry in the late 1990s—to light a fire under the people whose jobs depend on those numbers rising, not falling.

YOU, THE MARKETER

So where does this leave *you?* Presumably you've already taken care of Job One, which is coming up with some music that's ready to be heard, or will be ready soon. (This may not be your personal music, unless you're an artist or songwriter. It could also be music that you're representing as a manager, label owner, or employee of a large record company.)

Now that you have the music in hand, another big task looms before you. Your goal now is to make the music earn some money.

In your mind's eye is a transaction—an exchange in which someone willingly reaches into his or her pocket for money that will be given up in return for the pleasure of listening to, and owning, your musical product. That money will, in turn, travel down a channel of people, offices, and banks until it finally finds its way into your pocket.

Sounds great. But how do you make such a scenario happen?

The process of moving from the point of product creation to the other end of the commercial continuum—where you are on the receiving end of a sales transaction—is called marketing. And marketing is what you must do if you are to sell your musical product.

In addition, it is best to proceed according to a well-thought-out marketing program.

THE NEED FOR A PLAN AND A PROGRAM

"Build it and they will come." This statement, paraphrased from the 1989 fantasy film *Field of Dreams,* pretty much sums up the way many music people imagine success will come their way: "If I work hard enough on the music, eventually people will find out about it and start beating down the doors to get a piece of me."

But remember: the movie's title is *Field of Dreams.* If the movie were *Field of Reality,* the line would be: "Build something they want—then market and promote it—and there's a good chance they will come."

The point is, working on the music is only one part of the big task. The musical product will just sit there unless you also do the necessary marketing and promotion work.

With that fairly obvious point in mind, let's look at two contrasting ways of trying to sell a product: (1) using a "flying blind" approach and (2) using a more planned-out, systematic approach.

The "Flying Blind" Marketing Approach

One way to market a product is to release it blindly into the marketplace and hope it sells. In this scenario, the seller may have no proof or hard information indicating that there is any demand for the product. There may be no specifically targeted audience—no identified segment of the populace that research or experience has proven is likely to purchase the kind of product being released. The only basis for the sale is a gut reaction that "the time is right" for this sort of product. The seller purports to have a "finger on the pulse" of current tastes and trends and to know what kind of product will appeal. (In music parlance, the seller purports to have good "ears.") Armed with a product that is undoubtedly a good one (like so many others unleashed on the record-buying populace) the seller dives boldly into the market, fueling the effort with self-confidence, faith, and raw nerve. Promotion is aimed at informing "the public" about the product in a general way.

For example, you might be dealing with a recording of a new artist whose work you'd categorize as exceptionally good alternative rock. You also perceive that so-called alternative rock is currently popular. So you release the album with the sense that the album's quality will be self-evident and that people who purchase alternative rock records will find it appealing and will buy it. You place a few ads and hope that the project flies.

This "send it up and see if it flies" approach to selling is risky. For one thing, as "in tune" with current popular tastes as the seller might be, there is no way to determine with certainty how long those popular tastes will be in play. That disc you issued because it conformed to a current musical trend—such as alternative rock (which is a vague enough category to begin with)—may wind up in a market that has already turned to a new and different trend. Also, without relying on knowledge of a defined audience, your effort lacks focus: your advertising and publicity may end up being too randomly dispersed to effectively reach specific groups that might find the record appealing. And that "high quality" that you thought would set the record apart could get overlooked in the ongoing flood of equally high-quality competitive products.

Unfortunately, music and entertainment products are the kind most often released according to this model—and that is one of the reasons many of them fail. (Failure is expected. Thus certain companies take a scattershot approach to sales, where they release a large variety of records in the hope that among the many expected failures there will be a couple of hits. The more products, the more chances for success.)

The Planned-Out Marketing Approach

In contrast, the second of the two basic sales approaches involves more fine-tuning of the effort. The seller has evidence that a specific group of people—people from a particular geographic region or age group, for example, or who have specific lifestyle preferences—are inclined to buy the kind of product being marketed. Before the release, the seller finds out as much as possible about the buying habits and tastes of that group, and packages the product to match those tastes. The seller then makes sure that the product is distributed to outlets that cater directly to those people, and advertises and publicizes the product in media targeted to those buyers.

As an example, you might be in the fortunate position of having to market a record by a proven artist with a cult following. The first and second albums sold 50,000 and 100,000 units, respectively. The audience is made up mostly of college-age males located primarily in New England. It would be a reasonably safe market bet to focus distribution in college towns in New England, to set up tour dates in that region, and to advertise in publications that reach college-age males.

This approach to selling is far less chancy than the "flying blind" way. It involves proceeding according to some established guidelines to ensure an informed and—to the extent possible—*systematic* process of getting a desirable product to a receptive audience that has been made aware of the product and its benefits. This, more than the seat-of-the-pants approach, is what marketing is all about. When it comes to staging a marketing campaign, avoid winging it, and you'll have a better chance of winning it.

POPULAR PERCEPTION

The marketing of music is a loosely defined, make-it-up-as-you-go-along process.

Images abound of artists, managers, and record companies "winging it"—strategizing on a whim, exploiting momentary fads, and generating legions of one-hit (or no-hit) wonders.

ALTERNATE REALITY

More and more, the marketing of music is a carefully planned process, with specialists in the areas of artist development, sales, distribution, promotion, and publicity joining forces in a single, methodical effort to break an artist and build a long-term following.

THE FOUR P's OF MARKETING

The music field has its own unique marketing requirements, as do other fields. But there are some fundamental rules of marketing that apply to *all* fields, and it's helpful to be aware of them.

While the term marketing most simply translates as "selling," it has another, broader meaning. It's a meaning that has developed over the course of time as the focus of trade has changed from a "here's the product, now let's sell it" approach to another based on the idea, "here's a customer need; let's create a product to satisfy that need and then make the product readily available." Nowadays, marketing can really be said to encompass all activities having to do with transferring ownership of a product from the producer to the consumer in a way that meets consumer needs.

Today, marketing refers to an entire *program* for selling—a program consisting of several key components.

Those components have come to be known as the Four P's:

- Product
- Price
- Place
- Promotion

Product

The product is the primary means by which a producer meets a customer need. The *product* aspect of marketing refers to all activities related to product development. Product development involves ensuring that the product has definable selling points (that is, value) that can be conveyed to a definable group of people; that it offers something different from competitive products, or can be differentiated in some way; and that it has packaging that is appealing, economical, in conformance with legal and retail requirements, and relatively easy to produce. It's important to note that a given product has both a core benefit and secondary benefits. But we'll discuss that later.

Price

The price of the product must be set to achieve a balance of affordability to the audience, profitability for the seller, and competitiveness with similar products.

Place

The product has to be made available to, and easily obtainable by, the customers. This is really referring to *distribution.*

Promotion

All the steps that must be taken to increase customer awareness of the product and to convince customers of the product's value come under the heading of promotion. This includes advertising and publicity. It also encompasses special sales promotions such as incentive programs designed to boost sales within targeted time frames or under other circumstances.

The "Three W's and an H" Definition

As long as we're playing with letters of the alphabet, let's look at marketing in another way—in terms of Three W's and an H. The product can be considered the *What* of marketing. Distribution and placement can be thought of as the *Where*. Both promotion and distribution strategies can be boiled down to the *How*. That leaves one more W. Another crucial aspect of marketing is the timing—the *When*—of all the program elements, from production to distribution to promotion.

BEYOND THE FOUR P's: THE FINER POINTS OF MARKETING MUSIC

Music, as stated previously, has its own special marketing and promotion requirements. Not surprisingly, the typical music marketing effort is quite a bit more complicated than a simple set of Four P's would indicate. Music product development, for example, might involve coming up with several different product formats, permitting money to be earned from a number of different sources and in various different ways. More and more, the marketing function views music as a raw unit of information—digital information, nowadays—that can be presented in multiple configurations, adapted to any media, sent through a variety of distribution channels, and used to establish multiple revenue streams.

A single album, for example, can be sold as a CD, a cassette, and a vinyl LP. It can be combined with visual and text material in a multimedia format. A song from that album can generate sales from the original disc, a separate single, a movie soundtrack, a television commercial, and many other uses.

Similarly, promotion in music represents a complex effort that includes publicity, advertising, sales promotion, live performance, radio play, souvenir sales, television appearances, and more.

Music distribution involves not only retail store sales but just about any channel through which music is transferred to the consumer or reseller.

And after the marketing program has been set into motion, it must be carefully monitored. Where ineffective, the program will need fine-tuning. The plan must evolve according to market changes. Sales revenues must be managed.

Building the Perfect Marketing Machine

Whatever its final components, the marketing plan is created to achieve a goal. The goal, at its simplest, is to develop an audience base and to sell musical product. Along the way, a secondary aim is to build up the marketing program to the point where its momentum becomes almost self-perpetuating.

In music, as in many other fields, it is nearly impossible to completely separate the marketing categories of product, promotion, and distribution. As will be seen in later chapters, components of the marketing program tend to serve several purposes and to reinforce each other. Live performance, for example, is not only a direct source of revenue but also a promotion device, boosting retail sales of CDs. Television appearances generate both fees and publicity. Movie soundtracks do the same. When the components are working effectively, they function as a precisely calibrated system of interacting parts supporting a single money-generating engine, powered by audience demand. The engine's dynamics are summarized in the following illustration.

The marketing system fuels audience demand, generating sales. Success feeds energy back into the system, further boosting demand and sales.

Branding: Using the Machine
to Harvest Repeat Customers

As previously pointed out, the purpose of building this well-oiled machine is to generate sales. But is that all there is?

Marketing theory differentiates between the simple, one-time-only transaction—where all that matters is the immediate short-term sale (a kind of marketing hit-and-run)—and a "transaction" that is more lasting: the establishment of ongoing relationships with customers, so that there will be repeat sales to those customers over the long term. Ideally, customers will begin to view the artist (or occasionally the record company) as a *brand* that they can trust to provide music that they like.

This kind of long-term trust in a producer's products is often referred to as *brand loyalty*.

In music, building brand loyalty is an extremely important goal. In more familiar terms, it means *building an audience*. Establishing a base of loyal fans means having a core group of customers who are nearly guaranteed to buy your new CD or show up for your live appearance.

For an example of brand loyalty in the music business, think of the Grateful Dead and their fans. Deadheads, as the fans call themselves, have been a ready audience for any product linked to the Dead, from concert tickets and records to trinkets, books, and neckties. Even former Grateful Dead side musicians have been able to pursue successful solo careers based on the support of Deadheads.

Fortunately, music is ideal for establishing deep emotional connections between artist and audience. The connection is often felt on the most personal terms by the fan. Think of your favorite musical artist and you'll know what this means. The music and lyrics speak to you personally to the point where you feel a kinship with the artist. One fan of the British singer Morrissey described him as "the only one who understands." Another singer, Ian Dury, told a reporter for *Melody Maker* that "there's always one person on every gig who does your secret sign to you....They come up afterwards and get hold of you— always here, on the elbow, where it's really secure—and go, 'I know.'"

In many cases, the connection is such that the musical artist becomes an absolute necessity in the fan's life. In crassly commercial terms, this amounts to a one-to-one relationship between the seller and the buyer—the Holy Grail of marketing. It's the kind of "brand loyalty" that marketers of other types of products can only dream about.

Establishing that kind of audience loyalty and building on it is best done methodically, by thinking through and then following a multi-tiered marketing program.

COMPONENTS OF A MUSIC MARKETING PROGRAM

In music, the Four P's of marketing can be used as the basis for a more expanded set of building blocks for a marketing program. Again, the standard steps of traditional marketing may not always neatly match the requirements of the music business. But they can serve as a helpful point of reference. In an industry as volatile and mercurial as music, any tools that will help you steer a steady course are worth your consideration. With that in mind, use the following as flexible guidelines that you can adapt to your particular marketing situation.

Product Development

The nucleus of any marketing effort is the product. In music, a key product is, obviously, a new recording. (As discussed in the next chapter, however, the core "product" also includes the performer.) As stated previously, product development involves all activities devoted to making sure the product is saleable. This process includes identifying the target audience, identifying and enhancing the product's selling points, differentiating the product from the competition, choosing appropriate delivery formats, packaging the product effectively, and setting the right price.

At What Stage of Product Development Does Marketing Begin? Consider the following two scenarios:

Scenario 1. An artist comes up with a completed master recording and sells it to a record company. The company then sets out to identify a market for the already-recorded music and to develop a program for reaching the market.

Scenario 2. An enterprising label executive perceives a market—say, a market of adolescent female fans of the musical group Hanson. The executive then sets out to find and develop another artist who will appeal to the same market, and guides the artist to record an album of music most likely to be embraced by adolescent female fans of Hanson.

In the first scenario, the core product—the music—is created before the marketing begins. In the second, the *marketing guides the entire process,* including the creation of the product.

This begs the question: When in a project should the marketing process begin? Should it commence only *after* the product has been developed (as was once the norm)? Or should the marketing process begin *at the same time as,* or before, product development begins? In other words, should marketing be a consideration in the creation of the product itself? (The authors can already sense the artistic purists among you rising up in protest.)

Well, it all depends. In the case of "high art"—where the product is (much of the time) a self-contained creative expression unfettered by commercial considerations, the marketing would begin after. Captain Beefheart, for example, probably wasn't thinking about marketability when he created his left-field masterwork, *Trout Mask Replica*.

But in the commercial world, marketing is often an intrinsic part of the product development process. An artist is signed to a record label primarily because of his or her perceived sales potential. A set of tracks may be chosen for a CD on the basis of accessibility. In a classical concert series, "Mostly Mozart" is likely to sell more tickets than an Elliott Carter string quartet, and is thus chosen to dominate the programming. A jazz musician decides to join a rock band because she can earn more more money that way. Marketing decisions occur at any and every stage of product creation and dissemination.

POPULAR PERCEPTION

Marketing comes only after the music is already created.

The Beatles, for example, had songs written and a repertoire established before catching the ears of George Martin and issuing their first records.

ALTERNATE REALITY

When the Beatles assembled their repertoire and wrote their first songs, they did it at a time when they were playing in clubs and testing what worked and what didn't. To the extent that they chose material that they thought would be appealing, they were involved in self-marketing.

Where *you* begin the marketing process depends on your approach to your music. Are you interested purely in realizing your artistic ambitions, and then selling only as many copies as people may be interested in (hoping, of course, that that will amount to a lot of copies)? Or are you interested in sales from the start, in which case you would think hard about the sales potential of the music before you recorded or performed it?

But whether it's before or after the process of creating the product that you're thinking about sales, it's vital to ascertain the workability of the commercial idea before committing resources to a marketing effort. You have to know that the product has a chance in the marketplace— even if only a small chance.

With those considerations in mind, it's time for an overview of what happens in product development.

Defining the Target Audience. The workability of a given commercial venture depends on customers: Is there a group of people who will buy the product? If so, who are they? And how large is the group?

The group of people identified as the probable customers for the record is the *target audience*. The desired audience may be a mass audience. (The textbook terms for dealing with a mass audience are *market aggregation* and *undifferentiated marketing*.) Or the target audience may be only a portion of the mass audience. (The terms for this focus are *market segmentation* and *target marketing*.) Such a portion of the larger market may consist of people in a particular age bracket, people who live in a particular region, people of specific nationalities, people who fall into specific income brackets, people who subscribe to particular lifestyles, and so on.

For marketing purposes, it is essential that there be some sense of the audience for a given musical product. Ideally, the marketer should be able to define the audience precisely, in words, on paper. Otherwise the marketing effort is just a shot in the dark.

Determining the Product's Selling Points. Music speaks for itself, right? Sure—until you have to sell it. Then you need to take stock of the specific reasons why someone in the target audience would want to spend their precious money on it. Having a clear idea of the product's selling points—the matrix of qualities that the audience will find valuable and appealing—is vital for effective marketing. The selling points can be emphasized in the packaging, and used for sales "handles" and points to use in publicity and advertising.

When you begin to determine selling points, it's important to look beyond just the music. Music as a product is not just sound, and it's not even just music. It's also the performer and his or her personality and look; the lifestyle and philosophy expressed by the songs and stance of the artist. Music as a product can be a powerful symbol for the tastes and beliefs of a defined group of people.

Punk rock, for example, symbolized rebellion against the establishment, and against corporate rock in particular. Everything about punk rock's presentation, from ragged guitars to ripped T-shirts, underscored the symbolism. Those elements appealed primarily to listeners who imagined themselves as outside mainstream culture.

Successfully selling a product means having a handle on *all* its sales points, both overt (the music itself) and hidden (the underlying messages conveyed). The more you can define and communicate these aspects, the more accurately you'll be able to market the product to the correct audience.

In the case of a classical string quartet, for example, the *overt* selling points might be these: the group has won several prestigious awards; it performs adventurous new music; the members dress in outlandish style. The *hidden* selling point might be this: buying the group's recording will reinforce the customer's perception of himself as being culturally sophisticated and in tune with the avant-garde.

Differentiating the Product from Its Competition. Part of establishing a product's value involves setting it apart from the competition. Why would someone buy this jazz CD instead of another? What makes the product unique? Again, these are points that can be emphasized in both product packaging and promotion.

Packaging the Product. Having identified the product's audience and selling points to whatever extent possible, the marketer needs to answer the following question: Given the finished recording, what can be done to package it so that it appeals to the audience most likely to buy it?

The product packaging—the CD cover art, for example—can be designed to emphasize the qualities that target customers will find attractive. It can also be used to explicitly draw attention to the key selling points. The main design and selling points can be reused on ancillary material such as posters, retail display items, and souvenir merchandise. They can also be reinforced in advertising.

Visual appeal isn't the only factor in packaging, however. Other considerations are cost of production, speed of production, size and shape requirements for retail display, and legal requirements.

Pricing the Product. The price of a product obviously has important bearing on its sales success. A product may be priced so high that it is beyond the reach of the targeted customer. On the other hand, if it is priced too low, the seller may not earn a profit. And if its prices are different than those of similar competitive products, the sales effect could be very significant: increased sales with a lower-than-the-competition price; fewer sales with a higher-than-the-competition price. To cover all these bases, the seller has to balance three factors when setting a price:

the cost of production, the value of the product set by the customer, and the price of competitive products.

In music, this is made easier by the fact that pricing is relatively standardized: the top price of a new CD (as of this writing) is $17.99. The industry, collectively, has found this to be a workable price for covering costs and earning a profit; at the same time, it is a price that customers are willing to pay. So that for the music marketer, the focus in pricing will often be on keeping costs down to ensure maximum profit on the generally accepted price.

Distribution

Between the product and the customer lies the question of how to connect the two. The answer to that question is distribution.

It wouldn't do much good to know the audience if the marketer didn't then place the product in retail outlets that catered to that audience. It's an obvious point, but worth stating nonetheless: Sell the product in stores where people go to buy such products.

In the music field, this decision appears to be an easy one. Most record buyers buy records in large record stores. The process of getting records into those stores, however, is not quite as straightforward. Normally, the seller of a record must first secure the services of a distributor—a "middleman" whose job it is to serve as a one-stop for distribution to numerous retail outlets. The distributor buys from the seller at a discount off the retail price, and makes its money by selling to retailers at a higher price—a store wholesale price that allows the retailer to also make a profit.

The chain of entities involved in moving the product from the seller to the customer is called the *distribution channel*. Each part of the chain—the seller, the wholesaler, and the retailer—functions as a member of a team, and all stand to win when the team works well. There are a number of approaches to setting up distribution channels, and choosing the right ones—and the right channel members—is a crucial part of marketing.

If you are a one-person operation, or close to it, your approach to distribution may be to bypass the usual multi-member channels. You'll be setting up an order system through the Internet using e-mail and/or a toll-free phone number. You'll be visiting smaller music stores—possibly in person—to place CDs in their racks on consignment. You may be creating a brochure with an ordering coupon, which you will mail to names on a targeted mailing list obtained (by you) from an appropriate magazine, music organization, or commercial mailing list broker.

Music Promotion

An essential part of any marketing plan is a promotional strategy. Promotion boils down to informing the world about the product, persuading potential buyers of its value, and continually reinforcing public awareness of the artist and product. Without promotion, you could have all other components—product, distribution, and audience—in place or identified, and the enterprise would still go unnoticed by the public. In the world of music, promotion takes many forms, including live performance, radio play, television, free media coverage (publicity), and paid advertising.

Management of the Marketing Program

As pointed out previously, once the marketing program is in play, it can function as a well-oiled machine, with promotion and concerts fueling new record sales, and increased demand leading to more radio and television play, wider distribution, ever-expanding press coverage, and even more sales.

But the machine requires constant attention and fine-tuning. Changes in the market require changes in the marketing program. For example, if an artist's style of music goes out of fashion, there may be a need to adjust musical direction and to recast the tone and focus of promotion. Similarly, once a product is no longer "new," it will require a new set of tactics to ensure that it continues to generate sales. And finally, it may be that a product or artist is simply not catching on. The marketer has to have a sensitive hand on the pulse of the market to know when this is the case, and to accurately assess when to curtail active promotion and begin winding down the enterprise.

Management of the marketing program also means monitoring the incoming flow of money from the various revenue streams—that is, from retail sales, television use, movie use, and any other sources that have been tapped—and executing accounts payable to any subcontractors, vendors, and royalty participants. While in a large company it is the financial division that administers accounts receivable and accounts payable, the marketing people also monitor and scrutinize the sales figures. The numbers are the bottom line, the final indication of the success or failure of the product launch and marketing plan.

For a small company, this process may be hands-on and entirely do-it-yourself. As such, it can be an accounting nightmare, but think of it this way: if you're in the enviable position of administering accounts receivable for your up-and-coming music business, it's the best nightmare you may ever have.

With all these bases to cover, it's helpful to begin the process with a rough blueprint of elements that will shape the marketing plan and guide the overall program. It can serve as an ongoing point of reference— and can be revised at any time as needed. The following example outlines several of the items that can be included in such a blueprint.

PRODUCT MARKETING INFORMATION SHEET

Title of Product:

Name of Artist:

Format(s) of Product:

Price(s) of Product:

Brief Description of Product:

Targeted Audience:

List the main selling points of the product:

Describe what makes the product unique or different:

Where will the product primarily be sold?

List secondary market outlets (specialty stores and catalogs, direct mail, music clubs, special sales, and so on):

Describe the promotion, publicity, and/or advertising strategy:

The next chapters in this section provide more detail on how this chapter's marketing-program model can be used to make your music start bringing in money. The first order of business is to look at a basic music product—a piece of recorded music—and examine its role in the overall marketing scheme.

5

Defining the Basic Product and Its Audience

The most common way to sell music—apart from presenting live music in a concert or club setting—is to record it and distribute it in the form of a physical artifact.

Although new formats are continuously being devised, including digital files that can be transmitted across the Internet, the most widely accepted formats are still the compact disc (CD) and its older sibling the audiocassette. (The vinyl record, formerly the primary format, is now a little-used specialty item.) The great majority of potential customers purchase music in one of these formats, making the CD and cassette the primary revenue generators in the music market. Quite simply, they still provide the most effective means of reaching the largest number of customers. (Of total album sales in the United States as of fall 1997, according to *Billboard* magazine, 76.2 percent were compact discs, 23.5 percent were cassettes, and .2 percent were other formats, including vinyl.)

THE CORE PRODUCT

It's important to be aware of the difference between a product format and the core product.

On one level, a compact disc is a product. On another level it's simply a format for delivering a core product. The core product is, of course, music.

Music (as we'll frequently remind you in these pages) is a raw piece of information that can be formatted in different ways and marketed in different ways. (See Chapter 8 for a discussion of formats other than CDs and cassettes.) And music, as a product, has several different aspects. It consists of three components: (1) the performer, (2) the performance, and (3) the music composition.

The Performer

Performers appeal to audiences for their personalities, looks, and other characteristics. In a sense, the performer is the long-term product that marketers sell and promote, with records serving as short-term ways to generate income and build the career. Direct sale of the "performer" part of the product occurs through concert engagements, television and movie appearances, books, and any other context in which the performer as a personality is exposed to audiences.

Elvis Presley, as an example, was sold to the public through records, radio, television, and movies. Elvis, in that sense, was a product, and his records were by-products.

The Performance

Closely linked with the performer is the performance. The performance is the presentation of music by an individual artist or group. It is the audio expression of the performer's personality. People pay to hear a particular performer play music in a particular way. They like the sound of the voice, the style, the instrumentation, and other distinctive qualities. The performance, then, is a distinct product, and it can be exploited (used to generate income) in a number of ways: by being used on a CD, broadcast on the radio, presented in a movie or video, showcased in a commercial—the list goes on.

The Composition

The performer and performance are nothing, however, without the music composition or song. The song is a separate product all its own. It is intellectual property—a mental creation that earns money only when it is presented to the public in a performance, on a recording, or on paper. The song can be exploited in numerous ways: licensed to any number of different performers, licensed to producers of TV shows and movies, and sold as sheet music.

The Total Marketable Package

All of these components of the core product can be incorporated into CDs and tapes—the primary focus of most music marketing programs.

The question now is how to shape the marketing effort—starting with product development—so that the product will generate sales income and profits. The process will begin with an attempt to identify an audience and to find ways to make the product as attractive as possible to that audience.

THE ARTIST'S CHOICE: LEAVE THE MARKETING TO OTHERS, OR DO IT YOURSELF?

But first, a digression. Before embarking on frenzied pursuit of sales, bear in mind that if you are a musician, you may be standing at a major fork in your career road. There is a choice to be made between two different approaches to pursuing sales income (described in Chapter 1 as traditional and alternative approaches).

One way—the traditional way—is by getting signed to a contract with a record label and leaving the marketing to the label staff. In this case, your marketing job is to sell yourself to a record label so that you get signed, and then to cooperate with the marketing staff as they do their job. Your income, in this case, will be limited to your 10-to-15-percent royalty as a recording artist plus any royalties you're entitled to as a songwriter.

The second way to pursue sales income is to independently make and market your record. In this case, you'll be entitled to all sales profit, not just the 10-to-15-percent artist royalty plus mechanical (songwriter) income.

The benefit of the first approach—signing with an established record company—is that you'll be able to concentrate on your music and not have to concern yourself with the business side. In the negative column, you'll have a smaller stake in the sales income, while the record company will reap most of the financial rewards. But don't forget that with their seasoned marketing expertise, the label professionals may be able to sell more copies of a record than you would be able to as a fledgling marketer. Your 15 percent of the label's earnings could end up being greater than 100 percent of the earnings generated by a record you produced and marketed on your own.

On the other hand, one of the pluses of doing it all yourself is that the release will have your complete and undivided attention. It won't get lost or be overlooked amid a flurry of releases competing for your marketing attention—as happens with some established record companies. And, of course, you'll retain control over every facet of the enterprise, from creating the record to designing the album covers, press materials, and collateral.

But bear in mind that this seemingly momentous choice—signing with a label or doing it all yourself—may have already been made for you. Here's why: Today, the kind of new artist being sought by established labels is one who has built a strong local or regional following and has independently recorded an album that has generated sales and earned college radio play.

The process of getting signed to a record label has changed in recent years. At one time there was a reasonable chance of getting a demo tape heard if you sent it to a record company or music publisher. There was also a chance that label executives would sign an untested artist with the goal of developing him or her, over time, into a marketable performer.

Today, record companies are less likely to audition unsolicited tapes or to take a chance on an untested artist. Established companies are looking for artists who have already proven themselves in the marketplace.

Given that reality, chances are that one way or another you'll have to involve yourself actively in the marketing process—at least in the early stage of your career. So why not begin now?

CONVENTIONAL WISDOM

Signing with a major label is the next step after succeeding with an independent record.

Minneapolis-based Hüsker Dü successfully distributed albums on small labels. Then, in 1986, they signed with Warner Bros. Records, providing the band with access to broader distribution through Warner's corporate muscle.

UNCONVENTIONAL WISDOM

Sometimes it's better to remain independent.

Singer-songwriter Ani DiFranco continued to issue successful records on her own label, Righteous Babe, despite offers from major record companies. The hardcore band Fugazi did the same. Both enjoyed creative control of their music, and were free to market themselves as they saw fit.

ESTABLISHING THE PRODUCT'S MARKETABILITY

Marketing begins at the product development stage with an effort to determine the extent to which the product is actually saleable.

In some cases, as discussed in Chapter 4, this happens *before* the record is created, affecting the approach to creating the album or single.

For example, the singer Jewel was signed to Atlantic Records before she had released an album. The label's A&R representative, Jenny Price, saw in Jewel a performer whose strength was in winning over audiences in intimate live settings. Consequently, the record company made the decision to record an initial album that would emphasize this selling point.

"From the very beginning with Jewel we had an idea of how to very organically break her," Price told writer Bud Scoppa. "From the beginning of the recording process to the actual recording to the marketing plan to everything that came after—it all went along with that organic way we wanted to introduce her to the public....We wanted to make an honest and pure record with mainly just her and the guitar....The idea was to have people discover her as a live artist, which she is, so we decided to record the bulk of the record live...in San Diego at the Innerchange, this little coffeehouse where we'd actually found her."

If you are at the pre-recording stage of your enterprise, it would be well worth evaluating the market before proceeding. What you find out may have an impact on your recording decisions.

Whether you have a finished recording or are at the pre-recording stage, an essential part of establishing a product's marketability is ensuring that the product meets the following criteria:

- The music can be categorized for sales purposes.
- It has a targeted audience, and the potential audience is large enough to justify the cost—in money and effort—of producing and marketing the product.
- The product has selling points that can be articulated.
- The product can be differentiated from the competition.

Defining the Musical Category

It's important, for marketing purposes, to ascertain the musical category of your product. Is it country? Jazz? Classical? A mixture of several styles?

We can hear the artistes in the crowd protesting loudly: "Why all the labels and categories?" "The music speaks for itself. Let critics do the labeling." "If I could name my music, I'd have become a writer, not a musician."

The fact is, the marketing system depends on categories. Records are displayed in stores by category. If you don't let the record store know what kind of music you're selling, how will the retailer know which shelf to put it in?

Here's an exaggerated example: Your music is, say, a combination of classical composition, electric guitar sounds, and free improvisation, with some rock-like vocals thrown in. The artist in you decides to emphasize mystery in the packaging: the CD cover is completely black, with no text other than the artist name. The CDs are shipped to a store with little identifying information.

Where will the record store manager display the disc? In the classical section? In jazz? In rock? Or in a storage room, ready for shipping back to the distributor?

By labeling your music, even in the most general way, you're simply providing information that will help the retailer sell your product. And that's one of the goals of marketing.

If in doubt about where your music might fit in, go to the nearest entertainment superstore and look at how the music is categorized for shelving. One outlet used the following categories in 1998:

Pop, Rock, and Soul	Acid Jazz	Soundtracks
Hip-Hop	Oldies	Jazz
Electronica	Blues	Latin
Gothic	Country	New Age
Industrial	Folk	Reggae
Ambient	Gospel	World Music
Dance	Vocals (Pop)	Classical

Identifying the Audience

Identifying your audience, as precisely as possible, is a key step in the marketing process.

Professional music marketers have learned something about music audiences. Marketers of heavy metal records, for example, can identify the kinds of audiences most likely to buy their products. Marketers of new rock music know that their audience is mostly young, and perhaps youthfully rebellious. Marketers of classical music know that their core listenership has certain special characteristics.

The most successful marketers of products for targeted audiences have described knowing their audience so well that they feel they can almost reach out and touch them. Editors of a guitar magazine, for example, may know exactly who their readers are, because they have many of the same interests as the readers. They may know precisely the kinds of information that readers want, which makes them able to shape the magazine to precisely fit the readers' preferences (and which, in turn, may generate more sales).

Similarly, a band that has started out by building a local following has an excellent handle on its audience. The band has had extensive experience with direct feedback. They have literally touched their customers. They know who likes them and who doesn't. Thus they are in an excellent position to know the kind of "product" that fans will expect from them.

The band Phish, for example, maintains close ties with its audience through a newsletter, an official Web site, and a telephone hotline. Consequently, the Phish organization is able to accurately gauge the preferences of its listeners, and thus make artistic and business decisions precisely tailored to meet—or play off of—the fans' expectations.

Here's the rule: The more extensive the marketer's knowledge of target consumers' tastes and buying habits, the greater the ability of the marketer to make the product attractive to that target audience.

Of course, before pinpointing audiences' tastes and preferences, you have to figure out who your audience is.

How do you begin to identify a target audience? Start with the most obvious group: your family and friends. You can use these names as the first entries in a list you should assemble of core customers—people with whom you have a personal connection or who somehow indicate an interest in your music (we'll get into how they might indicate such interest a little later).

One-to-One Marketing. Over time, marketing as a science has increasingly emphasized the value of market segmentation (target marketing, or niche marketing) over undifferentiated marketing (mass marketing). The ultimate form of market segmentation is one-to-one marketing, where there is a direct one-to-one relationship between the seller and the customer. In one-to-one, the seller can learn precisely what the customer wants, and can customize the product to match the customer's need. This yields the most customer-satisfying product, and can lead to a long-term customer-seller bond, brand loyalty, and repeat sales.

The costs of this approach for a large producer have long been prohibitive. (It's cheaper and easier to develop one product with one marketing program for a large number of customers than to spend extra money and effort creating multiple products targeted at individuals.) But as a concept, it is valuable to bear in mind. It is also worthwhile to note that today the Internet is making one-to-one marketing more possible, because the World Wide Web's interactivity permits individual customers to submit detailed preferences to the manufacturer, and in some cases to specify customization of a product they wish to purchase. (An example of a customized music product is a CD made up of tracks individually chosen by the customer. SupersonicBoom!, an Internet-based company, offered this service to its customers.)

One-to-one marketing can be as simple as establishing some sort of direct communication or contact with customers. The value of this can clearly be seen in the realm of politics. During campaigns, politicians get out in crowds to shake hands with voters, and they do it for a good reason: a hand shaken is considered a vote taken. The direct contact establishes a personal bond, however fleeting. George Bush reportedly maintained a vast list of personal contacts—thousands of people he had met over the years—each of whom would receive, every year, a Christmas card signed by Bush. Bill Clinton, during his 1992 presidential campaign, became known for an uncanny ability to recognize (or appear to recognize) people he may have met only briefly years previously. It gave people a sense of intimacy and of connectedness with him; seeming armies of so-called FOBs (Friends of Bill) accompanied Clinton's rise to national prominence—and helped get him elected to the presidency.

How can you employ one-to-one marketing in your audience targeting? One way is to establish personal contact when you perform live. Go out of your way to meet people in the audience between sets. Shake hands. Ask people how they liked the music. And ask people to add their names and addresses to the mailing list that you should have set up near the main entrance to the venue. By taking these steps you are both identifying and building your audience base.

Mailing Lists. One of the most powerful tools for targeting audiences is the list of people who have indicated an interest in the kind of product you're selling. The names on the list can serve as a database of "likely prospects" to whom you can send product information, newsletters, questionnaires, coupons, and other marketing tools.

In music, your mailing list represents your core—make that *hardcore*—audience. You begin to assemble it, as mentioned previously, by listing your personal contacts. Then you bring the list to your live performances and ask interested audience members to sign it. Or you can put several blank name-and-address cards on all the club's tables, for customers to fill out. At the end of the night, you collect them; later you add the names to your ever-growing mailing list.

The table cards could also include questions about the customer's tastes and preferences, age, sex, number of records purchased in the past six months, and other matters. Examining this information will help you assemble a profile of the kinds of people who like your music.

Developing a customer profile—identifying commonalities in groups of people attracted to your music—will enable to you focus on that commonality in your advertising and promotion.

This kind of questionnaire is really an informal approach to market research. Sources of information about more formal market research methods are provided in this book's Appendix.

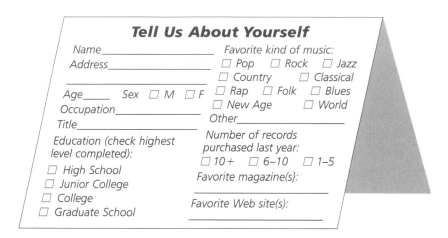

Tell Us About Yourself

Name_____

Address_____

_____

Age_____ Sex ☐ M ☐ F

Occupation_____

Title_____

Education (check highest level completed):

☐ High School
☐ Junior College
☐ College
☐ Graduate School

Favorite kind of music:

☐ Pop ☐ Rock ☐ Jazz
☐ Country ☐ Classical
☐ Rap ☐ Folk ☐ Blues
☐ New Age ☐ World

Other_____

Number of records purchased last year:

☐ 10+ ☐ 6–10 ☐ 1–5

Favorite magazine(s):
_____

Favorite Web site(s):
_____

Name-and-address table (tent) card to be filled out by club-goers at a live performance.

Researching Audiences of Music Similar to Yours. You'll need to sell the CD beyond the core group identified in your beginning mailing list. To accurately identify the wider audience for your music, so that you can effectively position the CD to reach that audience, you'll have to expand your research.

One approach to identifying your wider audience is to look at audiences that consume music similar to yours. Find out the characteristics of that audience, including age range, economic status, education level, geographical location, lifestyles, and cultural preferences. (Lifestyle factors are sometimes broken down into activities, interests, and opinions [AIO].)

Having identified the style of music you're working with, go to sources of information linked with that style: periodicals, record companies, and radio stations.

Look at magazines that deal with your type of music. Become familiar with them. Try to envision the readership by analyzing the tone and sophistication level of the articles, and by looking at the ads and imagining the people whom they are targeting. Are the ads appealing to young professionals with disposable income? To teenage girls? To find out more, you can call or write the magazine's advertising department and ask for a media kit. This gives the ad rates for the magazine, and supplies demographic information about the readership.

Similarly, you can request media kits from radio stations, which should include information about the audiences reached. Choose stations with formats that are appropriate for your music. Do this from your own knowledge and/or by checking such directories as the *Broadcasting and Cable Yearbook* and the *Gale Directory of Publications and Broadcast Media.* Some stations also maintain sites on the World Wide Web, where they provide information about the demographics of their listeners.

A good all-in-one source of information on U.S. radio stations and the kinds of music they play is Radio on the Web, located at www.gebbieinc.com/radintro.htm. (Gebbie is also the publisher of the hard-copy *All-in-One Media Directory.*)

Arbitron, a radio market research company, has a Web site at www.arbitron.com that provides basic demographic information on leading radio stations in the United States.

Two other sources of market information that deserve mention here are the following: MediaFinder, a Web-based library of media information that has listings of magazines, directories, mailing lists, and more (find it at www.mediafinder.com); and the Ultimate Band List, a more music-specific Web site with information on radio stations, record labels, magazines and e-zines, and record stores (its URL is www.ubl.com).

Estimating the Size of Your Audience (and Ballpark Sales Figures). In addition to researching the characteristics and locations of your targeted audience, you'll also want to begin estimating the size of the audience. There are several ways to ballpark this number.

Find out the circulations of the magazines that specialize in your kind of music. You can do this by requesting a media kit from each magazine's advertising department or by going to the library and checking such publications as the *SRDS Consumer Magazine Advertising Source,* the *National Directory of Magazines,* and the *Standard Periodical Directory.* Look up a specific magazine, and it should have the circulation count. (Make sure the directory is recent, or else you may be looking at outdated material.)

While you're at it, choose the magazine that most closely targets your market, and see if they will sell you their mailing (subscribers) list. (MediaFinder on the Web is a good source of information on music-related mailing lists.) Usually, you can buy mailing lists for around $75 per thousand names. This list can be invaluable. It consists of people who have demonstrated a strong interest in your kind of music, have spent money on it in the past, and are likely to spend money on it again in the future.

Research the sizes of audiences for radio stations that play your kind of music. You can do this by requesting the information from Arbitron, a company that specializes in radio and television market research (its phone number is 212-887-1300), or by looking in some of the sources mentioned in the previous section.

Past sales of specific records are also good indicators of the size of the market for your style of music. Choose an album similar in style to yours and find out what it sold. Since record companies don't ordinarily give out sales information to the public, you can find out how many copies a certain record sold by going to the local outlet of a nationwide record retail chain and asking.

If you know you'll be able to promote your record in a way that will cover all the audiences you've researched, you can consider the overall number you've assembled as the size of your targeted audience. (Don't add them all together: two different groups you've checked out—magazine readers and record buyers, for example—could consist of some of the same people.) If you'll only be able to promote within a limited geographic region due to money and staff constraints (as is typical with start-up ventures), reduce the estimated size of your audience accordingly.

Don't expect to sell to each and every individual in your targeted group. A rule of thumb in direct mail sales to a list of targeted customers is that you can expect from 1 to 10 percent of those people to make a purchase. Thus, if your estimated size of the target audience is 75,000, a reasonable sales expectation (assuming the customer group is effectively informed of the product) is 750 to 7,500 units.

Determining the Product's Selling Points

Once you have identified some common threads among the characteristics of your targeted audience, your task is to look for the product's selling points. These are aspects of the product that you feel will draw the interest of potential buyers. Essentially, you are answering the question, Why will these people buy this product?

Start with some of the obvious selling points. If the artist is a high-energy live performer known for drawing wild crowds, a selling point of the CD might be that it "captures all the energy of the live performances." For an artist known for writing sophisticated songs that appeal to an older, college-educated crowd, a selling point might be that the CD offers "more of the insightful, perceptive lyrics and heartfelt music for which [the artist] has been embraced by discerning listeners everywhere."

Here are some selling points from the real world: To sell Iggy Pop to a new generation of punk-rock fans, the sales point might be: "He's the Godfather of Punk, the original pioneer of extremism on stage, on disc, and in life." The band Asleep at the Wheel could be sold with the statement that "they have enjoyed 25 years of acclaim as the leading contemporary purveyors of western swing." The appeal of singer Shawn Colvin could be traced to her "expressive folk-pop vocals in the Joni Mitchell tradition." A selling point for Pat Metheny is that he's "a poll-winning guitarist whose compositions blend jazz improvisation, Brazilian rhythm, and rock textures."

After extracting the obvious selling points, look beneath the surface for the not-so-obvious ways the product might be attractive to the targeted audience. Remember that the musical product is only partly about music. It's also about lifestyle (recall the Beach Boys' sixties paeans to sun, surfing, and cars); social identification (Bruce Springsteen's evocation of working-class America); and various cultural factors (James Brown's "Say It Loud—I'm Black and I'm Proud").

The hidden selling point might be the way the product appeals to the customer's self-image—that is, self-image as a member of a particular culture, social group, or economic class.

Think back to the selling point cited above for the writer of "insightful, perceptive lyrics and heartfelt music...embraced by *discerning listeners* everywhere." The hidden selling point here is that purchasing the record will help the buyer to feel like a member of the club of sophisticated "discerning listeners."

Consider also the following example, from the world of high technology. In a 1997 newspaper ad, Apple Computer directly addressed its message "to the crazy ones": "Here's to the crazy ones. The misfits. The rebels. The troublemakers. The ones who see things differently. They're not fond of rules....Because they change things....We make tools for these kinds of people. Because while some see them as the crazy ones, we see genius."

In this case, Apple is apparently targeting its core market of creative professionals by appealing to their self-perception as unconventional and inventive. (The ad includes photos of Albert Einstein and Mahatma Gandhi, implying that Apple users are members of an elite group that includes these two.)

A rock group's "unseen" selling point might be that its grunginess and loudness will appeal to teenagers who want to rebel against their parents' old-fashioned tastes. A heavy-metal band's unseen selling point might be that its guitar screams appeal to aggression-spewing teen males. A singer-songwriter can be given an extra selling point by labeling him as "alternative," thus making him attractive to the masses of people who like to think of themselves as nonconformists. (One of the great marketing successes of the mid-1990s was the use of the word "alternative" to describe essentially conventional products so that they would sell to age groups noted for their rejection of so-called mainstream values.)

It's important to keep in mind the different ways in which the obvious, overt selling points and the hidden selling points will be used. The overt ones ("award-winning concert pianist") will often be explicitly stated in promotional materials. The hidden selling points will mostly be used as behind-the-scenes guidelines for linking the product—via visual and other means—with ideas, fashions, social groups, and activities embraced by targeted customers.

The following chart shows more examples of selling points matched to particular target groups.

Musical Product	Target Audience*	Audience Characteristics*	Product Selling Points
New-age piano music	Mature; counter-cultural	Domestic interest; health and spirituality focus	Unobtrusive; ambient; soothing
Young male pop group	Females aged 13–15	Concern with independence, appearance; onset of puberty	Musicians are attractive; songs are romantic
Punk rock with antisocial themes	Underemployed singles aged 19–24	Informal socializing; channeling anger at economic status	Angry, loud; provides role models
Electronic dance tracks	Young adults aged 19–24	Dance and club hopping; dating	Long, uptempo songs; good for dancing

* Audiences and characteristics are hypothetical examples.

After you have identified the key selling points, make sure you keep a record of them. You will be using them in product packaging, image building, advertising, and any other context that involves communicating with the target audience.

Differentiating the Product from Its Competition

In a print advertisement for the Brodsky Quartet, the classical string quartet that collaborated with Elvis Costello on the 1993 album *The Juliet Letters*, the headline labels the group as "The Garage Band of Classical Music."

What does this headline accomplish? Actually, three things at once: (1) it identifies the Brodsky Quartet as classical musicians, (2) it positions them as funkier than other classical music groups, and (3) it practically screams, "Hey, all you rock fans. This is the classical music group for you!" In essence, it sets the Brodsky apart from the usual, stereotypically buttoned-down classical group, and at the same time positions the Brodsky to appeal to an audience—in this case rock fans—outside the core classical market.

Figuring out how to do this—how to set your product apart from similar products—is another key task in the early phase of marketing.

Just as you peeled back the layers of the product to extract potent selling points, so should you examine the product for characteristics that make it unique.

The most obvious way to differentiate your product from the competition is to present some *evidence* that this music is the best—or near the best—of its kind. We say evidence because without it, any extravagant claims about the music may be perceived as hyperbole by the customer and viewed with distrust.

Commonly used evidence of superior quality includes listings of awards, excerpts from positive reviews, and endorsements by other musicians.

Another way to set the product apart is to focus on its difference from, rather than superiority to, similar works. Every musical product has its unique qualities: A band that generally fits into the punk rock mold may have an unmistakable undercurrent of surf music running through its sound. A jazz big band may have a leader who claims he was born on the planet Saturn. A classical pianist may have a special way she interprets Beethoven sonatas.

Your product, consisting of both music and performer, also has its unique qualities. Look for them.

After you have identified the key ways in which the product is different from the competition, keep a record of them. They may be used along with other selling points in product packaging and throughout the promotional campaign.

CHAPTER

6

Packaging the Product

"The most important marketing element is the packaging. It's the number one reason consumers make a purchase."

That's the majority opinion of a group of retailers surveyed by New Line Home Video, according to a marketing executive interviewed in *Billboard* magazine.

What do we mean by a product package? Obviously, we're talking about some sort of container in which a product is shipped and displayed. And more often than not, it's a container with visual design of some kind. Sounds simple enough. But actually, from a marketing perspective, packaging can amount to quite a bit more. In fact, it's a key part of the product development and marketing equation.

For illustration, look outside the music field for a moment. Take a batch of cornflakes. There are few things in life as vulnerable to crumbling, as indistinguishable from other similar products, and as plain boring to look at as a naked pile of cornflakes. Before they can be sold in a store carrying other brands of cornflakes, something has to be done to compensate for this sorry state of cornflake affairs (no offense to cornflake makers).

Here's some of what it takes: The flakes have to be packaged in a wax paper bag so they won't spoil, and then placed in a box so they won't be crushed during transport. The box has to be an appropriate size and shape to fit on the supermarket's cereal shelves. The label on the box has to be large and readable, so that people know what they're buying and who the manufacturer is. To meet legal requirements, information about nutrition and ingredients has to be printed somewhere on the package. A bar code has to be printed, so that the cereal box can be electronically scanned at the checkout counter.

And that's not all. Why would a customer choose this box of cornflakes over Brand X in the adjacent stack? Customers have to be given a reason. This can be done with the design, the "look," of the box. First, it's got to be visually attractive. Otherwise, the cornflake shopper may get the impression that the flakes themselves are not particularly attractive. Second, it has to be attractive to the right people. If the flakes are supposed to appeal to kids, the box should depict kid-friendly things like cartoon characters or their favorite heroes. If the flakes are aimed at adults, other images would be more appropriate. Finally, the design should in some way suggest the aspects of the flakes that make them special, different, and perhaps better than that Brand Z cereal down the aisle.

We're lingering here in the cornflakes world to emphasize that packaging involves a lot more than just popping a product into a container. Getting all the elements of packaging exactly right is a complex process that requires serious attention.

Just as with flake makers and their cornflakes, music manufacturers do not send their CDs naked into the world to fend for themselves. They give them protective clothing, identification, and attractive decoration.

THE PACKAGE AS MARKETING TOOL

From a marketing standpoint, the package is the image that the product presents to the outside world. It is the main means for communicating information about the product to potential buyers, and for emphasizing the aspects of the product that will appeal to the targeted audience. All of the marketing factors you have previously taken into account—from the product's selling points to the tastes of potential buyers—will inform your decisions about how best to package your CD or cassette.

In many ways the jacket of a music recording is a summation and a highly focused expression of the seller's (that is, your) beliefs about the nature of the music and how it should be presented in the marketplace.

That is why in the corporate world the jacket design process gets the concentrated attention of nearly all parties involved in the product launch, from the art director, the product manager, and the marketing manager to the recording artist (depending on the artist's clout). Such group efforts are famous for the conflicts that can arise between the parties. For example, the jacket designer's abstract rendering of the musical mood may run counter to the marketer's demand for simple, clear readability. But when the collaboration is functioning at a high level of professionalism, each party makes a constructive contribution of his or her expertise toward a common goal: that of creating a successful package that informs and attracts.

You, on the other hand, may not be in the position of working with a marketing staff, a staff art director, a product manager, or even a separate artist (after all, *you* may be the artist). What this means is that you'll have to oversee the creation of the design. As the head honcho in charge of product development, it's your responsibility to stay on top of everything that goes into designing an effective package.

KEY FACTORS IN PACKAGING DESIGN

As previously indicated, the aspects of the design that are meant to inform and attract are only part of the picture. The process of designing a package takes into account an entire range of factors, as follows:

- Physical requirements
- Information requirements
- Attractive, high-quality design
- Adaptable design
- Stylistically appropriate design
- Persuasive design
- Cost

Keeping in mind that for now you are working with the basic product configurations of CDs and cassettes, let's go through the key packaging factors one by one.

Physical Requirements

There are three main physical requirements for packaging: (1) the package must protect the product from damage during shipping and display and after purchase, (2) the shape and size of the package must be such that the product can be effectively displayed in the store, and (3) the packaging must permit clear identification of all components of the product.

Protection from Damage. Obviously, with all the handling of a typical CD prior to purchase, the packaging has to protect against smudging, scratching, and other kinds of damage. The standard packaging used for this purpose is as follows: for the compact disc, a plastic container commonly known as a *jewel box,* or sometimes just a cardboard box; for the cassette, a plastic container called a *Norelco box;* for a vinyl record (if chosen as a format), a paper or plastic dust sleeve and a cardboard or heavy-paper-stock jacket. All formats are covered with shrink-wrap.

Appropriate Shape and Size for Effective Display. The package has to easily fit in the standard racks and shelving units used by retailers. For this reason, packaging formats are standardized in the industry, and if you match your packaging to these standards, you will have no problems. Manufacturers and package producers will have this information.

Surfaces for Identification of All Product Components. The packaging has to provide areas for printing identification of all parts of the product.

In the case of CDs, this means including a *tray card*—a paper insert that fits under the plastic tray section of the jewel box and folds onto the spine (the thin edge of the box that is visible when CDs are stacked sideways). The tray card is meant to stay in position in the jewel box, and carries printed information about the CD. Compact disc packaging also includes a paper insert or booklet that slides into the front section of the jewel box and provides primary and detailed information about the music. Some of the information on the package may also be printed directly on the CD.

In the case of cassettes, packaging includes a printed insert called a *J-card*, which folds to fit inside the plastic container. Additional information is printed directly on the cassette shell (the plastic unit that houses the tape reels) or on a self-adhesive label applied to the shell. (See page 65.)

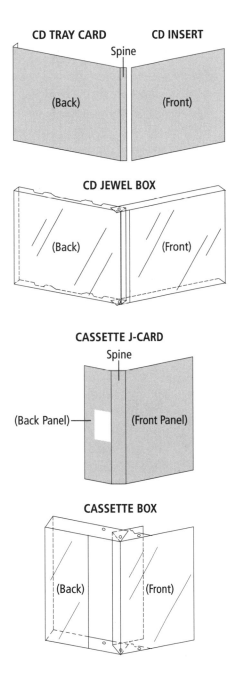

CD TRAY CARD   CD INSERT

Spine

(Back)   (Front)

CD JEWEL BOX

(Back)   (Front)

CASSETTE J-CARD

Spine

(Back Panel)   (Front Panel)

CASSETTE BOX

(Back)   (Front)

For vinyl records, the album jacket is used for primary information about the recording. Additional information, such as song lyrics, may be printed on the dust sleeve or on a separate paper insert that slides into the jacket. The record should have a paper label with identifying information.

Information Requirements

There's certain information that you need to include on the package, and other info that is optional, as follows:

Name of Artist and Title of Album. This information should ideally be printed on the front of the CD near the top, so that it will be readily visible to a customer flipping through a rack of products. This positioning is especially important for a new artist. For well-established or world-famous acts, there is quite a bit more leeway in the kinds of information to include and how visible you need to make it; sometimes a photograph is sufficient identification information.

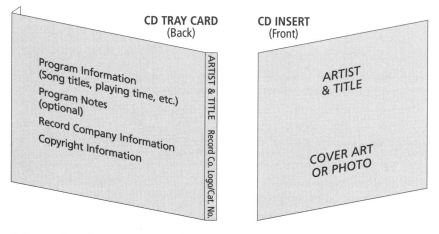

Information placement on packaging of a CD (above) and cassette (below).

Company Information. Display the name and address of the record company. (This is a legal requirement in most states.) And include the company logo, if you have one.

Trademark. Company names that are considered trademarked should include ™ after the name. If the trademark is registered with the U.S. Patent and Trademark Office, use ® instead.

For information about registering a trademark, contact the USPTO at 703-308-HELP or on the World Wide Web at www.uspto.gov.

Program Information. Provide a numbered list of tracks arranged in playing order. (For cassettes and records, supply separate lists for the different sides of the disc.) For each track, indicate the song title, writer(s), publisher(s), ASCAP or BMI affiliation (more about this on page 221), and playing time.

1. **Iggy Pop "The Passenger"** (4:42)
Courtesy of Virgin Creative Projects
Published by Bug Music (BMI)
Written by James Newell Jun Osterberg
and Denis Roderick Gardiner
2. **Lou Reed "Dirty Boulevard"** (3:32)
Courtesy of Warner Special Products
Published by WB Music Group (BMI)
Written by Lou Reed
3. **The Replacements "Alex Chilton"** (3:15)
Courtesy of Warner Special Products
Published by WB Music Corporation (ASCAP)
Written by P. Westerberg, T. Stinson, and C. Mars
4. **American Music Club "Johnny Mathis' Feet"** (3:42)
Courtesy of Warner Special Products
Published by I Failed In Life Music (BMI)
and Songs of Polygram International (BMI)
Written by Mark Eitzel

CONVENTIONAL WISDOM

You've got to include information about the tracks—their titles, playing times, and playing order—somewhere on the CD, cassette, or record package.

It's important to do this to make life easy for the listener who may want to skip around to different tracks—and for the deejay who might want to pick out tracks for radio airplay.

Copyright Information. Separate copyright notices must be provided for the compositions and for the recorded performance of the compositions. These indicate ownership. Copyright of a composition is indicated with the symbol © followed by the year of publication and the name of the owner (that is, the publisher); for example, © 1997 by John Doe Music, Inc. The performance copyright is the same idea, except that instead of a © you would use a ℗ symbol. The owner of the performance is generally the record company.

Copyright of the cover design should also be provided.

Catalog Number. Assign your album a unique number, to facilitate tracking throughout the ordering, distribution, and billing process.

Universal Product Code (UPC) and Bar Code. The Uniform Code Council (UCC) issues numerical company and product-configuration codes as a way to standardize computerized tracking of sales and inventory. On packaging, this number is expressed as a bar code: vertical bars of different widths representing the 12-digit number. At a store checkout counter, the bar code is scanned (via SoundScan technology), and a computer database is updated to reflect the sale. The information is usable by you, the retailer, and the distributor to accurately record sales, and by the SoundScan company to compile industrywide sales statistics.

While a bar code is not absolutely required, it is highly recommended, since so many retailers use the bar code scanning system.

The 12 digits of the UPC number represent the following information: The first six digits are your permanent company code, which you order from the Uniform Code Council, and which you will use on all products. The next four digits are numbers you choose for your specific product (for example, the Four Gone Conclusions' album *Ybo Arising*). The next digit is a standard configuration code that identifies the medium of the product (CD, audiocassette, videocassette, and so on). The UCC sends you a list of configuration codes at the same time it sends you your company code. The last digit is a "check character" that verifies the accuracy of the entire 12-digit code. It is supplied by the firm from whom you order the bar code.

Let's clarify that last point. When you schedule a product for manufacture, you have to order the bar code "art" for that product from a bar code supplier. (The UCC can recommend companies in your geographic location.) You provide that company with the UPC number containing your chosen four-digit product code and the configuration code. The bar code company then provides you with film of the bar code for incorporation into your package design.

In addition to including the bar code art on your product, you should print the UPC number itself on all sales materials, including price lists, invoices, and shipping labels. To avoid confusion with your separate catalog number, you might want to use the same digits for both the catalog number and the product portion of the UPC number.

Got all this? If not, the UCC will spell it out. You can contact the Uniform Code Council at 937-435-3870 or on the World Wide Web at www.uc-council.org. Their address is 8163 Old Yankee Street, Suite J, Dayton, Ohio 45458-1839. Be aware that there are special procedures for manufacturers of audio and video products. That's you.

Manufacturing Information. Indicate where the disc was manufactured, by country. For example: Manufactured in the U.S.A. (That's refreshingly straightforward, isn't it?)

Recording Technology Identification. You may use a standard code for identifying the technology used in preparing the recording. DDD means digital processing was used for all phases of production. ADD means analog technology was used for recording, and digital processing was used for both the mixing/editing and mastering phases. AAD means analog processes were used for both the recording and mixing/editing phases, and digital processing was used for mastering.

Ordering Information. You wouldn't want to pass up an opportunity to promote additional sales, would you? Be sure to provide the address, phone number, fax number, e-mail address, and/or Web address where a company catalog and other company products can be ordered. (And it wouldn't hurt to include an insert showing some of the additional products.)

The Spine. Since the spine is often the part of the package that is visible in a store's display, make sure the spine clearly shows the following information: artist name, title of album, company name, and catalog number.

The Disc or Cassette. The minimal information to print on the CD, cassette shell, or record label is the artist name and the title of the album. Beyond that basic information, you may include the following: the titles of songs, record company name, catalog number, side number or letter (not applicable to CDs), and copyright notices (both the © and the ℗). Additionally, you can include writer and publisher names, producer name, playing time, technical recording information (digital/analog information and the kind of noise reduction used), and just about any other information you'd like to include—as long as it will fit.

For CDs, you may opt to include the "compact disc" logo, which may be printed on the CD tray. One thing to bear in mind when considering any design to be printed directly on the CD: keep it *simple*. Silkscreening (the printing method used in this case) cannot adequately capture fine detail or subtle color treatments.

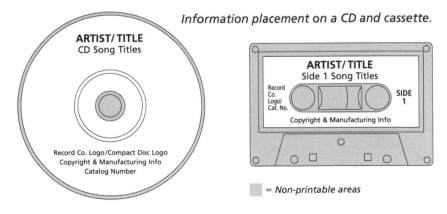

Information placement on a CD and cassette.

ARTIST/ TITLE
CD Song Titles

Record Co. Logo/Compact Disc Logo
Copyright & Manufacturing Info
Catalog Number

ARTIST/ TITLE
Side 1 Song Titles

Record Co. Logo/ Cat. No.

SIDE 1

Copyright & Manufacturing Info

= Non-printable areas

Program Notes. This is optional. Biographical information about a new artist is always worthwhile. In the case of a well-established performer, such facts wouldn't be needed since they're already common knowledge. Alternatively, or in addition, you could include complete lists of the contributing musicians and instruments played, lyrics of all the songs, and names of the producer and other supporting personnel.

And you don't have to stop there. This is your record, isn't it? Budget allowing (typesetting does cost money, after all), you could declare your undying gratitude to everyone from your Aunt Mildred to the cooks at the all-night greasy spoon near the recording studio. It's up to you. Just use a little bit of good judgment.

Attractive, High-Quality Design

A sixties rock star who shall remain nameless, and who had been out of the public eye for quite some time, staged a modest reappearance in the mid-1990s. He went on the road with a small band and performed a set of rootsy folk songs interspersed with a handful of his very well known classic hits. The music sounded terrific. He had also recorded a new CD, which you'd guess had the same high quality of his live sound. But there was a problem. The packaging of the CD was extremely sloppy. The photo used on the front insert was out of focus. The design looked as though it had been slapped together on a computer by an amateur after a few too many sleepless nights. It gave the impression that the music on the CD was equally substandard. In short, it made a good artist look bad.

The point is, whatever design approach you take, the packaging—illustration, photo, layout, typography, printing, and everything else—should be of the highest quality possible. It's the first impression you present to the public, and it should be a good one.

The way to ensure high quality is simple: hire a professional designer to create your graphics.

Adaptable Design

In addition to the album package, you may plan to create promotional material, either at the same time or at a later date. When creating a range of printed material, from album jackets and posters to bumper stickers and press kits, it's usually a good idea to use one design theme in all the elements. This helps to fortify the concept and image you want to present to the public. (Creating a single reusable design concept is especially important when you're trying to establish a strong brand identity, a concept that is discussed in detail later in this chapter.)

So for your CD and/or cassette release, make sure that the design used in the main product packaging is adaptable to other formats. Ideally it should look good at various sizes. (Keep in mind that if an image is very intricate at a large size, chances are the detail will get lost at a reduced size.) The main portion of the image should be usable in both horizontal and vertical formats. It also wouldn't hurt if the original color image also looked good in black and white, for those occasions when it is printed in a newspaper as part of an ad.

Adaptability is especially important when you're creating a logo, since you'll be using it on a wide range of materials. A logo is a symbol or image used to identify a commercial entity. When you meet with a designer to discuss the creation of a logo, have a list of every conceivable way it might be used, so that the designer doesn't go ahead and create something that looks good only on, say, a large, vertical, four-color poster.

Getting back, for a moment, to the issue of when to create additional material like posters, stickers, and promo matter, keep this point in mind: it's more cost-effective to produce and print all items at the same time.

A compact disc, a poster, and a brochure all using the same design.

Stylistically Appropriate Design

It wouldn't make much sense to create a high-tech, space-age cover design for a CD of Appalachian folk songs. Nor would it be wise to use an infantile depiction of cavorting cartoon animals for an album of Bartók string quartets (unless you knew that your audience had a taste for offbeat humor).

Make sure that the design of your package is appropriate for the music on the CD, as well as for your target audience. If the music is rustic, use a design that suggests rustic. If the music is gritty, urban rock and roll, go for an image that conveys urban grit. For humorous music, go with a visual idea that matches the concept of the humor.

A cover design that uses only type.

When you're operating on a tight budget— and most of us are—you may not be able to afford original artwork, custom photography, or lavish, full-color printing. Even so, you can convey a lot about style and mood using just typography and limited color. And stock photography can go a long way toward enlivening a design if original photos aren't an option.

When relying primarily on typography to get your message across, it is especially important to make sure the designer is absolutely clear about the idea and tone you wish to convey.

Persuasive Design

One step beyond appropriate design is *persuasive* design. Any package design that increases the customer's desire to buy the CD is effectively persuasive.

In the extreme, a persuasive design may be a design that panders. An album cover with a sexy girl in a bikini is meant to be persuasive. (Sex sells, knows the marketer, even though it may have nothing to do with the music.) A series of albums by the Ohio Players released in the 1970s all featured seductive photos of female models. The point was to get people to buy those records.

◀ *A CD cover using a sleek mechanical image is appropriate for the electronic sound of the band Fluke.*

Cartoonist R. Crumb's ▶ *design matches the old-time Americana that his band performs.*

◀ *Will Ackerman's soothing new-age guitar music is evoked by the spare design and abstract image on a 1998 CD.*

Original artwork © Michaela Harlow

A no-frills head shot ▶ *captures the raw energy of blues artist Shemekia Copeland.*

But there are plenty of other, perhaps less blatant, ways to attract consumers through package design. The idea is to use the design to emphasize the uniqueness and selling points of your music.

Here's an example of an album design that really worked, and helped sell the artist. The pop singer Cyndi Lauper first emerged in 1983. Her image was that of a slightly daffy, wildly garbed free spirit. The cover of her first solo album helped to build this image. The title was *She's So Unusual*. She was pictured on the jacket in a multicolored dress dancing alone against a background of vivid primary colors. On the back cover was a close-up shot of the soles of her shoes, which displayed sections of the Van Gogh painting *The Starry Night*. All of these images supported the idea of Lauper as effervescent and a little wacky— a persona that also came through in her music.

To use design in a persuasive way, start by recalling the music's selling points and unique qualities that you identified earlier in the marketing process. Then work with a designer to come up with visual ways to express those qualities. (Remember that you're not limited to pictures. You can always come right out and say it. Look at the title *She's So Unusual*.)

Here are some examples to get you thinking:

Artist/Album	Selling Point/Quality	Image
Bruce Springsteen, *Born in the U.S.A.*	Springsteen as American working-class hero	Springsteen in jeans and T-shirt in front of an American flag
Cocteau Twins, *Echoes in a Shallow Bay*	Atmospheric, mesmerizing music	Colorful, swirling abstract imagery
The The, *Infected*	Lyrics about urban decay, human suffering, and other dark topics	Abstract art of person screaming amid urban chaos
George Winston, *Forest*	"Rural folk piano" musical style	Simple photo of sunlit forest

A more subtle approach to persuasive design is to present images that are linked with the preferences of the targeted audience. For example, if the targeted audience is young professionals with disposable income, the artist might be depicted on the cover surrounded by the luxurious material rewards of financial success. This connects positively with the customer's economic aspirations, and establishes a bond between artist and customer. It can help to sell the record.

In the 1970s, singer Boz Scaggs departed from his blues roots and went for a sleeker, more polished, "uptown" sound. This was during the disco period, when urban glamour and glitzy nightlife were the rage. The cover of one of Scaggs' albums, 1980's *Middle Man*, seemed directly targeted at seekers of the upscale "good life": an urbane-looking, well-tanned Scaggs is shown in jacket and tie, lounging luxuriously with his head on a woman's elegantly stockinged leg.

The technique of appealing in a somewhat subliminal way to a target market's preferences and self-images is used mostly in advertising, and actually not too often in album covers. Here's why: record makers know that this approach can easily backfire. Audiences are often able to recognize a heavy-handed attempt at manipulation. As a result they may reject the artist permanently, even if they sense that the record marketers were the ones who were actually responsible.

On the other hand, there's nothing wrong with emphasizing values and lifestyles that are genuinely represented by the artist. If the artist subscribes to a school of thought or identifies with a particular social group, and expresses those affiliations on stage and disc, it's well worth communicating the fact to potential buyers who have similar preferences.

Cost

Another factor to take into account when creating packaging is cost. No surprise there. Generally, the more lavish and complicated the packaging, the more you'll have to spend.

The number of colors used in the design affects the cost: the more colors you use, the more expensive it will be to print. Also, special design elements like holograms and tin foil reflectors add significantly to the cost.

The more inserts you use, the more expensive it will be. And an insert with lots of folds or many pages will be more expensive than a simple one-page insert.

Any package formatting that departs from the standard formats will add to your cost. This would include odd-shaped record jackets, special printed slipcases for CDs, and custom boxes for sets of CDs or LPs.

You'll probably have a wish list of packaging and design preferences when you meet with the designer to plan. Talk it over with the designer to get an estimate of the cost, and be prepared to let go of your idea for a television-shaped album jacket stamped with a hologram of your smiling face.

SAMPLE COSTS OF PRODUCT PACKAGING*

COVER DESIGN AND PRODUCTION (for CD, cassette, and/or LP)

Design (CD, cassette, LP cover):	$500 to $9,000
Illustration or photography:	$500 to $7,000
Reuse† fee:	25–75% of standard initial fee for anticipated use

† Secondary use, as in advertising collateral

CD INSERT PRINTING
(Full-color outside panels, black and white on inside; includes separate tray card)

Quantity	1-Page	4-Page	8-Page	16-Page
500	$150	$250	$450	$525
1,000	200	300	500	575
3,000	450	550	700	1,000
5,000	600	650	1,000	1,250
10,000	1,000	1,200	1,800	2,250

CD MANUFACTURING (Includes jewel box, shrink wrap, and printing on disc)

Quantity	Initial Order	Reorder
500	$1,500	$800
1,000	1,800	1,500
3,000	4,000	3,750
5,000	5,500	5,000
10,000	10,000	9,800

CASSETTE J-CARD PRINTING (Full color)

Quantity	1-Panel	3-Panel	5-Panel
1,000	$60	$80	$100
3,000	180	240	300
5,000	300	400	500
10,000	600	800	1,000

CASSETTE MANUFACTURING

(Includes Norelco box, shrink wrap, and printing on cassette shell)

Quantity	Initial Order	Reorder
500	$650	$500
1,000	1,000	900
3,000	2,750	2,500
5,000	4,000	3,750
10,000	7,750	7,500

* All fees are averages as of 1997. Preparation of film for printing is a separate cost, and is handled either by a specialty service bureau or the printer. Contact vendors for current prices and fees.

VISUAL BRANDING

Effective packaging can help to build a brand identity, which in turn can build customer loyalty and help to ensure repeat sales over the long term. This is important if your product isn't just a one-shot deal and you're planning to release a string of records over time.

A *brand* is a collection of goods—such as a line of records—identifiable through a unique name, logo, and/or other design element. When that name and logo are printed on a product, the customer knows that the product is of a certain type or has a level of quality associated with previously purchased products of that brand. For example, buyers of Alligator Records products know they're buying the blues. Rounder Records customers know the company specializes in new folk music. Rhino Records listeners expect compilations of vintage tracks.

Branding can apply to an artist as much as to a company—more so, in fact, since audiences are more likely to build an attachment to an artist than to a label. (How many people do you know, for example, who will buy a CD simply because it is put out by Sony Records?)

The hope in creating a brand is to build *brand loyalty*. It works like this: The first several products issued under the brand name establish an identity (musical style or styles) and a level of quality. Succeeding products reinforce the identity and maintain the quality. Eventually, the customer begins to automatically link the brand with the style and the quality, and will respond positively to new products that carry the brand name and logo. The customer has developed brand loyalty.

A distinctive brand logo or design makes it easy for customers to identify, at a glance, any products marketed by the brand. (Think of the Rolling Stones' lips logo.) And, if the brand is well regarded, the logo gives the products a sales boost. In cases where you are trying out spin-off projects or new products that depart from your established identity, stamping them with the brand name and logo may help to get them accepted in a market where they would otherwise be viewed as unproven products of unknown origin. (The term for a new product category given the brand name of an existing category is *brand extension*.)

Establishing a visual brand identity doesn't necessarily mean all products have to look exactly the same. You can also use different designs that conform to an overall style. For instance, Windham Hill Records has often used photographs of landscapes or other natural subjects on its album jackets. Although the photos are different, the layouts are similar, giving all the albums an identifiably "Windham Hill" look.

Sometimes a logo alone, or another type of visual image, is sufficient to establish brand identity. The band Kiss used its distinctive logo on its various products. A rendering of a dancing, fiddling, or otherwise active skeleton shows up on a number of Grateful Dead album covers.

Establishing a visual brand identity is not a strict marketing requirement. In fact, if you're releasing a variety of very different products, it may not even be desirable. But just keep it in mind as another potentially useful ingredient in your marketing mix.

STEPS IN PACKAGE CREATION

Whether you're a marketer in a large company or doing everything yourself in a small firm, you'll be involved in some aspect of package development—even if just to put in your two cents about the design concept. Here's an outline of the creation process, from conception to physical production.

Deciding What Elements You Need (or Would Like)

At the outset, you need to envision your ideal set of package elements. Will you be producing only cassettes (the most portable and convenient of the available formats)? Do you want to press compact discs as well, even though they are more expensive? And what about vinyl records, which some people still prefer?

You then need to plan the package inserts. For CDs, you can choose to go with a cheap single-sheet insert and a tray card, or you might want to splurge and prepare a multi-page booklet. (Alternatively, you could go with a cardboard slipcase instead of a plastic jewel box with an insert.) For cassettes, you might opt for a simple single-panel J-card, or you may lean more toward something with multiple panels so you can print all the song lyrics or other information.

Then you'll think about color versus black-and-white art for the cover image—or perhaps a duotone photo, where the black-and-white photo is reproduced using black and some other color, to oftentimes eye-catching effect.

At the same time, you need to envision the style of design. For ideas, you can go to a number of art and photo sourcebooks. *American Illustration Showcase* is a good source of illustration styles, while *American Photography Showcase* serves the same purpose for photo images. An excellent book for showcasing a wide range of album design approaches is *The Ultimate Album Cover Album,* by Roger Dean and David Howells (Prentice Hall Press). It contains hundreds of album covers created over a 45-year period. Any of these books, and numerous others available in libraries and bookstores, can help to get your creative wheels turning. (Simply browsing in record stores can also be helpful.)

While thinking about the design style, make a decision about the kinds of information to include on the packaging. Simplicity could be the way to go. Or you might want to cram the package with text about the artist, the songs, the musicians, or other products available.

Choosing a Designer

You could save money by hiring your art-student friend to design the album cover. Or you could make sure you end up with a professional product by hiring an experienced pro. For reasons stated previously, going with a pro is the preferred route.

How do you find one? Start by checking the design credits on printed pieces you like and then calling the company that issued the printed piece and ask how to contact the artist. You might also check local chapters of the American Institute of Graphic Arts (AIGA) for information about its members. Additionally, you can get artist contact information—and view samples of their work—in such directories as *Creative Black Book, AIGA Annual,* and *Art Directors Annual* (though people listed in them may be beyond your budget). Lastly, you can check your local Yellow Pages and look under Promotional Design.

Once you have found a few names, set up appointments to meet with them and review their portfolios. Choose someone whose portfolio includes samples similar to what you're looking for in an album design. Consider also the designer's depth of experience in promotional design—especially music promotional design.

Before making a final decision, check some of the designer's references. Verify that they supplied satisfactory work, on time, and at the agreed-upon budget. (It's a plus if the artist is affiliated with a professional organization such as AIGA, since it indicates a high level of professionalism and adherence to established ethical standards.)

Initial Meeting with Designer

Once you have hired a designer, set up an initial meeting to discuss your design ideas.

In this meeting you'll lay out the types of elements you need designed, from CD folders to J-cards to LP covers. If a logo is to be created, now is the time to bring it up. The same is true of any collateral material—such as stickers, postcards, T-shirts, and posters—that you may wish to have designed at this time. Cover all the bases. There's nothing more annoying to a designer than spending time coming up with an idea only to find out later that you've decided to tack on a new element for which the idea won't work. Avoid this by having all your information available at the beginning of the design process.

Provide the designer with precise size specifications for all the elements included in the packaging. CD and cassette manufacturers will have information about all the proper dimensions along with specs for positioning of type. They will mail them to you on request, or you can sometimes download design templates from a manufacturer's Web site.

Clarify the form in which you would like to receive the finished design: electronic files on a removable storage medium such as a Zip or Jaz cartridge, camera-ready mechanicals, or final film. The form you choose will depend on the method of reproduction you will be using. The designer should consult with the vendor (whether the printer, T-shirt silk-screener, or other manufacturer) to determine the required medium or format.

In the initial meeting with the designer, you'll also discuss the budget. The designer, knowledgeable in the costs and technical aspects of graphic production, will be able to tell you what is and what isn't possible to achieve with your budget. He or she will also be able to suggest alternative approaches that would be affordable for you.

If possible, supply the designer with visual reference material. If you have a strong notion of the kind of design you'd like, provide examples of similar designs. Also, give the designer a sample of the music.

If you wish to include a specific photograph, provide it at this meeting. Also give the designer a copy of the text that you wish to have included. Provide it on a computer diskette if the designer will be using a computer-based process (nearly universally employed nowadays) rather than the traditional pasteup approach.

Don't forget to discuss the schedule. Set up deadlines for sketches, rough layouts, and delivery of final art.

Be sure to write down all terms of the agreement—including the schedule, form of delivery, fees, and rights granted (whether all rights to the art or only the rights for limited use)—in an official letter of agreement, a purchase order, or an "estimate and confirmation" form. An excellent source of standard contracts for graphic design work is the *Graphic Artists Guild Handbook: Pricing and Ethical Guidelines* (available from the Graphic Artists Guild at 212-463-7730).

Reviewing Rough Layouts and Sketches

At the next meeting, the designer will return with several options for the cover design, for your review and, hopefully, approval. The ideas will often be presented in the form of sketches. The presentation of the concept may include recommendations for illustration or photography (which might involve hiring a separate illustrator or photographer, whose work will be overseen by the designer) or possibly a simple type-only approach.

Important: if you approve a sketch or idea, make sure you really mean it. The second most annoying thing to a designer (actually, it's probably the first) is to proceed with a job based on your approval, only to have you change your mind later. That's why designers will charge you for partially completed work that you decide, after the fact, is "in the wrong direction." Therefore, think long and hard about that initial sketch. If you don't like it, it's expected at this stage that you ask for another. If you do like it, great. Let the designer know he or she has your full OK to go ahead and develop the idea.

Reviewing Photos and/or Illustrations

If you've agreed to use illustration or photography, review the recommended artist's portfolio before work begins, to make sure you like the general style and approach. After you've given the go-ahead, approvals of the art proceed as follows: In the case of photography, the designer will provide it to you for approval when it's done. For illustration, you'll approve roughs before giving the green light to rendering final art. The same caveat about sketches applies to this stage, only more so. Don't approve a finished piece of art and later decide it's "not quite right." If necessary, refine your vision further before moving forward and incurring more unnecessary costs.

Reviewing Layouts

Here's where the designer shows you the near-final layout, with all the items in place, from titles and text to images. You will either approve it or suggest changes, requiring a revised layout for your review.

If text changes are needed (for example, a song has been dropped from or added to the program), now is the time to provide the revised copy to the designer. (Do this as soon as possible, since any change in text has the potential for affecting the layout, and thus your costs.)

Completing the Production Phase

Following approval of the final layout the designer will prepare the final "output." This will be in the form of either an electronic file in a page-layout program such as QuarkXPress or Adobe PageMaker, or a physical board called a mechanical, which shows all the elements in their exact "camera-ready" positions, ready to be converted to film.

Preparation of Film

Your agreement with the designer may have encompassed creating film of the final art (from which the printing plate will be "burned" or etched). If so, all you have to do is get the film from the designer and ship it to the printer.

If the contract with the designer is only for final mechanicals, or electronic files on a removable storage medium, you'll have to arrange for film output yourself. Getting from the mechanical stage (the traditional method) to final film involves processes called stripping and color separation. Getting from electronic files (the currently favored method) to final film involves the following operations: image reproduction and manipulation (scanning, color correction, special effects, and proofs); digital prepress (trapping, registration, and film imposition); and output (final proofs and film).

Many printers (or even CD manufacturers) will provide these services as part of their package deal. If not, you'll need to find a separate "service bureau" to output the film. Don't go to a copy shop. Find a vendor that handles commercial art and performs digital prepress services professionally.

Checking Proofs

Whoever prepares the film—designer, service bureau, printer, or CD manufacturer—will provide you with a color proof of the art for your approval. This is your last chance to note mistakes. At this point, there should be no errors in the type or the position of the art.

Do pay special attention to the colors and "registration" of the images. (Images should be sharp and clean, with no double images. Blurring can result if the color separations that make up the final film are not precisely aligned in relation to each other.) If color fidelity is essential for your project, be sure to request a *color-accurate* proof.

Printing

Printing will be handled by a printing company or the CD manufacturer—your choice. If it is handled separately from the CD manufacturing, you will instruct the printer to ship the finished CD inserts and J-cards (and whatever else) to the manufacturer at the time they do the CD pressing and/or cassette duplication. The manufacturer will then assemble the finished packages and ship them to the location you designate.

Your designer may oversee the printing process, either by reviewing proofs or (if it's geographically feasible) via an on-site press check.

The Easy (and Cheapest) Way

Instead of having the separate parts of the packaging process handled by separate vendors, there is an easier and cheaper way. That is to hire a full-service CD manufacturer. Full-service companies specialize in producing the entire CD-cassette-LP package. You supply them with your finished master recording and your ideas for packaging, including all the text and any photos or art you wish to have included. The company will take care of package design, printing, CD and/or vinyl pressing, cassette duplication, package assembly, collateral design and printing, and shipping to your warehouse (or garage, as the case may be).

All the production steps outlined in the previous paragraphs will still occur, but the fact that they are being handled by a single supplier may make your life a whole lot easier.

Here's a cost comparison: If you were doing the CD design separately from the manufacturing, for a quantity of 5,000 you might pay over $8,000 (and that's with a low-cost designer). Alternatively, if you went with a full-service manufacturer, for a quantity of 5,000 you might pay $6,500.

Full-service manufacturing is cheaper, but you'll probably get a better design and more control over the process if you hire a reputable independent designer.

If you do decide to use a full-service supplier, research it very carefully, check their references, and review samples of their work.

CHAPTER

7

Pricing, Payouts, and Profits

At some point before setting a commercial recording project into motion, a few vital calculations have to be carried out. You need to look at your estimate of the audience size and translate it into a specific quantity of recordings that you expect to sell. This figure must then be factored in with a product price and your total costs to determine whether the enterprise will be sufficiently profitable. In other words, you have to translate your marketing plan into hard numbers.

PRICE

Watch out! It's easy to overlook the importance of the price factor in the profitability equation.

"What's to figure out?" you may be wondering. "The music industry's standard top retail price for a new compact disc is $17.99. I'll just go with that figure, get the product displayed in a store rack, and that'll be that."

If you were to take such an approach you'd be flying blind in the marketplace. This is not a wise idea in the crowded skies of the music industry. Plenty of your competitors are out there adjusting price points to achieve a variety of commercial ends, not the least of which is to make sure their products sell. You have to compete, and to do so you'll need to use all the tools available for fine-tuning a music marketing program. Pricing is one of the important ones.

To begin with, the price of your product is a "control" number you will use to calculate your profit after subtracting your costs. This calculation forces you to cast a cold eye on the grand marketing plans you've envisioned and view them strictly in terms of dollars and cents. Those numbers, you'll find, either work or they don't. And if they don't, you'll have to begin rethinking your plan.

Secondly, once you've worked out the numbers enough to get the marketing plan rolling, the price becomes an ongoing mechanism that can be adjusted upward or downward to increase short-term profits, to affect market penetration, or to influence market behavior in any number of other ways.

The Balancing Act of Pricing

In standard marketing theory, there are several factors that may be taken into account when you're trying to establish a product price as part of a profit calculation. The factors are sometimes referred to as the Three C's of product pricing: Cost, Competition, and Consumer.

Cost-Based Pricing. Calculating a price on the basis of cost means starting with what you've paid to produce the product and then establishing a price high enough to ensure a profit over and above your cost.

Competition-Based Pricing. Arriving at a price based on competition means looking at what competitors charge for your type of product and then setting your price to match or compete with it (to undercut it, for example). Your costs would be a secondary concern; if they were too high to permit your desired price, you would have to find a way to cut them.

Consumer- or Value-Based Pricing. Computing price on the basis of the consumer essentially means setting your price based on what the market will bear. If the consumer perceives a product as having a given dollar value, that's what you can charge for your product.

CONVENTIONAL WISDOM

Set your price as high as the market will bear.

If people will pay it, why not charge it? Ticket prices for concerts by world-famous performers are often set as high as possible, and customers still buy them.

BREAKING THE RULE

To make themselves available to all their fans, the hardcore band Fugazi refused to play in clubs that charged more than five dollars a ticket. What they lost in short-term sales revenue they gained in fan loyalty, which translated into a solid core customer base.

In the real world, working the price factor into your marketing equation means attempting to balance all of the above elements—cost, competition, and consumer. You have to base price on cost because the price has to be higher than the cost in order for you to make a profit. You have to be aware of the competition, because if your price is much higher than the competitors', their products may be chosen over yours. And finally, if your price is higher than consumers are willing to pay, then your product won't sell.

In the music business, to some extent, prices are standardized. (As of this writing, top prices for new CDs are $17.99.) So your balancing act will focus mainly on controlling costs and, as will be discussed, balancing cost with the estimated number of records you expect to sell and the level of profit you wish to achieve. But the place to begin "running the numbers" is most often in the area of your costs. Let's go there now.

COST

To figure out if you're going to make any money on a recording project, you have to look at what it will cost. Once you know that, you can determine how many copies of your record you will have to sell at a given price in order to *break even* (earn back all your expenditures). If that number of copies is more than you think you could reasonably sell, then you'll have to review your costs with an eye to making them lower. Either that, or raise your price. But raising the price might mean fewer people will buy the record. (Welcome to the real world of trying to make the numbers work!)

While providing specific dollar figures for the cost of certain items is beyond the scope of this book (and would probably be out of date by the time you read this), it's worthwhile to take a look at a breakdown of what you'll be spending on a project. Costs fall into five main categories: recording costs, packaging costs, manufacturing costs, promotion costs, and royalties.

These cost breakdowns are primarily for people involved or interested in the total manufacturing process. The rest of you can skip the next discussion and go right to the section on "Competition" (found on page 90).

Recording Costs

Recording costs aren't limited to the hourly costs of booking a studio. They include a range of items, which will vary considerably depending on how you approach the recording process.

Studio Time. The cost of using a professional recording studio can range from $35 an hour to $300 an hour. So that if you're recording a full album of, say, 10 songs and it takes you 15 hours a song (150 hours for all 10 songs), you're looking at a bill of $5,250 on the low end to $45,000 at the upper level.

Now, you may be the kind of hands-on pro who owns a project studio, capable of outputting broadcast-quality master recordings. If so, you've eliminated the need to pay for studio time for the individual recording project. (The cost of equipment is an expenditure, of course. But that cost can be amortized—spread out—over a number of projects for a period of years.)

Musicians. The cost of musicians depends on a number of factors. Your musicians may be band members or close friends who are willing to donate their time as an investment in the ultimate success of the record. In that case, there might be zero payment for the recording time. Instead, they would be given a percentage of the artist royalty, to be paid when albums sell. (Similarly, you may be the *only* musician, if you're one of those do-it-all types who can arrange, sing, play several instruments, and work out additional instrumental parts on a sampling synthesizer. In this case, obviously, no musician fee is paid.)

An alternative is to pay musicians hourly. The fee would depend on your budget, and on whether or not the musicians were members of the musicians' union (American Federation of Musicians, or AFM). If not working with union players, you could pay a low-ball hourly wage of, say, $25 an hour. If working with union musicians, you would have to pay union scale, which is around $100 per hour. ("Name" musicians can command up to triple scale, or around $300 an hour.)

If you estimate five hours of recording basic tracks for each of the 10 songs, you'd have a total of 50 hours for basic-track recording of, say, four musicians (drums, bass, keyboard, guitar). That would add up to 200 payable hours. Then figure five additional hours per song for overdubs, probably recorded by one musician at a time. Total overdub hours payable would be 50. Your total musician payable hours would be 250. At $25 an hour, your bill would be $6,250. At union scale, it would be $25,000.

An alternative to hourly payments would be a set fee for the entire job for each musician, depending on the extent of contribution.

Producer. The producer is the person who oversees and directs the recording and makes sure the final product is not only professional-sounding but the best possible performance that can be eked out of the music, the players, and the studio. If this person is you, your cost will be zero. If you choose to work with an outside producer, your cost could be anywhere from $200 per song (a total of $2,000 for 10 songs) or a low-end hourly rate of $30 ($4,500 for 150 hours) to a higher $1,000-per-song rate ($10,000 for the entire 10-song project). As we'll later see, some producers are paid via royalty. And at the very high end, they can earn upwards of $50,000 per album.

Engineer. For the person who operates the recording console and takes care of all the technical aspects of getting the music on tape, expect to pay a low-end figure of $25 an hour ($3,750 for the 150-hour project). More experienced engineers command $50 an hour and up. An alternative approach is to pay a flat fee for the entire project. If you are the engineer, again, your cost is nothing.

Tape. For a full album's worth of songs, you may need three rolls of 24-track tape (about $500 total) plus quarter-inch tape for two-track mixdown (around $25) along with numerous cassettes for work copies (say 10 cassettes, for a total of $50).

Now that we're in the digital world, other types of storage media are DATs (digital audiotapes), Jaz cartridges, and computer internal and external hard drives. For purposes of the present general budget calculation, however, we'll use only the costs of analog storage media (that is, tape).

Mastering. The final polishing and tweaking of the finished tape to prepare it for replication is called *mastering*. It includes evening-out the audio levels and tone and sonically "sweetening" the tracks. A ballpark fee for mastering an entire album would be $600 to $2,400. For purposes of our present calculations, we'll assume mastering costs are included in recording studio costs (although mastering is often done by a separate specialist).

TOTAL RECORDING COSTS

Item	Low End	Midrange	High End
Studio Time	0	$7,200 ($50/hr.)	$37,500 ($250/hr.)
Musicians	0	6,250	25,000
Producer	0	2,000	10,000
Engineer	0	1,500	7,500
Tape	600	600	600
TOTALS	**$600**	**$17,550**	**$80,600**

Packaging Costs

As discussed in Chapter 6, packaging costs vary depending on the designer fee, type of design used, lavishness of the production, and quantity of packages produced.

A low fee for a design would be $500. What you'd get would be a very basic, type-only treatment—no photos or illustrations. On the higher end, you might pay $2,000 for the services of a graphic designer plus $4,000 for an original photograph or piece of art.

Printing cost will depend on the quantity of units to be printed, the number of colors (black and white, two colors, or full color), and the complexity of the element (single CD insert versus six-page booklet, for example).

The cost of digital prepress and film output will often be separate. Because such costs vary widely depending on the specifics of the job, we won't list them here. Just be aware that it's another cost you'll be incurring, either through the printer or through a separate service bureau.

Let's say you're planning to press 10,000 CDs and 10,000 cassettes, based on your estimate of the size of your market.

On a bare-bones budget, you would opt for black-and white printing, a one-page insert and a tray card for your CD, and a one-panel J-card for your cassette. For the CDs, your cost could be around $600; for cassette, approximately $350.

If you were to spend more, you might opt for two-color printing, a four-page insert and a tray card for your CD, and a three-panel J-card for your cassette. In this case, your CD cost could be around $1,000, and your cassette approximately $650.

On the high end, you might go for full-color printing, an eight-page brochure for your CD, and a five-panel J-card for your cassette. Here, your cost might run $1,800 for the CD and $1,200 for the cassette.

TOTAL PACKAGING COSTS

Item	Low End	Midrange	High End
Design	$500	$2,000	$6,000
Printing of CD Insert and Tray Card	600 (b&w, 1-page)	1,000 (2-color, 4-page)	1,800 (color, 8-page)
Printing of Cassette J-Card	350 (b&w, 1-panel)	650 (2-color, 3-panel)	1,200 (color, 5-panel)
TOTALS	**$1,450**	**$3,650**	**$9,000**

Manufacturing Costs

The cost of manufacturing compact discs is relatively standard through-out the industry. For 10,000, you can expect to pay around $10,000. Cassette manufacturing cost will depend on the quality and length of the tape. Let's assume you're opting for very good (chrome-plus) but not top-grade tape. Your cost for 10,000 would be in the range of $8,000.

Promotion Costs

The topic of promotion is discussed in detail in Chapter 11. But for pur-poses of analyzing overall costs in the context of profit calculations, promotion expenses need to be summarized here. (Bear in mind that all dollar figures are rough estimates, and that actual figures will de-pend upon the suppliers that you choose.)

Press Kits. The press kit will be your primary promotional device. It ordinarily contains a minimum of the following: a folder, a photo, a biography of the artist, a fact sheet about the album release, a clipping of a newspaper or magazine article about the artist (if available), and, in most cases, a copy of the CD or cassette. (For details about press kits, see page 152.)

A low-budget presentation might include 100 sets, each with a folder without a printed logo ($150 for 100); a black-and-white photo-graph ($100 for the shoot, $100 for duplicates); a bio ($100 for writing); and clippings and a fact sheet. Add about $25 for 100 photocopies of the bio, clipping, and fact sheet.

With a middling budget, you might go for 500 press kits, each with a folder imprinted with a logo ($500, plus $150 logo design fee); a more expensive photo ($200 for the shoot, $450 for dupes); a bio by a more established writer ($200); and clippings and a fact sheet. Photo-copying would add about $120.

A high-budget press kit mailing might yield 1,000 copies of the following: a folder imprinted with a more expensive logo design ($850, plus $500 for the logo design); a yet-more-expensive photograph ($300 for the shoot, $850 for duplicates); a biography by a well-known writer ($300); and clippings and a fact sheet. Photocopies would cost approx-imately $240.

Collateral. Collateral material might include posters, flyers, promotional postcards, and bumper stickers.

A low-budget approach might involve printing 500 black-and-white flyers ($300) and postcards ($150).

On the more expensive side, you might opt for 1,000 units of each of the following: full-color 18-by-24-inch poster ($1,000), two-color flyer ($500), two-color postcard ($400), and two-color bumper sticker ($450).

On a high budget, you could choose to print 5,000 units of a full-color 24-by-37-inch poster ($3,500) and full-color flyer ($1,200), postcard ($2,500), and bumper sticker ($1,000).

Stationery. Whatever the budget, professional-looking stationery will be a necessity. The stationery set will include a main sheet with your letterhead, a blank second sheet, an envelope, and a business card. The whole package should cost around $550 for 1,000.

Newsletter. A newsletter sent periodically to people on your mailing list is a good way to keep in touch with your core audience. A simple two-sided sheet is all you really need. The cost of design might run about $150 per issue. On a tight budget you could either not do a newsletter at all or, instead, manually print out 500 copies on a laser printer for the cost of a ream of heavy-stock paper (about $18). For more money you could have 1,000 copies professionally printed ($350). On a higher budget you might opt for 5,000 copies, professionally printed ($950). When you calculate the cost, make sure to factor in that you'll be spending this money periodically—that is, each time you publish an issue of the newsletter. For now, let's assume one newsletter connected with the album release.

Mailing Lists. As previously discussed, mailing lists are vital components of your marketing plan. Lists of media and music industry contacts can be assembled by you for the cost of your time and energy. Customer mailing lists, on the other hand, can be rented (in the form of mailing labels) for about $75 for 1,000 names. If you're really pushing a direct mail campaign, you might opt for 5,000 names, at a fee of roughly $375.

Mailing Costs. Press kit mailing costs will run roughly as follows: $200 for 100 envelopes (at 50¢ each) plus postage (around $1.50 per package); $950 for 500 envelopes plus postage; $1,800 for 1,000 envelopes plus postage. These postage costs assume you'll be including a cassette in each press kit.

Postage will be an ongoing cost for mailing newsletters, flyers, and other material. For now, we'll assume $200 for a medium-budget promotion campaign, and $1,000 for big-budget.

Record Promotion. Initially, the cost of record promotion will be included in the press kit budget. When your marketing plan begins to pick up steam and the record appears to be attracting attention, you may want to hire an independent promotion firm. A fee of $1,500 per month is not unusual for this service. Let's say you'll hire a firm for one month if you are on a medium budget, and three months if you have more money to spend. (Really high-end independent record promoters can charge as much as $50,000 per single that they promote.)

Publicity Campaign. As your marketing campaign takes hold, you also may want to hire an independent publicist. Fees can range from $200 a week to $1,500 per month and more. On a limited budget, you might utilize the services of a publicist for a month. For a more concerted PR effort, a three-month commitment would be an option.

Advertising. Advertising is expensive. On a bare-bones budget, you may be doing none at all. For purposes of this cost calculation, we will set aside advertising and assume that it will be an option if there proves to be leeway in the overall budget.

Tour Support. To ensure that the recording artist builds an audience and thus helps to increase sales of a record, the record label will often provide dollars for tour support. Amounts vary widely. Let's assume that for a medium-budget project the amount will be $15,000, and for a higher budget, $30,000. (Bear in mind that costs will include hotels, travel, food, equipment, support staff, and other items depending upon the level of the act and the size of the tour.)

TOTAL PROMOTION COSTS

Item	Low End	Midrange	High End
Press Kit	$475 (100)	$1,620 (500)	$3,040 (1,000)
Collateral	450	2,350	8,200
Stationery	550	550	550
Newsletter	——	500	1,100
Mailing Lists	——	75	375
Mail/Postage	200	1,150	2,800
Record Promotion	——	1,500	4,500
Professional PR	——	1,500	4,500
Tour Support	——	15,000	30,000
TOTALS	**$1,675**	**$24,245**	**$55,065**

Royalty Costs

Royalties are percentages of sales dollars, or fixed fees, payable to certain participants in the project. They are monies that are earned at the point of either sales or distribution, depending upon the recipient. You will need to account for royalty payments as a deduction from estimated sales income. For retail sales of recordings, two categories of royalties come into play: royalties paid to the recording artist, and royalties paid to songwriters and publishers (mechanical royalties).

Artist Royalties. If you, the record company owner, are also the recording artist, outgoing payments of artist royalties will be zero. All profits go directly into your pocket. If, on the other hand, you are marketing an album recorded by a separate artist, you will be paying them a royalty on each copy of the record sold. A portion of the expected royalty is generally paid up-front to the artist in the form of an advance. Once the record begins to sell, the artist is paid no further royalties until the advance is *recouped*—that is, paid back to the record company (you) out of royalties earned on actual sales. After the advance is fully recouped, the artist is sent royalty checks for any additional sales.

For simplicity's sake, let's assume that for your recording project the artist's royalty rate is an even 10 percent of the suggested retail price. (In the more complex real world, percentages vary depending on the type of sale, as we'll see later.)

Mechanical Royalties. If you are recording songs by writers other than yourself, you will need to obtain what is called a *mechanical license* to use those songs. This license, obtainable through the Harry Fox Agency (more about which is on page 218) or from the music publisher, calls for payment of royalties by you for each copyrighted song you use on the album. Payment will be made to the Harry Fox Agency, who will distribute the payment to the publishers. (If the publisher is not a Harry Fox affiliate, you'll pay the publisher directly.) The current royalty rate is 7.1¢ per song or 1.35¢ per minute of playing time, whichever is greater, per record, tape, or CD made and distributed.

Note the word *distributed* rather than *sold*. While recording artist royalties are paid for records sold, mechanical royalties are paid for records distributed, *whether or not they sell through.* (This could mean that you distribute 10,000 copies, none of which ultimately sell. Yet you'd still have to pay mechanical royalties on those 10,000 copies.)

For purposes of our upcoming calculations, we're going to assume that half the songs on your proposed recording project are original (written by you), while five others are owned by other writers and publishers and will require that you pay mechanical royalties. The royalty you'll have to pay for each record distributed will be 36¢ (five songs multiplied by 7.1¢, rounded off). Got that? There's more explanation coming up soon.

The sum total of all your costs can serve as the basis for deciding on a retail price. If, for example, your cost works out to $5.00 per CD (including royalties), you'd want to set a price high enough so that you'd earn a profit over and above that $5.00. (And remember, the money you'll actually *receive* for the sale will be the distributor wholesale price—approximately 50 percent of whatever you set as the retail price. More about this in Chapter 9.)

COMPETITION

Whatever price you eventually come up with, it will have to be within the ballpark of standard pricing within the industry.

Currently (as of 1998), the standard top retail price for a new CD is $17.99. But a visit to your local record store will reveal that price points cover a range. There are "mid-priced" CDs, set at around $11.99, and "budget" CDs selling for $9.99 and lower.

For cassettes, the top price is currently $10.99. Cassette prices also vary, and can range from a $7.99 mid-price down to a budget price of $4.99 and lower.

Setting your price in relation to the industry standard means doing one of three things: setting it lower than (underselling) the standard price to potentially make the product more attractive; setting it higher than standard, perhaps to achieve higher profit while knowing that the customer will compare it to other prices; or simply meeting the standard.

CONSUMER

Whatever the price you choose, it will also have to be within the range of what consumers—your customers—are willing to pay. If a record has been on the market for some time and sales have begun to dip, it may be that customers will now buy the record only at a lower price. On the other hand, a recording artist with a fiercely loyal cult following may be able to command a relatively high price for a new album release. Gauging customer reaction to product pricing means having an intimate knowledge of the target audience and its relationship to the artist. (For example, an artist known for keeping prices low may lose core customers if he or she shifts policy and begins to charge top dollar for new products.)

POPULAR PERCEPTION

The lower the price, the more attractive the product will be to the customer.

The conventional wisdom is that if you lower the price of a product, it'll sell faster.

ALTERNATE REALITY

Sometimes a higher price implies *better*. The buyer may feel that if the record costs so much, it must be good. Related to this is the technique of *market skimming,* where the manufacturer initially sets the price high to earn back immediate cash, knowing that core customers will pay the high price for the privilege of owning the record as soon as possible. The seller is figuratively "skimming the cream" off the top of the customer base.

CALCULATING PROFITABILITY

It's time to take a close look at the kind of juggling that goes on when you try to balance the cost, quantity, and price of a record release (while keeping in mind the competition and the consumer) to make sure that you'll be able to achieve marketing and sales objectives.

We'll assume for the moment that the objective is simply to sell as many copies of the record as possible, as soon as possible, and at the highest price possible. (There are other types of marketing objectives, but we'll save discussion of those for later in the chapter.)

Remember that in the world of big-time record companies, the marketing person would not ordinarily be the one performing these calculations. In a small record label, however, where the owner may also be the marketing person (and the A&R director, product manager, CFO, receptionist, and coffee runner), this kind of number crunching would be part of the job. Either way—whether large operation or small mom-and-pop—it's helpful to be aware of this process. (But if you'd rather not clutter your mind with such details, feel free to skip ahead to "Additional Factors Affecting Price," on page 99.)

The essential purpose of the calculation is to make sure that expenditures and projected income balance out in such a way that there is a reasonable chance for the enterprise to achieve profitability (or at least stay within the realm of fiscal sanity).

Bear in mind that the components of any one project will be unique. The real-world calculations you'll apply to an actual project will undoubtedly differ in their specifics (recording costs, for example) from the ones presented here. Use the following example only as a general model of the kind of thinking that goes into "running the numbers."

Running the Basic Numbers

Here we go. We're assuming that you've found a promising recording artist whom you will have record five of your songs and five songs by other writers. On the basis of research, you have estimated that you'll be able to sell 20,000 copies of the record. (Don't forget it's an estimate only. See "Reality Check" on page 95.) Of your estimated 20,000 copies, you figure 10,000 will be compact discs and 10,000 will be cassettes. (In today's market, more CDs are sold than cassettes. But to simplify this discussion of calculating profits, we'll leave the numbers even.)

You'll start with the idea of charging the standard top price for each format: $17.99 for the CD; $10.99 for the cassette. (Starting this way means you're taking a competition-based approach—and a value-based approach, since you presume that customers will pay these prices.) For simplicity, we'll round off the CD and cassette prices to $18.00 and $11.00, respectively.

To calculate total receipts generated by sales of the full 20,000, you'll multiply $18.00 by 10,000 (CDs) and $11.00 by 10,000 (cassettes) and add them together. Your total would be $290,000.

But wait! You won't be selling at the full retail price. You'll be selling in bulk to a distributor at a *wholesale* price, which will be roughly 50 percent less than the retail price. (Although we're using 50 percent in this example, in the real world the amount depends on what you're able to negotiate—which is usually between 40 and 65 percent. More on this in Chapter 9.)

Let's try again, using wholesale prices. For CDs, you figure the wholesale price at $9.00 (that's $18.00 minus 50 percent). For cassettes, you'll get $5.50 ($11.00 minus 50 percent). Selling 10,000 of each will earn you $145,000.

Hold on, though. You will probably be giving away at least 500 copies free. (This is a low figure, but we'll use it for this calculation.) They'll be supplied to distributors and included in press kits you send to radio stations, reviewers, and what-have-you. So you need to subtract $3,625 (the rounded-off total sales income for 500 CDs and cassettes, which you will not be receiving) from $145,000. The remaining amount is $141,375.

Right about now you're thinking that $141,375 is not too shabby a return. True, but it's still not your final income. In fact, you won't know what you'll really earn until you subtract all your other costs.

Let's start by subtracting royalties. You've already figured on an artist royalty of 10 percent of the suggested retail list price. For a CD, that will be $1.80 ($17.99 × 10%). For a cassette, the royalty will be $1.10 ($10.99 × 10%). The total artist royalties due, if you sell out all 19,500 copies (artist royalties are not payable on those 500 free copies), will be roughly $17,550 for CDs (9,750 copies at $1.80 royalty per copy) and $10,725 for cassettes (9,750 times $1.10). The total artist royalties payable, then, will be $28,275.

Do the math: Sales receipts of $141,375 minus artist royalties of $28,275 equals $113,100.

Now you have to subtract mechanical royalties—the money you have to pay the Harry Fox Agency for the use of those five non-original songs. Remember that the calculation was 36¢ for each unit that you distribute (7.1¢ per song times five songs). On 20,000 units (500 freebies are considered "distributed" by Harry Fox, although many labels reportedly disagree), the full amount is $7,200. Subtract that from your ever-dwindling sales dollars and you're now down to $105,900 (that's $113,100 minus $7,200).

What about all the other costs: recording, packaging, and promotion? You need to subtract them, too. Let's assume you've planned on moderate expenditures for production and promo. Using dollar figures from the charts shown earlier in the chapter, you come up with these figures:

Recording Cost:	$17,550
Packaging Cost:	3,650
Manufacturing Cost:	18,000 ($10,000 for CDs plus $8,000 for cassettes)
Promotion Cost:	24,245
TOTAL:	**$63,445**

(For the sake of simplifying our example, we're not going to break out the separate CD and cassette packaging costs, though real-world accounting would require doing so. For now, you just want to get an overview of how total costs stack up against total receipts.)

Subtract $63,445 from your remaining receipts of $105,900 and you get a grand total of $42,455. This amount is called the *gross margin*.

What percent of $105,900 is $42,455? The answer is: just over 40 percent ($42,455 divided by $105,900). This is your *gross profit*, expressed as a percentage.

Here's a summary of the calculations:

Receipts for 19,500 units based on wholesale price	$ 141,375
Less artist royalty	– 28,275
Subtotal	**$113,100**
Less mechanical royalty	– 7,200
Subtotal	**$105,900**
Less costs of recording, packaging, manufacturing, and promotion	– 63,445
GROSS MARGIN	**$ 42,455**

Well now what? That depends on how you feel about your profit. You may want it to be higher. (Remember: you haven't yet accounted for your *overhead*—namely, ongoing costs like rent, utilities, and other expenses that would exist with or without the album project.) To increase your profit, you have a choice of raising your price, cutting costs, or manufacturing and selling more units. (If the latter, you'd be spreading your fixed recording costs over more units—recording costs stay the same, no matter how many copies you have pressed—and you'd be paying a smaller per-unit manufacturing cost. This would mean your overall cost per unit would be less, and your profit per unit would be greater.)

If you raised your price, you'd be going too high. (Remember that you started out with the top going price for new CDs and cassettes.) On the other hand, if you pressed more than 20,000 copies, you'd be exceeding the number of copies you estimated you could sell. (You might end up selling them, but you'd be taking a risk.) The third option, trying to cut your costs, would seem to be the appropriate action in this particular case.

What if you felt that the profit of $42,455 was *more* than you really needed at the outset? Here you'd have some interesting options. You could set your retail price lower, thereby making the product more attractive to buyers and potentially selling more copies. You could spend more on promotion, and even buy a few print ads. You could opt for a more lavish recording. Or you could manufacture fewer copies, thus reducing your overall risk.

Reality Check: Putting Estimates in Perspective

Bear in mind this very important point: Calculations of quantities sold and profits expected are, at this stage, *estimates only,* the purpose of which is to give you a general sense of the feasibility of your planned enterprise. What happens in the real world, thanks to the unpredictability of the music market, may bear little resemblance to the numbers you've put down on paper.

It would be a mistake to assume that you're really going to sell the total number of CDs and tapes in your estimate.

One industry safety measure is to try to delay placing an order to manufacture copies until actual distributor orders come in, then manufacture 10 to 20 percent more than the distributor orders, and reorder as inventory goes down. (Promo copies, of course, are manufactured ahead of time to use in creating demand for the hoped-for big orders.) As one industry veteran put it, "Hold on to your money until the last possible minute. Don't press on a guess of what you'll get orders for."

Return on Investment (ROI)

In the preceding calculation, you started with fixed costs, a fixed price, and an estimated sales quantity to calculate a profit.

Another way to analyze the finances of your project is to start with the profit. You focus first on a fixed *return on investment* (ROI)—that is, you establish a fixed profit percentage that is the minimum acceptable for the viability of your project. Then you calculate your price and costs to make sure that the ROI is reachable.

One way to do this is to use what is called a *target-return* approach. You estimate the number of records you expect to sell and determine the desired profit. Then you adjust price and cost to guarantee the profit. In our number-crunch example, you estimated 20,000 sales units. If you established 50 percent as your desired profit, here's what you'd come up with: Based on retail prices of $18.00 and $11.00 and net receipts of $105,900, a 50 percent gross profit would be $52,950. But, as you already discovered, your current production/promotion costs of $63,445 would allow a profit of only 40 percent. What to do? Either cut your costs by $10,495 or raise your prices.

Another approach is called *cost-plus pricing.* In this case you start with your fixed cost, establish a desired markup above the cost—say, 100 percent—and then set the price according to that markup. If, for example, you had a fixed cost per unit of $5.00 and you wanted to earn back a 100 percent markup on that cost ($5.00 $\times$ 100% = $5.00), you would need to sell each unit wholesale for $10.00. That, in turn, would require a retail price of around $20.00 to allow for the markups added to the wholesale price by both the distributor and the retail stores. (As you can see, in this case the ultimate price to consumer would be higher than the norm. You would have to do one of the following: cut costs, reduce your markup percentage, find a cheaper distributor, live with the higher price, or cancel the project.)

The problem with these approaches is that in the music industry it is exceedingly difficult to ensure a fixed return on investment. Trends come and go too quickly and audience tastes are constantly changing. To counter the unpredictability of sales, the best strategy is to keep costs down, find the best distribution deals, delay manufacturing until the last possible minute, try to sell the maximum number of records, and promote like crazy.

Break-Even Analysis

You can shed more light on the financial viability of your project by performing a *break-even analysis*—that is, determining how many CDs and cassettes you will need to sell in order to earn back your expenditures. This number of units is called the *break-even point*.

In your calculations, your estimated production and promo costs were $63,445 and your mechanical royalties were $7,200. One item that wasn't factored in was the artist *advance against royalty*—the amount the artist will be paid up front, to be recouped from royalties on sales. Since the general rule is that advances are nonrepayable (the artist gets to keep the advance even if it isn't fully recouped from royalties) you have to consider it an expenditure until it's recouped. Let's establish a $20,000 advance (roughly 70 percent of the expected $28,275 in artist royalty earnings).

Adding all these figures together, you come up with total expenditures of $90,645 ($63,445 plus $7,200 plus $20,000).

To break even, you would have to sell $90,645 worth of units. That would require selling approximately 6,250 CDs and 6,250 cassettes at retail prices of $18.00 and $11.00.

Bear in mind that when you lower the price, the break-even point increases (you'll need to sell more units to earn back your investment). When you raise the price, the break-even point decreases (it takes fewer sales to earn back the investment).

Given this information, you can decide whether it is better to try to sell more CDs and cassettes at a lower price or fewer units at a higher price. Your decision will depend largely on how you think price will affect the customer's decision to buy.

The Way the Industry Does It

If you were serving strictly as the record label—not the recording artist—there would be another way of calculating costs that would help to compensate you for the risk associated with large up-front expenditures. Surprising as it may be, you would be completely in keeping with standard music industry practice if you were to charge many of the production costs, and even some of the promotion costs, back to the artist. Yes, it's true.

Here's how it sometimes works: All recording costs are advanced to the artist, who pays them directly to the studio, musicians, and other participants. (In other cases the record label exerts more direct control over recording expenditures.) *These costs are then recouped from artist royalties.* In other words, the recording cost ultimately comes out of the artist's pocket, not the record company's (but only if the record is successful enough to generate artist royalties; if not, the record company loses the amount it advanced). The same applies to the payment for a producer. In the record-biz big time, producers are often paid via royalty—usually around 3 percent of the suggested retail price of the product. This amount may also be shifted to the artist's ledger. The artist might be guaranteed a 15 percent royalty, but he or she would be responsible for paying the producer's royalty (and advance) out of that money.

The charge-backs to the artist don't stop there. A portion of third-party promotion costs—ranging from 50 to 100 percent—may be recouped from artist royalties. The same is true for 100 percent of money provided for tour support.

It's also standard for a record company to deduct an amount of money from royalty-bearing sales receipts to cover the cost of packaging. This amount is usually 25 percent for CDs, 20 percent for cassettes, and 10 percent for vinyl records. So that if the retail price of a CD is $18.00 the "packaging deduction" would be 25 percent of that, or $4.50. The artist royalty would be calculated on $13.50 ($18.00 minus $4.50) rather than the full $18.00. In other words, *the artist is helping to pay for the packaging.*

In addition, record companies do not pay the artist royalties on "free goods," such as the 500 promotional giveaways in our original computation. This makes sense, because the companies themselves are not being paid for these records. In some cases, however, record companies routinely offer 15 percent discounts to retailers or wholesalers as a kind of sales incentive, but treat it as 15 percent of an order given away for free. Categorizing 15 percent as "free" means they only pay artist royalties on the 85 percent "sold." (If it was treated as a 15 percent discount on the full order, they'd have to pay royalties on 100 percent of the units.)

It continues. For a time, it was standard in some companies to stipulate that royalties be payable for 90 percent of records sold (not for the full 100 percent). Why was this? It was originally so that record companies wouldn't have to pay royalties on the estimated 10 percent of stock subject to breakage. But it became an industry habit. So that if 100,000 records sold, the artist would receive royalties for only 90,000 of them. Some companies still hold this policy.

On top of all this, royalty rates for CDs may be reduced rates—that is, they may be set at 75 to 90 percent of the rate paid on analog cassettes. (This is a holdover from an earlier practice of reducing rates for "new formats," even though CDs are no longer new.)

None of this is particularly good from the artist's perspective. But from the label's point of view, such deductions and charge-backs may be justified by the high-risk nature of the record business. Most records fail to recoup their costs. The labels have to protect their businesses somehow. They compensate for their losses on flops by ensuring maximum profit on those products that do end up selling.

Now let's see how our numbers play out using this approach.

ALTERNATE ARTIST ROYALTY COMPUTATION

Cassettes

Retail price	$ 11.00
20% packaging deduction	− 2.20
Amount subject to royalty payment	$ 8.80
10% royalty per unit	.88
× 9,750 units	8,580.00
Less 15% "free goods"	− 1,287.00
Total artist royalty	**$7,293.00**

Compact Discs

Retail price	$ 18.00
25% packaging deduction	− 4.50
Amount subject to royalty payment	$13.50
8.5% royalty per unit (85% of cassette rate)	1.15
× 9,750 units	11,212.50
Less 15% "free goods"	− 1,681.88
Total artist royalty	**$9,530.62**

The combined CD-plus-cassette royalty, rounded off, is $16,824. That's $11,451 less than the royalty calculated in your original number-crunch.

Of your original costs, $34,050 will, in this new computation, be recouped from artist royalties. (That's $17,550 in recording costs, $15,000 in tour support money, and $1,500 in independent PR and record promotion.)

Again, let's do the math to see what you'll earn:

Receipts for 19,500 units (at wholesale price) less 15% "free goods"	$ 120,169
Less mechanical royalty	− 7,200
Subtotal	**$112,969**
Less costs of production and promotion*	− 63,445
Gross margin	**$ 49,524**

* Includes a $17,550 advance to the artist to cover recording costs

But what about the artist royalty of $16,824? We've previously determined that recording costs, tour support, and some promo money—totaling $34,050—are recoupable from artist royalties. Since $16,824 is less than that, the record company keeps it. (In fact, the artist still owes the company $17,226 out of that $34,050, which the record company will recoup out of future royalties.)

So the gross margin remains $49,524, representing a gross profit of about 44 percent—a 4 percent increase over the results of your first calculation.

How you calculate artist royalties, and whether you choose to charge recording, packaging, and promotion back to the artist, depends on your sense of fairness and how you define your role as a record company. If you view the record company's role as simply providing administrative services, manufacturing expertise, and distribution clout, then you might justifiably charge back items that don't fall into these categories. Further, you may feel that maximum profit should be your compensation for taking the financial risk.

ADDITIONAL FACTORS AFFECTING PRICE

Earlier, we assumed your objective was to sell as many copies of the record as possible, as soon as possible, and at the highest price possible.

There are other types of marketing objectives, and they have an effect on the price point you choose.

Your objective may be *early cash recovery.* In this case, you would set a low initial price to maximize sales and cash early in the marketing program.

You might opt for a *market skimming* approach. Here, you would secure maximum early profit by setting a high price, based on the knowledge that core customers will want to be among the first to own the product, regardless of the cost. (Of course, you have to be certain these customers exist.)

Another possible objective is *market penetration,* where you set a low price to ensure purchase by a large segment of the potential market.

Mid-Priced and Budget Albums

You may encounter a situation where you want to boost sales of *back-catalog product,* meaning CDs and cassettes that have been on the market for a while, are no longer being actively promoted, but are still for sale. You can use a price adjustment to achieve such an objective. Generally, you'll sell these products as either mid-priced or budget items.

Mid-Priced Albums. A mid-price is one adjustment down from the standard price (that is, the suggested retail list price) of a top-line new release. A mid-price is used to encourage customers to buy older product that the company believes still has sales potential. An example is an early album by a still-popular veteran performer.

A mid-price is generally 20 to 40 percent below the standard price of a new release. Thus, a CD priced at $17.99 when new would be mid-priced somewhere between $10.99 and around $13.99.

Bear in mind, too, that artist royalties for mid-priced albums are usually 75 percent of the rate for a new album.

Budget Albums. It may be that an old album won't sell unless the price is reduced even further. In that case, you'd set the price at the budget level, which is generally under 65 percent of the new-release price. For a CD priced new at $17.99, the budget price would be any price lower than around $11.50.

Artist royalties for budget records are typically one-half to two-thirds of the rate for a new album.

If a budget record fails to sell, you have the option of slashing prices even further to encourage retailers to take your "excess inventory" off your hands.

8

Extending the Product:
Additional Delivery Formats

Sales of music come primarily from delivering the product to the market in the most widely accepted format. But a product's sales-generating capacity can be increased by creating product extensions—that is, by increasing the number of formats in which the product is delivered to the marketplace.

Think of different formats as different ways of packaging essentially the same product. Each different format allows the producer-seller to highlight or add features that satisfy the preferences of a specific segment of the customer base. Each additional format thus has the potential for attracting new customers to the product. It also increases the product's visibility in the marketplace by requiring additional retail shelf space and by getting the product into additional stores that specialize in the particular format.

How many different delivery formats are possible for a music product?

As previously discussed, the most popular delivery formats for music are the compact disc and the cassette. And within those formats, full-length albums (as opposed to shorter programs) account for the largest percentage of music sales (81 percent in the United States in the first three quarters of 1997).

Beyond those standard formats, the possibilities are many. They can be loosely separated into the following three categories:

- Audio formats
- Audiovisual formats
- New-media formats

While most additional product formats are generally not brought into the marketing mix until some success has been achieved with the primary format, it's important to be aware of them for when the time is right to create new revenue streams.

AUDIO FORMATS

Audio-only formats include vinyl records, singles and EPs, multiple-album sets, and audiophile recordings.

Vinyl Records

Before the advent of the CD and the cassette, the vinyl record was the leading format in which to sell recorded music. Today it has largely disappeared from the marketplace. (In 1997 vinyl records accounted for less than .2 percent of all U.S. retail music sales, according to a report in *Billboard* magazine.)

Nonetheless, some artists and specialty record labels continue to issue limited quantities of product on vinyl. The market, though small, consists of audiophiles who believe that the analog sound embodied in vinyl records is warmer and more expressive than the digital audio of compact discs. Such enthusiasts also have a fondness for vinyl's larger 12-inch physical format and packaging.

Additionally, vinyl records are still used in certain types of music promotion—especially promotion relating to dance-club music genres.

As of this writing, the retail price of a top-line vinyl record album is around $10.99.

Singles and EPs

Instead of or in addition to releasing an entire album, the music seller can choose to release fewer songs (or less music) at a cheaper price for the consumer. The options are singles and EPs (extended-play recordings). Both configurations can be produced in CD, cassette, and vinyl formats.

The definitions of the two configurations overlap somewhat. While 7-inch vinyl singles have traditionally consisted of two songs, one per side, CD "singles" may contain from two to five tracks, although one or two of those tracks may be remixed versions of other songs on the single. The format termed *EP* may range from three to six songs. If the EP is on vinyl it is generally in the same 7-inch format as a single, although EPs—as well as singles—are sometimes issued in the 12-inch format.

Singles and EPs are often used for promotional mailings, such as those aimed at radio program directors. (See page 161 for more about radio promotion.)

In terms of retail sales, the target market consists of customers who may resist buying an artist's complete album but are willing to spend less money to purchase a song that they may have heard on the radio or at a club. Their numbers are not insubstantial: retail sales of singles amounted to nearly 20 percent of total record units sold in the U.S. in the first three quarters of 1997.

As of this writing, the retail price of a vinyl or cassette single is $2.99. CD singles range in price from $2.99 (for two tracks) to $9.99 (for four or five tracks).

Multiple-Album Sets

A multiple-album set may be a two-disc release of new music. It might also be a five-disc compilation of previously released recordings. Whatever the musical content, multiple albums sell in significantly fewer numbers than single discs, simply because their prices have to be set much higher.

A rule of thumb when thinking about using a multiple-album format is that they generally only work if the artist is already extremely popular, with a core audience of customers ready to snap up a new release regardless of the cost. For example, in 1986 Bruce Springsteen released a five-disc collection of live recordings. Because of his popularity—and because there had been a pent-up demand for audio "mementos" of his famously exciting live shows—the set sold phenomenally well.

Obviously, the cost of repackaging old recordings into a set will be much less that the cost of newly recorded multiple discs, with correspondingly higher profits.

As of this writing, typical retail prices of two-disc CDs range from $24.99 to $35.00. A set of two cassettes may sell for $19.99. One chain record store had a 28-disc set of Julian Bream recordings selling for $279.99. The same store listed a 60-CD set of Bach cantatas for $599.99.

Audiophile Recordings

When an artist's popularity is already established, there may be a market for an audiophile release of one of the more popular albums. An audiophile recording is a special limited edition of an album, sonically processed to achieve the highest possible audio fidelity. Notable rock audiophile products include Donald Fagen's 1982 album *The Nightfly* and Guns N' Roses' 1991 recording *Use Your Illusion II*. The latter was priced at $29.99—approximately double the price of the original non-audiophile release.

Audiophile recordings are aimed at and priced for a niche market of loyal fans who also happen to be high-end audio enthusiasts. The niche is usually small—as are the numbers of audiophile recordings that are sold. It's best to steer clear of this format unless you are marketing a superstar performer or the main focus of your business is high-quality issues of, say, well-known classical recordings aimed at owners of high-end audio systems.

AUDIOVISUAL FORMATS

Most people who enjoy an artist's recordings also enjoy seeing the artist in action. An opportunity to do this—other than at a live appearance—is offered by audiovisual product formats. The most popular of these is the videocassette. A higher-end product is the laserdisc.

Videocassettes

A new artist is rarely in the business of selling videocassettes. Most of the videos on sale in retail stores are long-form videos, consisting of collected video clips or full-length concert performances. New artists simply don't have enough video clips (if any) to compile into a long program. (The creation of initial one-song video clips usually occurs after the artist has established some success selling records and gaining radio airplay. Years pass before enough clips have accrued to justify a video compilation.) Nor do new artists have the broad popularity necessary to create demand for a concert video.

But for established performers, video is yet another way to repackage music in order to generate sales. In this case the basic product—the recorded music—is given extra value with the addition of a visual component.

The audience segment that videos target consists of fans for whom the performer's visual appeal is of key importance. In some cases, those customers may be in addition to—not just a subset of—the record-buying segment of the performer's audience. For that reason videos have the potential of broadening the market. (See page 200 for more information on marketing videos.)

Laserdiscs

Laserdiscs, which at this writing retail for $24.99 on the low end and $39.99 on the high end, are the audiovisual equivalent of audiophile recordings. They consist of material culled from other audiovisual sources—such as movies—and present that material in a high-resolution format for home viewing. They are aimed at, and priced high for, customers who not only prefer high-quality video and audio but also own the special hardware needed to play laserdiscs.

The content of music-related laserdiscs is much the same as that used in videos: full-length concerts, video-clip compilations, movies (such as the Beatles' *A Hard Day's Night*), and documentaries (such as that based on Elvis Costello's 1992 album *The Juliet Letters*).

As with videocassettes, musical performances generally don't show up in the laserdisc format until well after the performer has become broadly popular.

NEW-MEDIA FORMATS

Recent decades have seen the arrival of powerful new technologies, generating new and intriguing formats for presenting music.

Such formats—at present, collectively termed *new media*—are dominated by digital communication products that make use of multiple data types and that permit a high degree of choice (interactivity) on the part of the user. For example, a CD-ROM (ROM stands for *read-only memory,* meaning you can read the data in a variety of ways but you can't alter it) is a digitally encoded disc that can incorporate audio programs, video material, still photographs, graphics, animation, and text. At the same time, it offers the user substantial leeway in choosing the order and combination in which those audio, visual, and text elements are heard and viewed. CD-ROMs are playable on CD-ROM drives that are either stand-alone units or built in to a personal computer.

Another new-media format is the DVD (digital video disc, or, confusingly, digital versatile disc). Like the CD-ROM, the DVD looks like a standard audio CD. And like the CD-ROM it can hold vastly more data—roughly seven times the storage capacity of an audio CD. It can store full-length movies, multiple audio albums, and a range of other data. The DVD format is being positioned by manufacturers as a potential successor to videocassettes, laserdiscs, CD-ROMs, and possibly even audio CDs.

Multimedia formats like DVDs and CD-ROMs are viewed as providing a richer entertainment experience than offered by standard formats, in terms of amount of information, audiovisual quality, and, in the case of interactive software, personal involvement of the user.

By definition, new-media products are somewhat experimental and not yet widely embraced by the market. They may or may not catch on. Until they do (or until they are proven a passing fad) their appeal is mostly limited to a specialty market of upscale, technologically savvy consumers with enough disposable income to spend on the equipment needed to play these products. (See page 199 for more information on new-media marketing.)

One of the problems with so-called new media is the lack of industrywide standardization of certain products' features and hardware requirements. Another problem is the sheer number of different formats that are introduced to the market on a regular basis. This state of affairs creates customer confusion and thus inhibits sales. In turn, content developers (record companies, for example) become reluctant to produce new products for all new formats. As a result, some formats fail to catch on and eventually fade from sight. Examples of onetime new-media products that did catch on are compact discs and, to a lesser extent, laserdiscs.

The moral of this story is: Spend money on manufacturing a new-media version of your album only after determining that the format has a well-established, large base of users.

9

Distributing Through
Stores and Their Suppliers

You may have a CD full of brilliant music. And you may have packaged it with eye-popping artwork. But the audio brilliance and visual dazzle will be lost on all but immediate friends and colleagues unless you take the next important step. The music has to be delivered to the public at large. And the term for getting it to the public is *distribution*.

Distribution is the "place" part of the Four P's of marketing: Product, Price, Place, and Promotion. (And, as long as we're dealing with letters of the alphabet, it is also the "where" of marketing's Three W's and an H: the What, Where, How, and When.)

Distribution is the part of the marketing program devoted to getting shelf space. It's where you make sure the musical product is displayed in locations visible and accessible to your target customers, so that they can purchase it—and so that you can make money. That's why your distribution scheme will be a cornerstone of your marketing effort.

It is also the first step in the marketing program where you'll confront a significant obstacle. So far, in the product development stage, nothing (other than budget) has stood in the way of your creating the ideal musical product you have envisioned. Now you'll face distributors and store personnel who need to be convinced your product has commercial potential before they'll agree to work with you. (For a potential way around this obstacle, see Part 3, Music Marketing and Promotion on the Internet.)

There are many approaches to distribution, including direct mail sales to customers (which is discussed in Chapter 10). In this chapter we'll look at the most commonly used and most profitable approach— that of conventional retail and wholesale distribution (translation: getting CDs, cassettes, and other formats into stores).

The notion of distribution sounds simple enough. But of course, nothing is particularly simple—in life or in the music business. In keeping with that axiom, the store distribution part of marketing involves several stages, and several different types of participants. In fact, store-based distribution involves a *chain* of participants, each of which moves the product (the CD, tape, vinyl disc, laserdisc, or DVD) one step forward on its way to the final customer. This chain of distribution entities is often called the *distribution channel*. For now, let's go right to the last and best-known segment of that channel: the retail outlet.

TYPES OF RETAIL OUTLETS

The *retailer* segment of the distribution channel is the segment that deals directly with the final customer. An example is the store on the street—the place where individual customers go to buy records. (Retailers are differentiated from *wholesalers,* which we'll get to in a minute.) As you probably know, there are many different types of outlets that carry recorded music.

Where do *you* want to sell your CDs and tapes? Let's go out on a limb and guess that you're more than willing to sell records wherever people will go to buy them. Fine. But before jumping headlong into the retail maelstrom, let's first identify some of the different store options, bearing in mind that there are probably a few types you haven't previously considered, including non-music stores that might be ideal for reaching your target audience.

At the top of the food chain in the retail sector is the large chain record store. As of this writing, Tower Records, Wherehouse Records, Virgin Megastores, Borders Books and Music, and Musicland are the principal players in this category. They're the department stores of the record world, handling large amounts of stock covering a wide range of musical styles, and dealing also in audiovisual products like videocassettes, CD-ROMs, laserdiscs, and DVDs.

The chain stores have outlets across the United States and in other countries, and they service the largest number of music customers. Tower Records, for example, has outlets in the U.S., Europe, Asia, the Middle East, and South America. Musicland, which also owns Sam Goody and other sub-chains, has about 1,500 stores in the U.S., the United Kingdom, Puerto Rico, and the Virgin Islands. Borders Books and Music runs 150 stores across the U.S. and, as of this writing, is growing rapidly. Barnes & Noble, the bookseller, also sells music in many of its 450 superstores.

It's important to note that chain stores—because of the quantities of product they purchase and the resulting lower prices they can offer customers—control most of the retail market.

VERTICAL AND HORIZONTAL INTEGRATION

One of the giant entertainment chains, Virgin, is a case study in the organizational system known as *vertical integration,* where a single company will control all links in the commercial supply chain—creative, production, and distribution. Virgin, for example, not only runs a record label, through which it creates new product, but also owns more than 60 Virgin Megastores in the United States, Europe, Japan, and Australia. This enables Virgin to distribute its own product and thereby maximize its profits at each stage of the enterprise.

Sony is an even more striking example. Not only does it create the *content*—the entertainment property—through its Sony Records label and Sony Pictures film studio, and distribute the properties through Sony retail stores and movie theaters, it also manufactures the *hardware,* from CD players and VCRs to televisions, with which buyers listen to and/or view the content at home.

A related system is *horizontal integration,* involving the merger of similar—perhaps formerly competing—businesses under a single corporate owner.

Both vertical and horizontal integration characterize the structure of the media conglomerates—from Viacom and Disney to Time Warner and TCI—that dominate the 1990s entertainment industry.

It's truly a quantum leap from these entertainment megacompanies to the next type of retailer on our list. Struggling alongside the retail giants are smaller, independent record stores, sometimes called mom-and-pops. The typical mom-and-pop has a much smaller stock than a chain store, a more limited musical selection, and a smaller customer base that is drawn from the immediately surrounding neighborhood. They are said to offer more personal service and, often, expertise in a particular musical area or genre.

That pretty much sums up the most obvious places to sell records. How about some less obvious ones? You've probably noticed that chain stores of other types, like Sears, Wal-Mart, and Kmart, sell limited selections of records—mostly chosen from current top sellers and mainstream music releases. These general-goods stores can serve as a way to reach customers who don't ordinarily frequent record stores.

And you've probably come across the occasional specialty music store, the small retailer that supplies specific types of music—say, reggae, jazz, electronica, or gangsta rap—to aficionados of those styles. For many small record labels, these are excellent places to make product available to targeted customers.

Further off the beaten path are non-record stores that cater to specialty customers. These stores occasionally carry music product that fits the theme of their primary products. For example, a store that specializes in new-age products—gifts, crystals, and books of "fantastic" art—might also carry recordings of new-age music. Craft and health-food stores might also sell albums of acoustic music. Stereo equipment stores might feature a selection of audiophile recordings. The resourceful marketer will seek out these nontraditional outlets as a way of broadening distribution and reaching customers who might not otherwise become aware of the product.

GETTING PRODUCT TO THE RETAIL OUTLETS

Now the fun begins. How do you get your product into the racks and shelves of these retailers? Answer: With a lot of effort. So much effort, in fact, that an entire segment of the music business is dedicated to relieving creative and other non-sales personnel of this immense responsibility. Businesses that cover this sector of the commercial music industry are called, not too surprisingly, *distributors*. They are the middlemen (and women) who specialize in taking shipment of product from record labels and making sure it gets into the proper retail outlets. The chain of distribution, in its simplest form, is shown below.

The Do-It-Yourself Method

Since lining up distributors takes a certain amount of salesmanship (and is helped by having a track record of previous sales), small, fledgling labels often start out by trying to handle local distribution on their own.

Here's an example: You may have heard of Danny Gatton, the Washington, D.C.-based guitar whiz who died in 1994. Both prior to and after Gatton's death, his mother, Norma, ran her own label called NRG Records. NRG issued product that consisted entirely of Danny Gatton music. Mrs. Gatton started in 1977 by pressing a thousand 45s, taking them around to local record stores, and asking the owners if they'd be willing to sell some. She kept at it over the years, working out of her garage, taking orders for CDs and tapes from individuals over the telephone, shipping to specialty record stores, and finally hooking up with a couple of large distributors. Sales in 1996 exceeded 25,000 units.

Another case is that of the Boulder, Colorado, band Big Head Todd and the Monsters. For their initial album, they pressed 2,000 compact discs and cassettes combined—all they could afford at the time. They personally delivered them to record stores, and would check back weekly to see what sold. (The band eventually achieved enough success with two independent albums to attract the attention of a major label, and went on to release a platinum-selling CD.)

If you are a beginning music marketer handling a small quantity of CDs for an equally small label, the do-it-yourself route may be where you launch the distribution process.

Hands-On Techniques

Here's one way to approach your hands-on retail distribution: Start by making a list of all the small record stores that operate in the vicinity of your home base. These are your prospective retail "accounts." (The small stores will be more open to stocking your product than large chain outlets would be.) Then use the following steps to get your product through their doors.

Prepare an Information Sheet. Before contacting the stores, prepare an $8\frac{1}{2}$-by-11-inch information sheet on your company letterhead. (This item is roughly equivalent to the "distributor one-sheet," described later in the chapter.) It should list such vital data as the name of the album (or single), the name of the artist, product formats available and their respective retail prices, the product catalog numbers and UPC codes, the name of the record label along with its address and phone number, some biographical facts about the artist, listings of past and upcoming concerts in the area, and a summary of radio activity (if any). In addition, if the artist has been reviewed or featured in the print media, photocopy one or two of the articles (positioned neatly on another sheet or two of $8\frac{1}{2}$-by-11-inch paper) and staple them to the main information sheet. The purpose of all this is to show that you're a professional and you mean business. And, as much as possible, you want to demonstrate to prospective buyers that the music you're peddling is saleable.

Visit Stores in Person. Just as professional sales reps do, you'll need to visit these prospective accounts in person. In each case, ask to speak to the manager or the product buyer. Explain who you are, and that you would like to know if the buyer would be interested in stocking some of your CDs and tapes to sell on a *consignment* basis. This means that the store pays you nothing for the records unless they sell. If they do sell, the store keeps a percentage of the sales receipts (50 percent is not unusual). (Consignment is far from an ideal arrangement for you the seller—retailers tend not to put much effort into selling products in which they haven't invested cash—but it is a way for start-ups to begin building a distribution track record. And it's best to get used to the arrangement, because, as you'll soon learn, even the mainstream industry's payment system is a kind of consignment.)

Assuming that the store's buyer hasn't abruptly cut you off in mid-sentence, describe the recording artist and his or her activities in as succinct and convincing a way as possible. For example:

> "This is [the artist's] first full-length CD. He [or she] has been play-ing in the area for several years, most recently at [name the venue], and has developed an extensive following. Local appearances are booked over the next few months at [name some more venues]. The act will be plugging the CD at these engagements. Also, [local radio station] is currently playing one of the CD tracks. In addition, we're planning some advertising in the local press, and we'd be happy to list your store in the ads."

The point is to communicate the key selling points without monop-olizing the manager's time. Offer a copy of your information sheet as a source of more-detailed product information.

If the store is interested in stocking your product, ask if they would be willing to display any of your promotional material. Also offer to create a rack divider with the artist's name on it, so the discs don't get stashed with many others in a general alpha letter section.

Make this entire process as easy as possible for the store manager. Whatever aspects you can handle yourself—such as tacking up a flyer—you should offer to do. And be professional and self-confident in your interaction. Remember: you're not there to beg for help; you're offering a reasonable opportunity for both of you to make some money.

Put It in Writing. Be sure to put your agreement in writing. Specify the time period after which unsold goods are to be returned to you. Specify the condition the merchandise must be in if the retailer returns it. Specify the retailer's promotional activities, if any. (Usually there are none, but if you can convince the retailer to put down a deposit on the merchandise, recoupable from sales, you will have created an incentive for them to put some effort into promotion.) And, obviously, specify the percentage of sales income each party is to receive.

Expand to Non-Music Stores. After you have visited all the record stores on your list, make a separate list of non-record stores that you feel cater to a clientele that would be interested in your music. (Remember the new-age store mentioned earlier?) Then pay each a sales visit, as you did with the record stores. Keep in mind that CD sales in these types of stores will be significantly boosted if the store actually plays the CDs as background music. That's worth a suggestion to the product buyer—as is the fact that customers often don't realize that CDs are for sale in such non-music stores, making some sort of display notice a near-requirement.

Build Business Relationships. Once you have placed CDs in a store, think of it as the beginning of a business relationship that will require a certain amount of ongoing attention. Make sure that you keep in frequent touch with each of your new accounts. Stop by the stores weekly, or at least monthly, to check on sales. If discs have sold, you can request payment at the same time as you offer to replenish their stock. You can also provide updated performance information and offer stores the option of displaying new flyers or posters. (For more tips on working with record stores, see the Don VanCleave interview on page 284.)

This door-to-door sales approach may not be for you. You may already be at a stage where professional distribution is an option. But if you're starting out and taking the do-it-yourself route, think of it this way: You're laying the groundwork for a future sales pitch to a distributor. Being able to say "We sold X amount of records in X local retail outlets over several months" can be an important buying incentive to someone who has the capability of lifting you to the next stage in the retail hierarchy.

That next stage is having a distributor pushing your product.

TYPES OF DISTRIBUTORS

As mentioned previously, distributors are the go-between entities that transfer product from the record label to retail outlets. They are *wholesalers* insofar as they distribute the product to entities other than the final consumer—in other words, to other businesses in the distribution channel. There are a number of different types of distributors, some of which are wholly owned divisions of established record companies, and some of which are independent operations.

Major-Label Distributors

Just as sales in the music industry are dominated by major record labels, so is the record distribution system dominated by a handful of distribution networks directly affiliated with those major labels. As of this writing, there are six of these major-label distributors: BMG, CEMA,

MCA, PolyGram, Sony (formerly CBS), and WEA. Each has numerous warehouses near major metropolitan areas, where they store product from manufacturing plants and distribute it to large chain record stores, one-stops (defined below), and rack jobbers (also defined shortly).

The major-label distributors also handle the product of each label's subsidiary companies and partners. BMG, for example, distributes Arista, RCA, and Windham Hill Records; CEMA handles Capitol, EMI, and Virgin; MCA moves records from MCA and Geffen; PolyGram distributes A&M, Mercury, and Motown; Sony distributes Columbia and Epic; and WEA handles Warner Bros., Elektra/Asylum, and Atlantic.

Independent Distributors

Independent distributors are just that: business entities that are not affiliated with the major labels. (They may, however, be branches of large indie labels. For example, the independent distributor Faulty Products was, at one time, an extension of Miles Copeland's I.R.S. Records.)

These operations vary in size. Some may encompass several different offices spanning the U.S. continent. Others may have two or three offices covering a multi-state region—the Northeast, Southeast, Midwest, Southwest, and/or Northwest. (In recent years, local and regional distributors have largely been replaced by national operations.) All of them specialize in smaller, independent record labels, taking delivery from the labels' manufacturers and distributing product to many of the same entities reached by the major labels: one-stops (explained on page 115), chain stores, and smaller mom-and-pops.

Some independent distributors offer specialization in particular musical genres, or in specific types of products. It could be a "boutique" distributor handling alternative rock, hardcore, ska, and roots music. Another might focus on oldies. Yet another on classical music. Still another on ethnic music. There are indie distributors that specialize in cassette singles, indies that focus on imported product, indies that claim expertise in children's and educational music. The point is that, in aggregate, they offer retailers a more diverse selection than can be ordered from the six major-label distributors. And they provide distribution services for the smaller specialty labels that don't have access to the major network.

Independent labels who go through the indie distributor network often do business with several different distributors, each handling its own retail and wholesale accounts.

Because indie distributors have close ties to small, specialty retailers, a trend has arisen in which major labels buy in to these distribution firms. This provides the majors with access to "fringe" audiences they would not otherwise have the expertise to reach.

One-Stop Distributors

One-stops are operations that stock a wide variety of musical product that they obtain from the major-label and independent distributors described above. They provide "one-stop shopping" for retailers looking for a range of products that they can buy in small quantities—quantities too small for the larger distributors to be concerned with. Thus one-stops are essentially *sub-distributors,* buying in bulk from the majors and selling in small numbers to mom-and-pops and specialty stores. They may fill back-catalog orders for major record chains, and may service the record departments of large book chains like Barnes & Noble. One-stops also provide musical product to jukebox operators—which means that jukebox income for record companies comes from sales through one-stops (rather than directly from jukebox operators).

Rack Jobbers

Recall the earlier mention of chain general-goods stores along the lines of Kmart, Wal-Mart, and Sears. Some of them sell musical product. But rather than maintain their own staff to stock and manage a music section, they may obtain such service from independent entities called rack jobbers.

Rack jobbers purchase records from large music distributors. They sell them by leasing sales space in department stores, discount stores, and other outlets, essentially setting up and managing a record department in a store that wouldn't otherwise have one. They pay the store rent and/or a percentage of sales income and then keep the profit.

The records chosen by rack jobbers are the most mainstream, broadly popular titles available—the ones currently situated high in the popularity charts (for more about charts—especially the ones published in *Billboard* magazine—see page 236).

Rack jobbers play an important role in the distribution system: they specialize in retailing beyond the sphere of music specialty stores, and thus help to get records to a wider audience.

Chain Stores

The large chain stores discussed previously—Tower, Musicland, Virgin, and others—can also be considered sub-distributors. They run central offices through which they buy product from the major labels and distributors. These central offices then ensure that the product is distributed to all the individual retail outlets in the company chain. Naturally there are going to be differences in the inventory requirements of different local stores due to varying regional tastes. The companies deal with this by using centralized, computerized inventory systems that track individual store sales and automatically order new stock in product categories that are selling well in those stores.

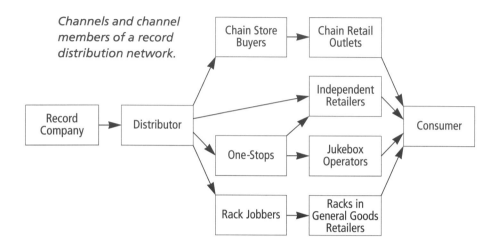

Channels and channel members of a record distribution network.

SERVICES THAT DISTRIBUTORS PROVIDE

You may be wondering why you need the services of these middleman entities. What do they do that justifies their added markup to the price of a CD or tape? In other words, what is their reason for existence? The answer can be summarized in two words: convenience and clout.

Rather than you having to deal directly with the scores of retailers that you wish to have sell your product, you can work with just a few distributors, and let them handle the details of mass dissemination. That's the *convenience* part.

The *clout* part is this: Chances are you're an individual or a small label with a limited track record of sales. With all the other record labels vying for store rack space, why should retailers choose your product? Just because you say it's good? They'll need more convincing than that. And that's where distributors come in. For the most part, they have longstanding business relationships with the stores. They are familiar with what sells and what doesn't. Their acceptance of and confidence in your music will go a long way toward convincing retailers that your product is worth a shot.

Record chains, in particular, tend to deal only with approved suppliers, and with as few of them as possible. A one- or two-record label is unlikely to be approved as a vendor. Thus chains may be off limits to small labels that wish to sell to them directly—an excellent reason to seek representation by an established distributor.

So the main service that distributors provide is to stock your product, get it into retail or other outlets, and pay you when the product sells.

A key part of this job is convincing the retailers to accept your product. The distributor's sales representatives contact individual accounts (which might include one-stops and rack jobbers in addition to retail stores) in person, by mail, or via telephone. They provide buyers with their catalog of products (including your CDs and tapes) along with other product and promotional information culled from materials that you have provided them (including one-sheets, which are described a bit later). They provide information about prices, different types of discounts, and in-store promotion preferences. They then take orders. Later, they keep in touch to make sure the order was received and to monitor the progress of sales.

In addition, distributors can provide you, the record label, with information about sales promotion packages—such as prime display space—offered by retailers. (See page 126 for more information about prime retail display space.)

For some distributors, the basic service stops there ("basic service" including accounting and payment to you, of course). Other distributors provide more.

Some, although very few, offer promotional services beyond simply promoting to the retailer. They supplement the efforts of the record label (you) by helping with radio promotion and publicity. Most distributors help set up what is called co-op advertising, where store and record label are promoted together in print ads (more about which on page 175).

In general, however, the reponsibility for promotion falls on the shoulders of the record label, not the distributor.

A miniscule number of distributors offer more extensive services. One distributor, for example, provides what it calls its "label management program," in which it guides "the growing record label through every step of the process, from the mastering stage through the artwork, UPC bar code and labeling, manufacturing, printing, radio promotion, retail promotion, publicity—and ultimately distribution itself."

If you're working with a major-label distributor, it would have the capability of providing both pressing and distribution services, as well as marketing. More about this a little later in this chapter.

WHAT KIND OF DISTRIBUTOR
IS RIGHT FOR YOU?

The kind of distributor you choose will depend on the size and extent of your enterprise. A well-established label may be best served by partnering with one of the major-label distributors. (See "Other Distribution Arrangements" on page 128.) A small specialty label, on the other hand, will seek the services of one of the independent distributors, with expertise in the label's style of music.

Let's backtrack, for a moment, to the process of hand-distributing to local stores described earlier. If you have done this for a while and have achieved some success—selling a respectable number of discs both in-store and on gigs, for example—you might be ready to move up to the level of working with a professional distributor.

A distributor or one-stop *that handles product such as yours* would be the most appropriate type of entity to contact first. Later, you might add distributors to cover a greater range of accounts, thus creating your own national or even international distribution network.

HOW TO FIND A DISTRIBUTOR

The process of researching distributors can be relatively straightforward.

If you're starting out locally and have been dealing directly with record stores, ask them the names of distributors they work with.

If you have friends or acquaintances who are involved in the record business, ask them for recommendations.

Billboard, the weekly home-entertainment trade magazine, publishes a yearly directory called *Billboard's International Buyer's Guide.* It contains a state-by-state listing of a large number of distributors. Several of them supplement their listing in the directory with advertisements, which offer more-detailed information about their specialties and services.

Many distributors have set up information sites on the World Wide Web. You can type in the keywords *record distribution* and get menus with links to the home pages of specific companies as well as to a variety of additional information sources. On Yahoo! (the leading Web search engine, or directory service), you can find companies by going to the main section heading Business; then clicking on Companies; then Music; then CDs, Records, and Tapes; and finally Distribution.

The Association for Independent Music (AFIM) puts out an annual directory that lists independent distributors. It also runs an annual convention. If you attend, you'll be able to meet directly with a number of distributors who handle indie labels. Bring along your promotion material and sample tapes, and you may be able to get some distribution interest right at the convention. If not, you'll at least come away with expanded knowledge of the distribution system and its participants.

The important thing in finding a distributor is making sure that they handle the kind of music you are trying to sell. Specialists in your genre will have an inside track to the customers most apt to be interested—that is, your target audience.

HOW TO APPROACH A DISTRIBUTOR

The step after finding a distributor is approaching them to see if they would be interested in working with you. Approaching a distributor is essentially a process of selling them on the value and commercial potential of the product you're offering. They'll be investing time and energy in the distribution process, so they'll want to be sure that the effort has a reasonable chance of paying off in the form of sales—both to retailers and to the end customers. (A product isn't really considered sold until it sells to the final customer.)

POPULAR PERCEPTION

If a CD "ships platinum" it means it's a big success.

It's not unusual for retailers to order huge shipments of new releases by well-known artists.

ALTERNATE REALITY

The release may ship from distributor to retailer in large quantities, but it may not sell to the final customer in large quantities. When this happens, unsold copies are sent back to the distributor and the record company, with no money earned for those copies. A record isn't a success unless it sells through to the public.

Preparing a Sales Presentation

Because finding a distributor involves selling, you'll need to carefully prepare your presentation to any prospective distributor. Just as you would do in selling directly to a record store—or even in trying to get a recording deal with a major record label—you have to take stock of all your promotional assets and assemble them into both a concise piece of printed communication and a brief list of talking points.

A FEW BUSINESS ESSENTIALS

Before focusing on selling your product, you'll need to take care of a few business essentials.

The first is to obtain a **Fictitious Name Certificate** for the name of your venture. You can obtain one by filling out a simple form at your local county clerk's office. This establishes your exclusive right to use your chosen name in your geographic area. (At some point, you may want to register your business name as a trademark. To find out information about this process, contact the United States Patent and Trademark Office at 703-308-HELP or on the World Wide Web at www.uspto.gov. To verify that your name is available for trademark registration—that is, it hasn't already been registered by someone else in your trade category—you can conduct a trademark search either through an attorney or by checking patent and trademark databases provided free at selected public libraries, which are listed on the USPTO's Web site.)

The second task is to obtain a **seller's permit,** also known as a **resale license,** if you work in a state that assesses sales tax. This ensures that you will collect and pay tax for each item that you sell to the public. It also entitles you not to pay state tax on materials you purchase from suppliers (such as packaging materials). You can obtain a seller's permit through your state board of equalization.

The third is to set up a unique **catalog number** for your release. Additionally, you should obtain a **Universal Product Code (UPC)** from the Uniform Code Council at 937-435-3870 and bar code film from your local bar code supplier. (See page 63 for details about UPCs and bar codes.)

The promotional information that will be most impressive to a distributor is a track record of successful sales. If you have sold a few hundred or, better, a few thousand discs on your own (on store consignment, by direct mail, and at concerts, for example), emphasize the fact. This will support your claim of future saleability.

If you have no track record of sales, your job is going to be harder. To convince a distributor to work with you, you'll just have to assemble whatever selling points you can to bolster your case. Particularly valuable is current radio play, current touring, and media coverage in the form of newspaper and magazine articles.

Bear in mind, too, that most distributors want to know not only that you're serious about promotion and that your record will sell but also that you plan to have a continuing series of releases. They want to be sure you'll be a reliable customer and won't suddenly pull out of the business, leaving them holding stacks of unsellable records. For this reason you should probably steer clear of the label business if you're intending to sell only one record.

Distributor One-Sheets

The form in which you will present your product information and sales points to the distributor is called a one-sheet. The one-sheet is an $8\frac{1}{2}$-by-11-inch sheet of paper containing two kinds of information: (1) the basic factual information about the product (such as the title and UPC code), which the distributor will enter into its computerized accounting records, and (2) the important sales points that will convince the distributor to buy the product (and which the distributor, in turn, will use to convince retailers to buy the product). Specifically, the following information should be included:

- Record company logo (if any) and contact information
- Album title and artist name (and logo, if available)
- Product catalog numbers and UPC numbers for all formats (CD, tape, and so on)
- Suggested retail list price for each format
- Release date, both to retail and to radio
- Brief description of the artist and the album (including all noteworthy information, such as the names of any well-known participants, whether producer, songwriters, or musicians)
- Artist's track record of previous sales
- Record company's track record of previous sales
- Description of the artist's audience, and size of following
- Touring or live-performance plans to support the release (including schedule)
- Radio airplay plans (including independent promotion) and schedule
- Publicity plans and schedule
- Advertising plans and schedule
- Additional marketing and promotion plans and ideas
- Names of other distributors that will be handling the product

After you have prepared your one-sheet, you're ready to begin contacting prospective distributors. Make contact by phone or by mail, and try to set up an appointment to discuss the product.

Remember that you are competing with a glut of other independent labels trying to get distribution. You've got to do everything you can to "sell your product to the seller"—that is, the distributor.

DISTRIBUTOR FINANCIAL ARRANGEMENTS

What kind of financial arrangements will you need to make once you have received a positive response from a distributor?

Here, in general terms, is how distribution deals work: The distributor agrees to buy an established quantity of your product at a discount off the suggested retail list price. That discount is negotiable depending on the size of the order and your company's clout, but it generally runs about 50 percent (although it can range from 40 to 65 percent). Thus, if your retail price for a CD is $17.99, the price for the distributor—called the *distributor wholesale price*—may be $9.00 (that's 50 percent of $17.99).

In addition, you may need to supply the distributor with a number of free goods, as an incentive they can use to secure a sale to retail. The number of free goods is often 15 percent of the total order. (For more information on free goods, see page 97.) The distributor will undoubtedly want some additional free copies for promotional use.

Promotional copies of recordings are given by the distributor to retailers, who generally use them for in-store play. (You should punch holes in, or otherwise mark, the artwork of promotional product to ensure that it doesn't get returned by the record store for credit.)

Now here's the catch: the distributor does not necessarily pay for all the records it orders from you. It only pays for the records shipped out of its warehouse to retailers—minus records that end up not selling through to consumers.

Furthermore, it doesn't pay for these shipped records immediately. There is usually a negotiable billing schedule of 30, 60, 90, or 120 days. The length of time you can negotiate depends on your clout, and chances are (if you are a small start-up label) you won't have much bargaining power at the beginning. However, you can provide incentives—in the form of discounts off the distributor wholesale price—for early or prompt payment. Typical discounts are as follows: 10 to 15 percent off for cash on delivery; 10 percent off for payments within 30 days; 5 percent off for payment within 60 days; 2 percent for payment within 90 days.

(Be aware that some distributors may count the days till their payment date not from the actual order date but from the last day of the month in which the order was placed.)

When payment comes due, there is a further deduction. The distributor will hold back a *reserve fund* as a hedge against records that are returned unsold. More about this shortly, but first let's take a look at the arrangements between the distributor and the retail outlet, and how they affect you.

Impact of Arrangements Between Distributors and Retailers

The retailer buys from the distributor at what is called the *store whole-sale price,* which is the list price minus a negotiated percentage. The typical percentage is between 40 percent and 25 percent off. (That means that for a $17.99 CD sold to a distributor at a 50 percent discount and then sold to the retailer at a 30 percent discount, the distributor will make $3.60 per CD and the retailer will make up to $5.40, depending on whether it offers a discount price to consumers.)

The retailer agrees to pay the distributor within a negotiated time period (often 60 days) for the quantity of product shipped. (Discount incentives to pay earlier—like the ones given by the record label to the distributor—may be offered.) Like the distributor, the retailer will with-hold a percentage of the payment (a reserve fund) to cover unsold goods.

The lag time between shipment and payment at the retail level is the reason the distributor doesn't pay you immediately. Essentially, the distributor wants to get paid by the record store before it pays you.

Returns Policies

It's entirely possible that some of the records stocked in retail will not *sell through*—that is, customers won't buy them. Here's what happens if records don't sell through: Retail stores are allowed to return 100 per-cent of unsold or defective product to the distributor for full refund or credit. (The retailer's reserve fund set aside to cover unsold goods, usu-ally capped at 20 percent of the original shipment, will be applied to the refund or credit.) When the distributor receives the returns, and is unable to sell them elsewhere, it can then send them back to you for a full refund or, more typically, full credit toward purchase of other product. This arrangement is in fact spelled out in your distribution agreement: *100 percent of unsold goods are returnable to you.* And the distributor withholds up to 20 percent of its accounts payable to you as a hedge against any returns.

Here are two scenarios—good case and bad case—that might un-fold from this arrangement.

Good case: You sell 5,000 CDs to a distributor on a 60-day pay-ment schedule. The distributor sells them to retailers on a 45-day payment schedule. The CDs all sell through quickly. The retailers do their part and pay the distributor in full within 45 days. The distributor then pays you in full within 60 days and places an order for more CDs. Because you have been paid, you can afford to pay your manufacturer and have more copies pressed for the distributor. Everyone is happy.

Bad case: You hire a manufacturer to press 5,000 CDs on a delayed-payment schedule of 120 days. You sell these CDs to a distributor on a 90-day payment schedule. (You figure that when the distributor pays you, you'll have enough time to pay your manufacturer.) The distributor sells only 3,000 of the CDs to retailers, on a 60-day payment schedule. Sixty days pass, and the CDs have sold to customers only in dribs and drabs. The retail stores get cold feet, and ships everything back to the distributor as unsold goods (paying, of course, for the units that did sell through). The distributor receives the returned shipments to its warehouse. It tries to sell them to other retailers but fails. Having paid you nothing so far, it decides the product is a loser. Per its agreement with you that allows it to return 100 percent of unsold goods, it ships back to you all the returns received from the retailers, along with the 2,000 that it wasn't able to move in the first place. Your warehouse (or garage, as the case may be) is now inundated with boxes of returned CDs that couldn't be sold. You receive a paltry sum from the distributor for the several hundred that did manage to sell through. Suddenly the bill comes from the manufacturer for the cost of pressing the full 5,000 copies. Because of the poor sell-through and the 100 percent return policy, you don't have enough money to pay the total amount. You pay what you can and then—in a spasm of fiscal panic—you shut down your business.

What can you do to prevent such a disaster? For one thing, don't manufacture a greater number of CDs and tapes than you think can reasonably be sold. (If possible, wait until you get an actual order from the distributor before pressing.) Be conservative—at least initially. If your first order does sell well, you can always go back and order more. This assumes, of course, that you have the money to do so. To make sure you do, focus like a laser on the distributor's payment to you, first negotiating a payment schedule that allows you enough time to pay for repressings, and second, staying on the distributor's back to pay you within the established time frame (not always easy).

Techniques for Ensuring Payment

This brings us to a common pitfall for independent labels: the problem of distributors not paying on time—or simply not paying at all—thereby putting the label in a financial squeeze when its bills come due.

For example, one San Francisco-based independent label secured a pressing and distribution deal (a concept explained later in this chapter) with an independent distributor. When it came time for payment, the distributor went out of business, leaving the label with empty pockets.

Small labels with no clout are the most vulnerable to this problem.

The only way to handle this is to use any leverage that is available. The most effective is having a product that is selling well, so that the distributor wants to order more copies from you. In this case, you would make a reorder contingent upon the distributor paying you in full for copies already shipped.

To increase the likelihood of this happening, limit the quantity you initially provide to the distributor. That way, sell-though would occur more quickly, prompting the distributor to request a reorder sooner than it otherwise would.

Before making a deal with a distributor, be sure to check references and get opinions of the distributor's business practices from other clients.

WHAT YOU NEED TO PROVIDE TO THE DISTRIBUTOR

When the distribution process gets under way, you'll be doing your part if you provide the following elements:

Invoice. A notice of payment due is mailed to the distributor separately from the shipment. It should contain the following information: invoice date, invoice number, distributor's purchase order number, product number (UPC or catalog number is standard), brief product description, ship date, unit price, quantity ordered, total amount due, and due date (terms of payment). The purpose of this is to enable the distributor to correctly cross-reference the bill to the order on their accounting system. (This may be obvious, but there you have it.)

YOUR COMPANY NAME
Street Address
City, State 00000
Country
TEL. NUMBER   E-MAIL ADDRESS
FAX NUMBER   WEB SITE URL

INVOICE

Invoice Date:
Invoice No:
Purchase Order No:

SOLD TO:
COMPANY NAME/ACCOUNT NO.
Street Address
City, State 00000
Country
Contact Person/Contact Phone

SHIP TO:
COMPANY NAME/ACCOUNT NO.
Street Address
City, State 00000
Country
Shipped via:

PRODUCT NO.	DESCRIPTION	DATE SHIPPED	UNIT PRICE	QUANTITY	PRICE
0000000	Description	00/00/00	00.00	00,000	$ 000,000.00
0000000	Description	00/00/00	00.00	00,000	$ 000,000.00
0000000	Description	00/00/00	00.00	00,000	$ 000,000.00
0000000	Description	00/00/00	00.00	00,000	$ 000,000.00
0000000	Description	00/00/00	00.00	00,000	$ 000,000.00
0000000	Description	00/00/00	00.00	00,000	$ 000,000.00
0000000	Description	00/00/00	00.00	00,000	$ 000,000.00
0000000	Description	00/00/00	00.00	00,000	$ 000,000.00

TERMS
Net 30 days

Subtotal	$ 000,000.00
Shipping	$ 000.00
Federal Tax	$ 000.00
State Sales Tax	$ 000.00
TOTAL	$ 000,000.00

Packing Slip. Each shipment that you send to the distributor (or order a manufacturer to send) must be accompanied with a packing slip. It contains all the vital information about the shipment, including a description of what was ordered, the distributor's purchase order number, and a list of the shipment's contents.

Other Items. As mentioned previously, you'll also need to provide the informational one-sheet. If you plan to have the distributor assist with in-store promotion you'll also want to provide them with display items like posters, banners, and anything else that might be used by the retailer to attract attention to your product.

SECURING PRIME RETAIL DISPLAY SPACE

Naturally, you'll want your product displayed in very visible sections of the store, rather than just in the racks. Promotional space in stores includes table space near the front of the store, end caps (which are prominently featured display stands), wall displays, window displays, and listening posts.

There is huge demand for the limited amount of promotional space in stores. (There are way more companies clamoring for space than there is space to accommodate them.) And what happens when demand increases? You guessed it: people pay large amounts of money. Today record labels must pay for the privilege of having their products featured in store displays and listening posts. How much? For a single store they might pay several hundred dollars per CD release. For a national campaign, the cost would run into many thousands of dollars. ("Payment," by the way, is usually in the form of a credit to the retailer's account with the distributor, who then subtracts the amount from its account with the record company.)

Bruce Iglauer, the president and founder of the blues label Alligator Records, describes his approach to securing display space:

> "There are a number of things we do. First of all we do play this game. We spend anywhere from ten to twenty thousand dollars on a new release for price positioning, listening posts, end caps, and anything else related to retail placement.
>
> With Borders, they have a thing they call a gondola, which is a free-standing display rack that costs a thousand dollars a month to be in. Sometimes it's a sale table; sometimes it's a front rack when people walk into the stores; sometimes it's a listening post. So we spend money there."

It's possible for labels to arrange deals in which substantial discounts are offered on shipments in return for promotional space in the store combined with co-op advertising in local media. (For more about co-op ads, see page 175.)

Small labels with no budget are essentially denied access to in-store promotion. Fortunately, some independent retailers have banded together to address this problem. The Coalition of Independent Music Stores (CIMS) has instituted a policy of employing custom marketing initiatives to promote developing artists. Their programs include "adopting" several artists each month and promoting their releases with in-store play, displays, and sale pricing.

SUPPORTING THE DISTRIBUTOR'S EFFORTS

Once you have established a relationship with a distributor, treat it as an ongoing one.

Support their efforts by keeping your part of the bargain. Follow through on the marketing and promotional plans you described in your one-sheet.

Also, keep in touch. Keep the distributor informed about your unfolding plans. Supply them with press clips when they become available. Let them know about local radio coverage, including interviews. Keep them abreast of your act's performance schedule. Knowing when and where a performance is to occur will allow the distributor to provide retailers in the area with extra stock of the product and promotional items, so they can meet any increased customer demand.

Be liberal in supplying promotional items to the distributor—especially copies of your recording. Having an ample quantity will help the distributor sell your product.

When possible, establish personal contact with the sales representative who handles your material. Provide that person with detailed information about the product. Make the salesperson feel involved in your success effort. This will be appreciated, and will make the product stand out in the salesperson's mind rather than get lost in the vast quantity of product he or she handles.

It can also be a good idea to go straight to the stores. Staff at Alligator Records, says Bruce Iglauer, regularly call retailers just to check in:

"For example, I have two people who do nothing all day but call retail stores. And the irony of that is that we don't sell to retail stores. We sell through distributors. We're a real independent company. We don't sell around our distributors at all. But we call up stores and just talk to them about our new releases, about artists coming into town, about numbers on SoundScan reports. We talk about radio play in their market or other media in their market. We invite them to gigs, basically greasing them. Shmoozing them. Getting them to remember our product, talking to them about bringing titles in. I don't think that there's anybody else at our level of the independent industry who works so closely with retail. **"**

OTHER DISTRIBUTION ARRANGEMENTS

It's possible for independent record labels to enter into business relationships that go well beyond simple distribution agreements as described above. They include label deals, pressing and distribution deals, and joint ventures.

Label Deals

In this arrangement, the independent record label or production company provides finished product to another more-established (or "major") label, which then handles distribution and possibly marketing and promotion. The distributing label's name may appear on the product in addition to, or instead of, the producing label's name. Payment occurs in one of two ways: (1) the distributing label pays a royalty to the producing label, or (2) the distributing label buys at the distributor wholesale price minus a percentage (usually 20 to 25 percent) to cover distribution costs, and pays only for products sold. Costs of manufacturing, packaging, and marketing are covered by the producing label.

The value of this to the indie label is that the clout of the distributing label will increase the likelihood of sales to retail and prompt flow of payments back down the distribution channel.

Pressing and Distribution Deals

This arrangement involves the indie label providing the distributing label with the recording masters and finished artwork. The distributing label manufactures the products, sees that they are distributed, and possibly handles marketing. The payment options are similar to those for label deals.

Joint Ventures

A joint venture involves the producing label and the distributing label splitting costs and profits. After monies are received from retail, the distributing label deducts an amount to cover distribution, and payments are made for production, manufacturing, packaging, promotion, and mechanical royalties. The remaining amount is the profit, which the two parties split.

For example, in 1997, Reader's Digest Music, which had previously been selling music exclusively through direct marketing, expanded into store retailing by setting up a joint venture with Warner Bros. The agreement involved both companies producing the recordings and Warner handling manufacturing, promotion, and distribution.

CHAPTER

10

Direct Marketing and Non-Store Sales Methods

Successful marketers rack their brains to find and exploit every possible means of reaching customers. Part of this task is seeking methods that will supplement (or in some cases replace) standard retail store distribution.

Why would a music marketer feel the need to supplement or even replace standard retail store distribution? Record stores, after all, are visited by a very large segment of the music-buying public. There are at least three answers: (1) other distribution methods may allow access to customers who do not regularly shop at record stores, (2) other distribution methods may permit more precise targeting of prospective customers, and (3) the marketer might not have access to retail store accounts, due to lack of distributor interest in the product.

A notable utilizer of "alternative" marketing methods is Windham Hill, the well-known record company that specializes in so-called new-age music. In its early years of operation, the label had difficulty cracking the standard channels of record store distribution. Consequently, it was forced to develop off-the-beaten-path approaches, which included sending catalogs of its products directly to names on the label's mailing list. The silver lining was that these alternative channels—the label also placed their CDs in bookstores, health-food stores, and other specialty outlets—enabled Windham Hill to focus on its market niche and eventually develop an unusually loyal base of customers. Along the way, they gained a clear understanding of the "customer profile" of the typical Windham Hill buyer, enabling them to market more effectively by distributing through outlets connected to their special interests. (In an interview in *On Achieving Excellence*™ one of Windham Hill's founders described the label's market as "25- to 45-year-olds, many of whom are intimidated by record stores, where there's all this loud music blaring [and] some kid behind the counter with a weird haircut.") Success in its niche market eventually gained Windham Hill access to mainstream record stores and the mass market.

As Windham Hill discovered, and as many other small labels have found out, there are a number of effective sales channels outside the realm of retail store distribution.

Direct marketing, for example, accomplishes just what its name suggests: it employs techniques for bypassing the traditional wholesale-retail distribution chain and offering purchasing opportunities to core customers directly. For some small companies that specialize in niche markets (specific segments of the population, rather than the mass populace), direct marketing is the *primary* marketing method.

Record clubs offer another means of marketing music outside the retail distribution system.

Yet another way of reaching potential buyers directly is to sell CDs and other product formats at live performances.

These are just a few of the common additions to the music marketer's distribution repertoire. You're encouraged to uncover more, but first, let's get the creative juices flowing by looking at these main categories in detail.

DIRECT MARKETING

Direct marketing is any method of creating buying opportunities by providing information about the product directly to the customer and including in that information a way for customers to place an order. The most common types of direct marketing are direct mail and direct-response advertising. The advertising may be in print or via broadcasting. (Direct marketing can also be carried out on the Internet, details of which are covered in Part 3.)

Direct marketing is really a combination of distribution and promotion. The promotion part is providing information about the product along with persuasion and incentives to buy. The distribution aspect is the customer request to purchase and the fulfillment of the order.

Direct Mail

For the small label, the most available method of distribution is direct mail, which eliminates the need for an outside distributor. It involves creating an informational brochure, promotion piece, or catalog and mailing it to names on a targeted mailing list.

The mailer should include instructions for ordering the product via mail, telephone, fax, e-mail, or the World Wide Web.

Use of Mailing Lists and a Customer Database. The key to successful direct mail programs is having a targeted list of customers. Part of this list will consist of *core* customers—people who have indicated strong interest in your music by signing your mailing list at performances, filling out tent cards, returning business reply cards that you've included in CDs, and subscribing to your newsletter (if you have one). Another part of the mailing list will consist of likely prospects—people who fit the profile of your typical customer as closely as you can determine. These are names that can be obtained for a fee from music magazines specializing in your style or from commercial mailing list brokers. (See page 53 for more information on mailing list sources.)

As you collect names, enter them into a computer database program. This will allow you to maintain an easily updatable customer list, into which you can insert comments about product preferences of individual customers. Certain programs also have a "mail merge" function, which allows you to automatically print out mailing labels, saving hours of valuable time. (Check your local computer software store or the Internet for recommendations of specific programs.)

Bear in mind that response to targeted mailings follows relatively predictable patterns, running between 1 and 10 percent. If you have a very good core-customer list—a list of bona fide fans—a 10 percent response would be a smashing success. For the "likely prospect" portion of your list—the names purchased from a commercial mailing list broker, for example—a successful response would be in the range of 1 or 2 percent. If you had a mailing list of 80,000 names (a not-unusual number for an enterprising niche marketer), 800 to 8,000 responses would indicate an effective effort.

Flyers and Brochures. If your direct mail program is aimed at selling a single product, such as a new CD release, the most effective mailing tool would be a simple flyer or brochure.

In designing the flyer or brochure, you have two goals: (1) to get the customer to want to buy the product, and (2) to make it as easy as possible for them to order it. For example, providing a postage-paid return envelope will eliminate finding an envelope and buying a stamp as impediments to making a purchase decision.

On the simplest level, you could create a one-page flyer with a tear-off order form. (For details about what kind of information to include on an order form, see "Order Forms" on page 138.) The bulk of the flyer would promote the product, as in the example on the following page.

Include the following basic elements in the promo section of the flyer: the name of the artist (and logo, if available), a photo of the product or a graphic element pulled from the CD cover design (if affordable), the album title, item or catalog number, announcement of availability, and descriptive copy.

Additional elements might include an eye-grabbing headline, an endorsement quote from a magazine or individual, and a quote from the artist, commenting on some aspect of the album.

However you choose to promote the musical product, be aware of the following time-tested formula—often called the AIDA formula—for successful direct mail:

- Grab **a**ttention (the "Look at this!" part of the promo).

- Spark **i**nterest ("Imagine this...").

- Create **d**esire ("Here's what it can do for *you*").

- Call to **a**ction ("Order now!").

One-page flyer with an order form.

Among the year's top 10!
—SOUND SPACE

BATBOYS

FLY BY NIGHT

Hurry—Take Advantage of Our Special Discount for Preferred Customers!

Call 1-800-000-0000 or visit our Web site at www.oooooo.com
LIMITED-TIME OFFER—ACT NOW!

ORDER FORM

Name____
Address____

Mail to: 666 Main St., S.F., CA 00000

Qty.___ × $10.00 = ____
Sales Tax ____
Shipping ____
TOTAL ____

Ship To Address____

Method of Payment:
☐ Check   ☐ Money Order
☐ VISA   ☐ MasterCard
Card No.____
Expiration Date____

Whatever approach you take (and tone, wording, and style will vary tremendously depending on the music and the targeted audience), the attention-interest-desire-action elements are at the heart of every direct mail piece. (For more about copy and headlines, see the section on "Direct-Response Advertising" on page 140.)

Since the flyer in this example is meant to be simple, you would just fold and seal it, stamp and address the reverse side, and mail it as is without an envelope. (Any mailing piece that can be mailed without an envelope is called a self-mailer.) In this case, you would not provide a return envelope.

If you mail the flyer in an envelope you would then have the option of inserting either a self-addressed, postage-paid return envelope or a self-addressed return envelope requiring the customer to add postage.

A convenient but more expensive mailer is a one-page flyer with a detachable return envelope built in. You address the *back* of the return envelope to your customer and add your postage. The *front* of the return envelope (which is not visible when you send the mailer out) is printed with your business address and a box for a stamp, a "No Postage Necessary If Mailed in the United States" message, or a bulk rate indicia. (See "U.S. Postal Regulations and Rates" below.)

The non-envelope portion of the flyer may be both a promo piece containing additional product information and an order form that the customer can then fill out and return to you in the envelope provided. (For an example of an order form with return envelope included see the photo on page 139.) It is worth noting that this type of mailer requires more complex manufacturing, and should only be handled by a printer who specializes in it. Local printers or print brokers can refer you to qualified printers, or you may consult the Printers section of the Yellow Pages. Be sure to compare estimates from several printers and get samples of similar jobs they have handled in the past before making a final decision.

U.S. POSTAL REGULATIONS AND RATES

The United States Postal Service has a number of regulations governing the format and design of business reply mail and return envelopes. For details, see the booklets *Designing Letter Mail* and *Designing Reply Mail,* published by the U.S. Postal Service. Find out more at www.usps.gov.

If you will be relying heavily on direct mail in your marketing program, you should learn about procedures for purchasing a permit for postage-paid reply cards and envelopes. Also find out about bulk rates available for business mailings (also requiring a permit) as well as special postal rates that apply to records and books. Call your local Postal Business Center for detailed information.

Since the U.S. Postal Service has strict requirements regarding size and weight of mailing pieces, it's a good idea to consult with your local postmaster about the components of your planned mailing—*before* you spend money producing the pieces.

There are a number of variations on the single-product mailing piece. Here are just a few:

- A postcard. It can provide information and also be used as an order form to be placed in an envelope and mailed back to you.
- A letter plus an order form.

- A glossy, heavy sheet of $8\frac{1}{2}$-by-11-inch stock that folds once into an $8\frac{1}{2}$-by-$5\frac{1}{2}$-inch mailer. The customer address goes on the outside back. The outside front delivers the main message. The inside contains more promo and an order form that can be removed.

- An 11-by-17-inch sheet that folds over into an $8\frac{1}{2}$-by-11-inch "brochure." Stapled in the center is a business-reply-mail envelope. One panel of the brochure serves as an order form, which the customer can cut out and insert into the return envelope. Two panels are devoted to the product announcement and promo. Finally, the piece folds again into an $8\frac{1}{2}$-by-$5\frac{1}{2}$-inch mailer that can be taped closed. The customer address prints on one of the exposed panels.

- A more elaborate piece that could include a glossy, full-color information sheet, a personalized cover letter (which can be laser-printed) on company letterhead, a separate order form, and a postage-paid reply envelope.

The envelope in which you send the mailing can also be an important promotional tool. It might include an attention-grabbing headline to make the recipient want to open it. It might be in a special shape or size to make it stand out from other mail (although this can be expensive).

Another point to bear in mind is that you want the customer to pay *before* you send them the product. What does this mean for the design of the brochure or flyer? It means that if you expect a buyer to send a check or money order, make sure you provide the means to send it—either a return envelope or instructions to use their own envelope.

There are many other possible mailer sizes and folding styles. It is beyond the scope of this book to list them all. For more information, refer to one of the many available guidebooks that focus on direct marketing. A good one is *The Do-It-Yourself Direct Mail Handbook,* by Murray Raphel and Ken Erdman (Philadelphia: The Marketer's Bookshelf, 1986).

The only limitations to mailer design are your imagination and your budget. Remember: the simpler the mailer, the cheaper to produce.

Newsletters. Another effective approach to direct mail sales is to use a newsletter. The beauty of this is that the recipient will not so readily toss it out as junk mail. The fan will receive it as a valuable source of information about the artist, or label, or whatever the subject may be. Contained somewhere in the newsletter is product information and an order form.

The people managing the rock band Phish send out a newsletter, *Doniac Schvice,* several times a year, reaching many thousands of fans. Most of the publication deals with Phish news, like upcoming tour dates and recording schedules. It also contains a letters section, for that "interactive" touch. In addition, a tear-out order form is included, with which fans can order T-shirts, stickers, posters, and hats.

Catalogs. Catalogs are the direct mail tool of choice when you're trying to sell a line or a series of products rather than just one. If you're starting up a label and you get to the point of needing to produce a catalog, congratulations. You must be doing something right to have come this far.

For an example of effective catalog marketing, let's look again at Windham Hill, which won a Gold Award from the magazine *Catalog Age* in 1995. The label mails out catalogs several times a year to customers on its mailing list. The cover and a sample spread from their Autumn–Winter 1996 catalog are shown on the facing page.

For the cover, they used a photo that reinforces the label's image. Its subdued, cool, atmospheric quality reflects both the ambient aspect of much of the label's music and the graphic approach used on many of their album covers.

Inside the full-color catalog are clear, straightforward profiles of each current release and several "backlist" products.

Each profile includes the artist name, album title, a capsule description, format(s) and price(s), catalog number (they call it an "item" number), and a reproduction of the album cover. Where the artist has previous albums, they are listed after the new-product profile.

On *every* spread is a reminder of the toll-free number for ordering products by telephone. (A detailed discussion of toll-free phone numbers can be found on page 139.)

The order form is designed as a separate insert in the center of the catalog. Attached to it is a tear-off return envelope. (See page 139.)

In some of their catalogs, Windham Hill encloses a CD sampler.

Overall, the Windham Hill catalog presents its information clearly, attractively, and in a way that conveys the substance of the label's product line. Like the music, the tone of the catalog is understated, devoid of splashy, slam-bam histrionics—just the way their customers like it.

In contrast, the Ralph Records "Buy or Die" product catalog (shown on the facing page) has a slapped-together, idiosyncratic tone that matches the convention-bashing ethic of the Residents, the guiding force behind the label.

For your catalog, provide the kinds of product data used by Windham Hill and Ralph Records. Though different in design, both provide all the standard information that should be included in a catalog.

Beyond that, make sure your catalog design matches the company and product image you are trying to convey.

Windham Hill cover
© 1998 Morton Beebe & Associates.
Used by permission.

Ralph Records catalog
© 1994 Ralph America.
Used by permission.

Covers and internal page spreads
of two product catalogs. One uses a straightforward, conventional design style (top), and
the other uses a funky, unconventional approach.
Each of these catalogs employs a design that
is appropriate for its product line.

Order Forms. The essential tool of the direct mail piece is the order form. It can be simple or complex, but it must contain the following minimal elements:

- Space for the customer's name and address (pre-printed, if possible).
- Space for the customer to write the "Ship To" name and address (usually the same as above).
- Your mailing address, fax number (if available), and toll-free phone number, if any (see "Setup and Use of Toll-Free Phone Numbers" on page 139).
- Space for the customer to list the item(s) ordered. This should include separate spaces for the item number, item title, price per item, quantity ordered, subtotal price (unit price multiplied by quantity ordered), state sales tax (if applicable), shipping and handling fee, rush charge (if applicable), and total amount due (subtotal + shipping/handling + tax).
- For the customer's reference, a list of shipping and handling fees for different amounts ordered; for example, $4.50 for orders up to $19.99, $6.00 for orders between $20 and $49.99, $7.50 for orders from $50 to $79.99, and so on. You determine the shipping and handling charges by combining the postal fee with reasonable labor costs for packing.
- Information about discounts (if any).
- Expected delivery date (for example, "Allow 4 to 6 weeks for delivery"). (See "The FTC Mail-Order Merchandise Rule" below.)

THE FTC MAIL-ORDER MERCHANDISE RULE

The Federal Trade Commission (FTC) has specific regulations governing stated delivery dates of mail-order merchandise. If you fail to ship within your stated time period, you must seek the customer's consent for a delayed shipment. If you can't get consent, you have to refund the money paid for the unshipped merchandise.

For more information, consult the FTC's Web site at www.ftc.gov.

- Space for the customer to indicate payment method. Typical options are check or money order. (Indicate that it should be made payable to your company.) If you are set up to take credit cards (see page 140 for more information), provide space for the type of card, the card number, and its expiration date.
- Space for the customer's signature.

- A code (in numbers and/or letters of your choice) that tells you where the customer got the order form. Each type of mailing piece and each separate print ad should be assigned its own code (printed on the piece). This will enable you to determine how many orders each type of mailer or ad generated and therefore how successful each was.

Tear-out order form used in the catalog of an established record company. Note the built-in return envelope.

Setup and Use of Toll-Free Phone Numbers. If you wish to provide customers with the means to order by telephone, you'll need to set up a toll-free phone line (otherwise known as an 800 number, or an 888 number). When you do, you'll pay a monthly service charge plus a per-minute usage charge whenever a customer calls you. That is, you, not the customer, will pay for the call.

You can set up service by calling the business service office of your local telephone company. Typical rates are around $5.00 for the monthly charge and a 10¢-per-minute usage charge.

There are companies that specialize in these services and that offer competitive rates for toll-free lines. Before choosing a service provider, do some comparison shopping via the Yellow Pages and the Internet.

Credit Card Payment. It's common knowledge that people are more likely to make spur-of-the-moment purchases if they can pay by credit card than if they have to take the time to write a check. If you want to provide this capability, you should set up a credit card processing system.

To do so, have your bank set you up with a business account for merchant credit card processing. There are also commercial services, called credit card processing agencies, that can help you set up and use a system for accepting cards from all the major companies. Whether you go through a bank or a dedicated service, they will provide you with computer software for registering each transaction.

Credit card transactions will then work as follows: When a customer orders by credit card, the funds are transferred to your account, usually within 30 to 60 days (although some banks offer next-day availability of funds). The bank or processing service may charge you a setup fee, a service fee, a fee for a monthly statement, and a fee for purchasing or leasing software.

Discounts and Other Purchasing Incentives. Sometimes it's not enough just to inform the customer about the product. In order to nudge the customer over the final hurdle to decide to buy, you often have to give them something extra, a special break of some kind, a bit of added value.

The most typical form of incentive is a discount. For example, you might offer 10 percent off the retail price if the customer places an order by a certain date.

Another way is to offer an extra item—such as a T-shirt, poster, or copy of your newsletter—for free if they buy within a given time period.

Direct-Response Advertising (Print)

Placing ads in magazines and newspapers can be very expensive—and even distasteful to some people. "I don't like advertising," Windham Hill's Anne Robinson once admitted, "because I don't think it's inherently honest. Second, we didn't have the money. Third, it's hard to sell music in a print medium."

Actually, though, when you compare the cost of an ad in a magazine that reaches 40,000 people with the cost of mailing a brochure to 40,000 people, the ad may be the more cost-effective, and easier, choice. This is especially true if you are promoting a single CD release. (For a full line of products, you'll need a brochure or catalog.)

In direct-response advertising, the goal is to ignite a purchasing decision and provide a response mechanism—an easy way for the customer to place an order. Usually the response mechanism is a toll-free number to call or a tear-out order form.

Choosing the Right Publication. The most important choice you have to make is whether to advertise in a publication with a small but very targeted readership or a mass-market publication with a larger but less definable group of readers. For example, if your music has a Brazilian jazz flavor, putting an ad in *Brazilian Jazz Now!* magazine might not get you to a lot of customers, but you'll know for certain that they are positively inclined toward your type of sound. Advertising in *Women's Wear Daily,* on the other hand, will get you a huge audience; but for all you know only a very small percentage of that group listens to jazz of any kind, let alone yours. These are extreme examples, and most often the decision will be less cut and dried. But it is one you'll have to make. For a tiny company, the decision will be easy: the targeted publication will be all that you can afford.

Whatever you choose, make certain that the publication does reach a demographic that matches your typical listener. Here's a good fit: advertising a Grateful Dead album in *Relix,* a magazine written by Deadheads for Deadheads. And here's a bad one: advertising the Flower-Power Peace and Love Ensemble in *Soldier of Fortune* magazine. You get the idea.

One way to save money is to set up a cooperative deal with the magazine. You pay them only for actual orders received from the ad. The magazine gets to keep 50 percent of the receipts. This is called *per-inquiry (PI)* advertising.

If you're running ads in several publications, assign each a separate code and print it on the order form. That way you'll know which magazine generated the sale, enabling you to make better-informed advertising decisions in the future.

Headline and Copy Guidelines. As pointed out previously, the heart of any direct-response piece (and this includes print ads) is the AIDA formula: grab attention, spark interest, create desire, and call to action. When writing headlines and copy, there are numerous other rules to consider (and to break, if it serves the purpose of your sales approach). Here are some of them:

- A headline should hook the reader. As much as possible, it should be about something that matters personally to the reader— something that relates to an emotional need (being popular with friends, for example) or appeals to self-interest. (It's been said that there is one headline *guaranteed* to interest John Doe the reader. That headline is: "This Ad Is All About John Doe.")
- A headline should also be easy to understand, and it should be written for the right audience.

- The body copy (that is, the main copy that follows the headline) should speak directly to the customer, as if you were talking one-on-one. Try to keep an image of the ideal customer in mind as you write.

- The body copy should relate logically to the headline (that is, explain the headline or answer the question the headline poses).

- Copy should be short and simple—unless the product demands more-detailed information.

- Avoid using long words, and try to use words that create mental pictures and sensations—so that readers *experience* what you're talking about.

- Avoid exaggerated claims, overblown adjectives, and hype.

- When possible, provide proof of quality by using endorsements.

Direct-Response Advertising (Broadcast)

You've seen the ads on television late at night as you're starting to doze off in your easy chair. A familiar hit from the 1980s will jar you back to consciousness in time to see a lengthy list of song titles crawling up your TV screen: "I Want a New Drug" by Huey Lewis and the News, "Rhythm of the Night" by DeBarge, "Karma Chameleon" by Culture Club, "Wake Me Up Before You Go-Go" by Wham!. The announcer is peddling the complete three-CD set, *Eighties Essences,* for "only $29.99!" Your finger twitches on the remote but the announcer's voice stops you: "And if you order now, you'll get a special bonus CD, *The Nebulous Nineties,* for $5.00 off the regular price! That's right! An $11.99 value for only $6.99! Call, toll-free, 1-800-765-4321 now while supplies last!"

You're on that phone like a cat on tuna.

Well, maybe not. But ads such as these do tend to generate very healthy sales.

The ad described above would have been placed by a company that obtained licenses to the original songs for the purpose of compiling them into an "eighties" package. Most TV ads for music are those that are selling such packages.

Financially, TV and radio ads tend to be way out of reach for the small marketer. (Although one of the authors recalls once seeing a local TV spot for a guitar teacher. It ran at about 3:30 a.m.)

If you're able to afford broadcast ads and they're appropriate for your product, the guidelines for providing information, incentives, and response mechanisms are essentially the same as for direct mail and print ads (minus the tear-off coupon, of course).

CATALOG MARKETING
THROUGH OTHER COMPANIES

Another approach to distribution (and promotion) is to have your musical product advertised in the catalogs of other companies.

These may be music catalogs, such as Collector's Choice Music, or general-goods or gift catalogs that also include music recordings.

The concept of the latter is similar to selling your music in general-goods retail outlets or specialty retail stores that reach your targeted audience—except in this case the channel is mail order. Catalogs that fall into this category include *Signals* (the gift catalog affiliated with Public Television).

Generally, the catalog company buys product from you at your wholesale price and sells at the retail price.

To get your CD listed in one of these catalogs you'll have to contact the catalog's product buyer and send them promotional information so that they can evaluate whether they want to include it. The key, of course, is choosing a catalog that reaches the appropriate audience.

LICENSING TO RECORD CLUBS

Record clubs are mail-order organizations that offer members regular opportunities to purchase, directly from the club, the products of a variety of different record labels. A club will usually offer prospective customers first-time membership deals of several initial recordings for free or at a nominal price contingent upon agreement to buy a specified number of additional recordings over a given time period. A typical arrangement is this: After the customer becomes a member, he or she will periodically be mailed a description of a "featured selection" or a "selection of the month." If the customer does nothing, he or she will automatically be sent the recording and charged for it. If the customer does not want to buy the recording, he or she must mail a cancellation card back to the record club within a specified number of days.

Record clubs generate a very large percentage of total mail-order music sales. The leading clubs are BMG Music and Columbia House.

A record company will license its recording to the club, which will manufacture copies from the master tape. The club pays the record company a royalty on each copy sold (a typical arrangement is $9\frac{1}{2}$ percent of receipts on 85 percent of the total number sold through to the customer, less a packaging charge).

A substantial number of copies distributed by the club are free goods. That's because many are sent out free as part of the initial membership deal, and other monthly mailings are simply never paid for by customers. This matters to record companies because they receive no royalties for free copies. For this reason, labels sometimes include in their contract a stipulation that free copies will not exceed a certain number. (That number, by the way, is typically high: 100 percent of the number of records sold.)

The benefit of the clubs to record labels is that it helps them reach a segment of the marketplace to which they may not otherwise have had access.

To place a record with one of the clubs, contact the club directly. You will need to send promotional material as evidence of your product's commercial viability.

SELLING RECORDINGS AT LIVE SHOWS

Perhaps the most immediate form of distribution outside the retail realm is selling your recorded product at live performances. You're pitching the product (the music) as you perform it, and if the audience likes the sound they can buy a copy of the CD on the spot.

A key benefit is that the profit for the seller is higher than in retail—even if discs are sold at a discount to customers. One owner of a small label pointed out that "if you're a band selling [CDs] at gigs for $12, it's cheaper for buyers, but you're still making about $10 profit on each. You can pay for the pressing in about 200 CDs—that's pretty easy to do if you're a gigging band."

Bear in mind that once an artist has achieved substantial commercial success and is performing to large audiences, the record company may prohibit sales of CDs at concerts because of the potential for cutting into retail sales.

11

Promoting the Product

Somewhere, a recording of music that could ignite the next big cultural craze is sitting in CD form on a record store shelf, awaiting purchase. But will customers buy it? Will sales transactions occur, setting the star-making machinery in motion—and eventually putting money in the pockets of the people who created the work?

Not necessarily. Not unless the seller makes customers aware of the CD's availability and of its value as a purchase. Without customers having that awareness, the CD will end up as little more than a piece of random plastic lost in the industrial scrap heap.

That's where promotion—the last of the Four P's of marketing—comes into play. Promotion, in brief, is activity designed to stimulate demand for a product.

Promotion starts with the product selling points identified during product development (see page 54) and translates them into appealing messages and a marketable image (Aerosmith as rock-and-roll bad boys, for example). It then makes use of the entire media system—print, audio, visual, and multimedia—to communicate the message, project the artist's image, and broadcast the sound in as many ways, and to as many potential customers, as possible.

In music, promotion has several components, including publicity, radio play, television exposure, sales incentive programs, live performance, and advertising. Each of these types of promotion, in turn, has its own set of components.

A complete promotion program makes use of all available tools, techniques, and outlets. In the case of a new CD release, for example, a promotion campaign might involve the following activities:

- Convincing magazine, newspaper, and Web 'zine editors to write articles about the artist and the new CD

- Setting up interviews on radio and television
- Featuring the CD on Web sites (as detailed in Part 3, page 249)
- Scheduling in-store appearances to sign autographs
- Placing ads in publications that reach the targeted audience
- Convincing radio music directors to add the music to their playlists
- Making sure the music is featured at store listening posts
- Getting the music played in non-music stores frequented by target customers

The goal, of course, is to boost not only one-time sales but also multiple sales over the long term. That means that promotion has to be an ongoing, long-term process, not just a one-shot effort.

Whether you are able to make use of all available promotion methods will depend on your resources, both human and financial. But whatever your capabilities, you'll be devising a campaign that draws from options detailed in the following discussion.

PUBLICITY

The most available form of promotion is publicity, because it is free. Publicity is the process of increasing public awareness of the product by getting editorial coverage in the media (as opposed to paying for ads). It's about gaining exposure through magazine articles, record reviews, photos in the news, and other means. In short, publicity is the art of attracting attention via the information outlets that consumers routinely use.

The value of publicity is straightforward: When people read or hear about a musician or recording, they develop not only an awareness but also an opinion of the subject matter. If that opinion is positive, there is increased likelihood of a sale.

The publicity seeker has a three-part job: (1) get the most possible coverage of the artist/product in a broad range of media, (2) get coverage in the most appropriate media, and (3) attempt to control the content of the coverage.

Getting *the most possible coverage* translates into reaching the largest number of people. Getting *coverage in the most appropriate media* means not overlooking the publications and programs that cater directly to the target audience. And *controlling the content of the coverage* means making sure that articles communicate the desired message. (Publicists can do this to a surprising degree, by funneling article ideas to "sympathetic" editors and by suggesting desirable "angles" for articles, to cite just two ways.)

Interdependence of the Media and the Publicity Seeker

The importance of the media to the marketer is substantial. The media provides the mass communication channels through which marketers can publicize their products. The media also provides feedback—via reviews—about how the product is perceived in the marketplace. (The marketer can, if so inclined, use this feedback to suggest changes in future products, such as a different musical or lyric direction in an artist's future recordings.)

But what about the other way around? What's the value of the CD marketer to the media? Is the marketer-publicist always in the weaker position of having to beg for media coverage? Actually, no. And here's why: Media people have a job, and that job is to feed the public's giant appetite for information. In the music world, the public hungers for facts about new music and about artists and their lives, opinions, and personalities. That information—the subject matter—comes from the music makers and their representatives. Without it, the media would have nothing to report or write about. The publicist provides news about upcoming releases, which the media then reports. The publicist also provides the media with access to the artists, for interviews and in-depth features. The media, in other words, *needs* the publicists for its lifeblood.

Interdependent relationship of the mass media and the record industry, involving a trade-off of product information and exposure to the public.

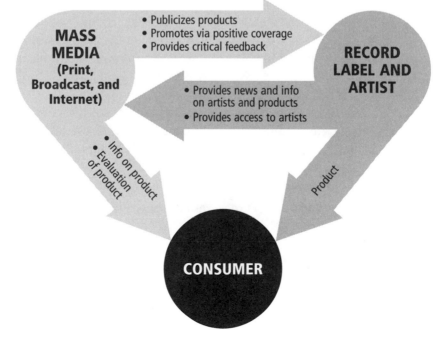

The point is that the media and the record seller have a mutually beneficial relationship. And awareness of this interdependency can guide the publicity seeker's attempt to get coverage. "What type of article can I suggest that would be of interest to this editor and his or her readers?" is the thought that should be foremost on the publicist's mind when planning a pitch.

The Media and Its Participants

Media is the collective term for the agencies of mass communication. Its individual participants—editors, reporters, critics, columnists, and commentators—are often described as the gatekeepers of public opinion. Their job is to monitor the constant worldwide flood of new data and report only the information deemed most appropriate for targeted readers, viewers, and listeners.

What kinds of media should you target when trying to get publicity? That will depend on the kind of audience you are trying to reach. Each media entity has an intended audience, whether it be a mass audience or a small group interested in a specific topic.

The communication outlet you choose for your publicity campaign will be drawn from three main categories: print, Internet, and broadcast.

Print Media. Newspapers and magazines publish information about music from a variety of perspectives, depending on the audience. Print publications of value to publicity seekers fall into the following categories:

- **Daily newspapers.**
  Audience: general readers from a national, regional, or local base.

- **General interest, lifestyle, and entertainment magazines** *(People, Interview, Details, Allure, Entertainment Weekly, Cosmopolitan, Vogue, Vanity Fair, Newsweek, Esquire, GQ, Playboy, Ebony, New Yorker, Time,* and others).
  Audience: broad national readership that conforms to the particular editorial focus; for example, *Time/Newsweek* to general readers, *People* to mostly female readers, *Entertainment Weekly* to pop culture consumers, *Esquire/GQ/Playboy* to men, *Cosmo/ Vogue* to women, and *Details* to young, upwardly mobile men.

- **Newsweeklies** *(Village Voice, Boston Phoenix, SF Weekly, Bay Guardian,* and others).
  Audience: young, urban, sophisticated, culturally aware readers from national, regional, and primarily local bases.

- **Music and pop culture magazines** *(Rolling Stone, Spin, Vibe,* and others).

Audience: young, affluent adults with strong interest in pop culture and music.

- **Genre-based music magazines** *(downbeat, JazzIz, Flipside, Option, Country Music, The Source, Rap Pages, Metal Edge).*
  Audience: fans and aficionados of specific musical genres.

- **Promotional magazines** *(Pulse, Request).*
  Audience: customers of chain record stores.

- **Magazines for music hobbyists and professionals** *(Keyboard, Guitar Player, Guitar World, Modern Drummer, Computers and Music, Electronic Musician, Mix, and Musician).*
  Audience: players of instruments, recording engineers, and other active music makers.

- **Magazines for record collectors** *(Goldmine, DISCoveries).*
  Audience: collectors and aficionados of "oldies" and rare discs.

- **Trade publications** *(Billboard, Gavin Report, Radio and Records, The Music Trades, Hollywood Reporter, Variety).*
  Audience: music industry professionals, including record company personnel, radio program directors, music promoters, managers, and marketers.

- **Fanzines** *(Tiger Beat).*
  Audience: pre-teen and teenage fans of new artists.

Internet. The World Wide Web has spawned a host of publications that are essentially hybrids of print and broadcast. Many combine text coverage of music (news, feature articles, and reviews) with audio and video clips. Publicity outlets on the Web include the following:

- Web-based music magazines (like SonicNet, MTV Online, the Rolling Stone Network)

- General interest Web 'zines that include coverage of music-related subject matter

- Web editions of many of the publications listed in the "Print" section above

Broadcast Media. Deejays, veejays, commentators, and talk-show hosts on radio and television often have musical artists as guests or interview subjects. (In terms of radio, we're talking here not about airplay of the music itself—discussed in the "Radio Promotion" section of this chapter [see page 161]—but about coverage of the artist or music in the form of news, commentary, or interview.) Some outlets also have a music news or trivia feature. Programming of value to publicity seekers is generally of the following types:

RADIO

- Commercial talk radio, with occasional musical guests
- Commercial music radio, providing occasional interviews with musical guests
- All-news radio, with occasional coverage of music and entertainment news
- Variety programs featuring musical guests ("Prairie Home Companion," for example)
- National Public Radio programs occasionally featuring musical guests ("Fresh Air," for example)
- College radio programs, featuring interviews with musical guests

TELEVISION

- Network late-night talk shows ("The Late Show with David Letterman," "The Tonight Show," Conan O'Brien, and others)
- Network morning news programs, with occasional musical guests ("Good Morning America," "The Today Show")
- Network prime-time news "magazines," occasionally covering music topics ("60 Minutes," "Dateline," "Primetime Live," "20/20")
- Network prime-time "showbiz" news programs ("Entertainment Tonight")
- Network daytime talk shows, with occasional musical guests (Oprah Winfrey, Rosie O'Donnell)
- Cable talk shows, with occasional musical guests
- Cable music programming (MTV, VH-1, The Box, Black Entertainment Television [BET], Country Music Television [CMT], The Jukebox Network, The Nashville Network)

Types of Media Coverage

The kinds of articles or information that editors choose to provide depends on editors' intimate knowledge of what readers want. And what readers want tends to fall into the following categories:

- News, about current or upcoming products and ongoing career activities (for example, a change in musical group personnel, or a switch to a new record label)
- Performance schedules (as provided in entertainment calendars)
- Personality profiles, with in-depth information about an artist's life, opinions, beliefs, and tastes

- Reports on broad musical styles and trends (for example, the increase of interest in female pop artists in the late 1990s)
- Reviews of recordings and live performances

Tools of the Publicity Seeker

Before setting out to publicize a new release, you the publicist have to become familiar with the standard tools of the trade, and learn how to use them like a pro. The key items include reference tools, such as media lists. They also include the press kit—your primary "calling card" for getting the attention of media representatives. Finally, they include press releases and public service announcements, the simplest devices for getting instant exposure.

Media List. First, you'll need to identify the media people and businesses to contact when sending out information about your release or other product. You'll do this by assembling a media list—a database of names, addresses, and phone numbers of publications, radio programs, television programs, and Internet "webcasters" that would be open to covering a product such as yours. The list should also include the names of individual editors, reporters, critics, commentators, and producers who would be your personal contacts when pitching items and stories.

(This, by the way, is your second important list, the first being your mailing list of fans and other target customers. See page 51 for more information on mailing lists.)

If possible, store the media list both on paper and in a computer database for easy updating. And guard it with your life. It takes time and energy to assemble one of these lists, and when you do, it will be a one-of-a-kind, custom list for your product—not something you want to have to dig frantically for when preparing to send out a pitch.

You could begin building a list by phoning newspapers and appropriate magazines based in your region and getting the names and addresses of their current music critics or arts and entertainment editors. If you don't mind paying for a few long-distance calls (and considering what is at stake, you shouldn't mind at all), do the same for the most prominent music media entities around the United States. You can supplement this start-up list with information from such sources as the *Gale Directory of Publications;* the *Standard Rate and Data (SRDS)* directories *Consumer Magazine Advertising Source, Newspaper Advertising Source, Community Publication Advertising Source,* and *TV & Cable Source;* and the Internet's www.mediafinder.com. There are many others, researchable through the library and the Internet.

Once you've assembled a basic list, you'll need to keep it up to date. Job turnover in the media world is high, and the editor who loved your last concert may no longer be working at the same publication. Whenever you become aware of a new name, or an individual's move to a new organization, update your list. And most important, keep notes on your list about the individuals who have reacted positively to your product, as well as the people with whom you have established positive relationships. They will be key allies to contact in future publicity efforts.

Press Kit. The essential tool for presenting your product to the media is the press kit. It is the standard device employed by marketers and publicists when disseminating a substantial amount of information in a single mailing. It can be used to promote an individual CD release, a newly formed music group, an entire company, or any number of other newsworthy products or entities.

Whatever the musical product being promoted, the press kit is its "ambassador" to the press, and the kit's professionalism and quality will have a direct reflection on how the product itself is perceived. For that reason, the kit should be made as attractive and informative as possible.

The typical press kit is made up of the following elements: a jacket, with pockets on the inside for inserting other elements; a cover letter (also called a pitch letter); a fact sheet; a bio or product description; publicity photographs; press clips; a cassette or CD (if that's what's being promoted); and additional attention-grabbing items (optional).

Let's investigate these press kit components one by one.

The **jacket,** as described in the book *The Billboard Guide to Music Publicity,* is, "in a media sense…the sexy costume in which your client goes onstage. It's the part of the kit that gives the crucial first impression." The jacket is a combination of an attractive cover and a holder for all the other press kit items. The front is often decorated with a printed or stick-on logo, or it might have more elaborate artwork or a full-color photograph. On the inside, it has pockets or fold-up flaps, into which are inserted the bio, press clips, and other items. The standard size of a jacket is 9 by 12 inches.

(Bear in mind that there's a growing trend in the music business toward *not* using jackets in press kits, due to their cost and to a desire to conserve paper.)

The **cover letter,** or **pitch letter,** is the first item that is read—it's the introduction to the press kit—and the greeting should include the name of the individual recipient. (There are computer programs that allow you to merge a standard letter with names and addresses on your media list when printing, so that each letter will be personalized.) The format of the

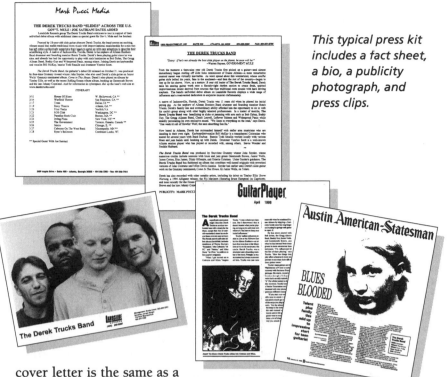

This typical press kit includes a fact sheet, a bio, a publicity photograph, and press clips.

cover letter is the same as a standard business letter. It should be written as clearly and concisely as possible, opening with a statement of what the letter is about ("I'm writing to let you know about Artist A's new CD release") and why it would be of interest to the recipient ("a step in a new musical direction that your readers will want to know about"). The remainder should expand on why the topic would be of interest, and the letter should close with an invitation to action ("Contact me if you'd like to work on scheduling a story for your publication [or program]. I look forward to speaking with you about it in the near future"). Under your signature, print "Enc." to indicate that there are "enclosures" (other press kit items) included for review.

A **fact sheet** is a simple one-page list of key facts about the product. It is perfect for use by a busy radio or TV commentator who has to interview a guest but hasn't had time to do background research. The fact sheet provides the main discussion points at a glance. The sheet is also useful in print media for quickly fact-checking an article.

At the top, print "Fact Sheet" followed by the name of the product or artist. In a vertical column on the left side of the sheet, print bold item headings, like Title of New Album, Title of Single, Style of Music, Band Members, Record Label, Unusual Facts, or any other items that you think would be important to note. Next to each heading, print the corresponding information, in short-and-sweet form. At the bottom of the fact sheet, print the name and phone number of the person to contact for more information (Contact: Bob Roberts 212-111-0000).

The **bio,** or product summary, is the central nervous system of the press kit. It is the fleshed-out description of the subject at hand, namely, the artist or product being promoted. It will not only be read by numerous decision makers who may know nothing about the topic, but may also be printed word-for-word by small newspapers who want to run an article but are short on writers. For these reasons, the bio needs to be publication-quality—a concise, informative, and entertaining piece of copy.

In form, the bio should consist of the following:

- An *introductory statement,* communicating the essence of the product's uniqueness (or persona, in the case of an artist). The nut of this statement is the *key selling point* that you identified during product development and have since translated into an image or easy-to-communicate concept.

- A *summary of current activity,* quickly providing the reader with information about the new CD, upcoming tour, or whatever else you consider to be the immediate focus of your current promotion.

- *Historical background.* Here's where you flesh out the story. When did the musical group first get together? Why did it form? What were some of the key events in its development? Who helped them? When? These kinds of topics can be addressed here.

In this bio promoting a new CD, the key selling point is that the artist is "a living American music treasure."

(HIGHTONE RECORDS)

RAMBLIN' JACK ELLIOTT

Perhaps more stories have been told about Ramblin' Jack Elliott than any other contemporary American music artist; but one thing's for sure: he is a living American music treasure. A major figure in the folk movement of the 1950s, Ramblin' Jack has been called "a wandering, true American minstrel" by playwright Sam Shepard. He learned his craft from the legendary Woody Guthrie, with whom he became a close friend. He has influenced several generations of singers, from Bob Dylan and Tom Waits to Beck and John Wesley Harding. His 1995 album, *South Coast,* won the Grammy Award as Best Traditional Folk Album. And now, with the debut of his HighTone Records CD, *Friends of Mine,* Jack has crafted his most ambitious work in a long line of creative visions.

Much has been said about Jack's early life: he got the cowboy bug at the tender age of nine; he ran away from home at 15; he learned cowboy songs and banjo from a rodeo clown; and, upon returning home, found an old guitar and started practicing.

Around 1951, Jack heard his first Woody Guthrie recording and—thoroughly inspired—sought out Guthrie himself. For the next few years, the two traveled the country together, as Jack absorbed the style and essence that made Woody Guthrie such an original

music icon. In 1954, after Woody was hospitalized for the disease that killed him in 1967, Jack continued to travel, playing the gospel according to Woody.

In 1955, Jack went to Europe, where he developed his own style and turned on a new audience to Guthrie's music. Upon returning to the States in 1961, Jack found the folk music boom in full swing and himself as one of its heroes. He lived in Greenwich Village in the early '60s, where he played the famous folk venues at the center of the folk revival. In 1965, he moved to California, and in the mid-'70s he joined Bob Dylan's Rolling Thunder Revue. Jack received the Bill Graham Life Achievement Award at San Francisco's Bay Area Music Awards in 1996.

As the title *Friends of Mine* suggests, Ramblin' Jack is joined on this CD by his friends: Guy Clark, Nanci Griffith, Arlo Guthrie, Emmylou Harris, John Prine, Peter Rowan, Rosalie Sorrels, Tom Waits, Jerry Jeff Walker, and Bob Weir. The songs on *Friends of Mine* demonstrate the breadth of American music roots—folk, blues, country and western—that encompass the style of a true American: Ramblin' Jack Elliott.

- *Additional information.* For readers who make it this far, this paragraph can be a source of nonessential information that fills out the picture of the artist or product. Special interests, unusual or influential experiences, favorite recording techniques, bits of philosophy—all are potential mentionables in this section.

- The *closing passage* should draw the bio to a satisfying conclusion. One way to do this is to restate the opening idea in a new way. Another is to end with a quote that provides a sense of summary or finality.

Speaking of quotes, they should be used liberally throughout the bio. Words taken directly from the mouth of the artist or another personality tend to add liveliness to these kinds of written pieces. If possible, use one per paragraph. (A pertinent quote is often used *directly after* a point made in the text, to provide amplification of the point. But avoid repetitively alternating text and quotes.) The quotes can be obtained through an interview with the artist or from past articles.

Putting together quotes is only one part of the bio preparation process. Whoever is writing the bio—and it could be a hired freelance professional or you the marketer—will have to start by gaining thorough familiarity with the musician, the music, and the image or main message that has been developed by the marketing team. This is done in several stages: (1) reading past literature about the artist and music, including magazine articles and any promotional material already developed; (2) interviewing the artist to find out as much as possible about his or her personality, musical approach, and background; and (3) listening to the music. Overall, it's essential that the image presented in the bio is in sync with the image presented in all other promotional materials.

A **publicity photograph** is another essential part of the press kit. The standard format is 8-by-10-inch black-and-white glossy. (Sometimes it's worth providing a color slide for use on magazine covers or in color interiors. But since it is expensive, do it only for established acts or when you are reasonably certain of getting coverage.)

The tone, style, and mood of the photo should support the image and personality of the artist or the character of the music. If the selling point of the music is that it is charming and upbeat, the photo should be charming and upbeat. If the chief sales point is the artist's guitar technique, show her with a guitar. If the song lyrics deal with the problems of living in the city, show the artist against a stark urban background. In sum, make the photo clearly convey the intended image at a glance.

Use a professional photographer with experience in the music business. You can find one by skimming through music magazines and looking at the credits for the photos that you like, and then calling the editorial office to find out how to contact the photographer(s). Another way is to consult such directories as the *Recording Industry Sourcebook, American Photography Showcase,* and *Click.*

When discussing the shot with the photographer, make sure you clearly communicate the idea you would like the shot to convey. If the final product conflicts with your intended message, then you will have wasted your money.

The photographer will own all rights to the photograph except for those that you explicitly purchase. Your basic payment will cover publicity uses—that is, use in promotion packages and "editorial uses in regular issues of newspapers and other regularly published periodicals and television news programming." For other uses, such as on album covers and in advertising, the photographer will normally require a higher fee. It's important to state your intended use when you first hire the photographer, and to put it in writing.

The publicity stills that you distribute should show, at minimum, the name of the artist or product, the name of the manufacturer (that is, the record label in the case of recordings), and the copyright date and owner (the photographer, unless you have purchased the copyright as part of the agreement). The name of the photographer should always be shown.

In addition to photos, a fact sheet, and a bio, you'll want to try to include **press clips** in your press kit. These are simply sample reviews or positive articles written about the product, which you cut out, tape neatly to a sheet of $8\frac{1}{2}$-by-11-inch paper (with the publication name and dateline at the top), and photocopy.

Finally, you might wish to include **additional promotional items** that will help to make the package memorable for the recipient. These might include buttons, stickers, or trinkets of various kinds. Since editors receive (and often toss) so many of these items, it's best to avoid them unless the item is truly imaginative. At the very least, it should be closely tied in with the concept of the band or product.

Press Release. When publicists set out to inform the media about a specific event, such as a new product launch or an upcoming tour, they use a tool called a press release. This straightforward, single-page (except for complex topics) device is designed to spark interest, hopefully resulting in a magazine article or some other type of media coverage.

The format of a press release is as follows: The phrase "For Immediate Release" should be typed at the upper left corner, followed by the date.

(An alternative place for the date is at the beginning of the body copy, used with the location. Example: "New York, July 9, 1998.") In the upper right corner, type the name of the contact person followed by his or her telephone number. Start the announcement with a succinct headline, typed in capital letters and centered above the body copy. The "lead" or opening text should summarize the topic, covering the "Five W's and an H" (Who, What, When, Where, Why, and How—not to be confused with the marketing Three W's and an H mentioned in Chapter 4). An explanation, with pertinent details, should follow.

A sample press release announcing a change in band membership is shown below.

FOR IMMEDIATE RELEASE   CONTACT: LUANN S. MYERS
JULY 9, 1998   954-111-0000

I MOTHER EARTH, MULTI-PLATINUM CANADIAN BAND, PART WITH LEAD SINGER
Search for Replacement to Span U.S. and Canada

TORONTO, ON, CANADA—Canadian recording artists I Mother Earth have announced a parting of the ways with singer Edwin. The decision was a mutual one, the result of the parties moving in different directions.

This development comes four months after the band's decision to exit their domestic recording contract with Capitol Records, a division of EMI-Capitol Music Group North America. The band remains on the EMI label in Canada and will be shopping another U.S. deal once a new singer is in place.

I Mother Earth have enjoyed platinum sales status in Canada with 1994's *Dig* certified platinum and the more recent *Scenery and Fish* approaching the triple-platinum mark. The band has also received numerous Juno and Much Music nominations and awards for their recording achievements, videos, and innovative Web site. Since the departure was confirmed on April 23rd, Canadian sales of both CDs have reached new highs.

Top U.S. radio programmer and former WXTB/Tampa operations manager Greg Mull, who was instrumental in developing the band's presence in the States, commented: "I Mother Earth proved to be one of the most exciting bands to break in the nineties. Tampa is one of the many markets where IME broke big and remain big. While I am saddened to see the original lineup of the band change, I Mother Earth are a solid unit, and I anticipate an outstanding third album. Along with their other longtime supporters, I look forward to the announcement of a new singer."

I Mother Earth are currently writing their next album and holding auditions for a lead singer.

Mailings for Entertainment Calendars. Listings of concert and club dates in "calendar" sections of newspapers and magazines and on radio are the most basic form of publicity. To get listed in print, send a simple notice showing the name of the act, the venue, and the date, and include a publicity photo. For radio do the same, but add a copy of your fact sheet.

Public Service Announcement (PSA). Public service announcements are simple notices of upcoming nonprofit or charity events, and they are sent out to noncommercial electronic media. A public service announcement should be no longer than one paragraph, covering the Five W's and an H. It should include a short headline and should also provide the name and phone number of the person to contact for more information.

Publicity Tactics and Techniques

The approaches used in generating publicity are as numerous as the products routinely pitched to the buying public. In music, the differences in approaches will depend largely on whether the artist or product is new on the market or well established, and on whether the publicity campaign will be local, regional, or national. Jim Pettigrew's book *The Billboard Guide to Music Publicity* offers detailed information about how to conduct campaigns under these different circumstances. The following discussion is limited to broadly applicable tactics and techniques.

Learn About the Product and the Audience. The first task in any publicity campaign is to gain a clear understanding of the product's (the artist's or the CD's) selling points and sales "hooks." Equally important is having a clear picture of the targeted audience. This information should be obtainable by interviewing the artist and others involved in the enterprise, and by reviewing paperwork prepared during the product development phase of the overall marketing campaign (see Chapter 5).

Target the Right Media. When planning gets under way, it's vital to aim for the appropriate media. Create a custom media list of the magazines, newspapers, Web 'zines, and broadcast programs that your intended customers read and watch. And that doesn't only mean music-oriented media. *Target all possible media outlets.* If you know the non-musical interests of your audience, you can plan to reach the audience through specialty publications and programs that cater to those non-musical interests. For example, if you know that the audience of your speed-metal band includes a large number of hot-rod enthusiasts, it would be appropriate to pitch an article about the band to the editor of the top hod-rod magazine.

CONVENTIONAL WISDOM

Put heavy emphasis on getting esposure through specifically *music*-related channels and high-profile entertainment outlets.

The major labels and other industry giants aim first at mainstream music and entertainment outlets like *Rolling Stone, Spin,* and "The Tonight Show."

UNCONVENTIONAL WISDOM

Niche marketers and small labels can succeed by going *outside* the standard media channels.

One independent marketer takes the following approach: "Look at the targeted demographic consumer...see what else they're interested in, and aim at exposing the music through these other areas of their lifestyle."

Time the Coverage for Maximum Impact. Aim for media coverage that coincides with live performance dates, or with the release of a new CD. In the case of live dates, send press kits to local media well before the date, and offer editors press passes to the performance.

Think Like an Editor. Publicists have an important and constructive role to play in the media realm apart from simply promoting their products. They feed story ideas to editors and writers who are in constant need of new content. Publicists are sources of information. For that reason, you, the publicist, should be able to put yourself in editors' shoes. Learn to speak their language, since part of your task will be to work with them to make articles happen. Know what makes an article interesting to readers. Be able to extract interesting "angles" from the activities of the artist you're representing, so that when you pitch an idea to an editor you're offering something more specific than just another "great band with a new CD." For example, you might pitch an article about an unusual event in an artist's life, or a non-musical interest or activity of the artist that matches a magazine's focus.

Start with Who You Know. When ready to contact the media, focus first on columnists, editors, writers, and commentators with whom you have had previous positive contact. Short of that, start with the "best bets"— the people whose writings (which you know about from regular reading) indicate a preference for the kind of music you're promoting.

Before contacting them, come up with angles about the product that would make good subjects for articles in their individual publications. In other words, tailor your pitch to each individual as much as time allows.

Make your pitch by telephone to these people. If they're interested, tell them you'll supply any materials or information that they need.

Follow Up. After mailing press kits to the names on your media list, follow up by telephone with as many of the recipients as possible. Ask if they received the press kit. Offer to provide additional material, such as photos and extra CDs. Find out whether they are interested in covering your act. If they would like more time to think about it, make a note of that, and follow up with another call after a mutually agreed-upon interval.

Also follow up after a concert that a writer has attended as your guest. Make sure that all went smoothly. Ask if the writer needs any additional material or would like to schedule an interview with your artist.

The key in following up is to be helpful. Approach it as an opportunity to assist the editor in doing his job.

Work with the Editor. The concept of working in partnership with editors is an important one in the world of publicity. The most effective publicists have a reputation for being informative, responsive, and ready to meet editors' needs for interviews, photos, copies of CDs, and whatever else is called for. When you contact people in the media, offer to work with them on developing story ideas. Mention the availability of the artist for interviews. Ask if color slides or other items are needed. In short, make the process of preparing an article or story as easy for the editor as it is within your power to do.

Establish Positive Relationships with People in the Media. This will occur naturally if you follow the previous guidelines in this section. Having good, mutually trusting relationships with professionals in the media sector will help immeasurably in any publicity effort. Being able to phone up and "run an idea by" a familiar editor is several shortcuts past the anonymous cold call and the faceless press kit added to the editorial slush pile.

Stay Abreast of the Media. New information channels, from underground 'zines to midnight talk shows, come and go with startling speed. If you blink, you may miss an outlet that would be perfect for promoting your act. So keep your eyes open. Read trade magazines to stay on top of the changing mediascape. Surf the Internet for new music sites. Regularly peruse new and old publications to get a handle on their latest slants, and to learn about the interests of their writers. And when you find important new information, update your media list.

Independent Publicists

At a certain point in the success curve of your enterprise, your publicity needs will become more than you or your staff can handle. It is at this point that you should consider hiring an independent publicist. Indie PR people are professionals who are intimately familiar with the tools and techniques of getting exposure for clients on a regional, national, or international basis, and who know how to coordinate their plans with those of other personnel involved in the promotional campaign (such as artist management, record company staff, and radio promoters). Publicists can be put on retainer for as long, or as short a time, as they are needed in a campaign.

You can find the names of publicists by asking around and by looking in directories like the *Recording Industry Sourcebook.*

RADIO PROMOTION

In popular music, radio airplay is a near-essential promotion tool. It ranks among the Big Three of commercial activity in music, the other two being record sales and live performance. Having a number one hit single in *Billboard* magazine's Hot 100® popularity chart—a measure, in part, of radio airplay—has long been considered one of the highest achievements in commercial music.

In classical music, jazz, and other commercially marginal genres, radio play is not as much of a factor in promoting sales of recordings, simply because those types of music get less radio play. Where there is radio play of one of these non-pop recordings, of course, it provides a vital boost to retail sales.

The promotional value of radio play is easy to understand: Listeners get exposed to the music, and if they like it, chances that they'll buy the recording improve.

There are cases of performing artists making money without benefit of mainstream radio hits. One of the best examples is the Grateful Dead. The band became one of the top concert draws in the world, despite having only one top-40 radio hit in nearly 30 years of recording.

But the general rule is that radio is an important part of the marketing puzzle, even if it's airplay outside the commercial top 40.

If a recording will be well served by exposure over the radio, what can the marketer do to make sure it happens? The answer is: promote the record to radio stations. (Although radio play is itself a form of promotion, the term *radio promotion* refers to the task of convincing radio decision makers to play the record.)

First off, marketers have to be aware of the architecture of the radio industry, including the types of broadcasters in operation and the kinds of programming they offer. With this information, marketers will be better prepared to target the stations that cater to the artist's targeted customer.

Types of Radio Broadcasters

The radio industry is subdivided into two main sectors: commercial and noncommercial.

The commercial sector consists of national radio networks (such as ABC), regional radio networks, local independent stations, and syndicators. (Syndicators are production companies that package programming, which is then sold or licensed to radio stations. Shows may include announcers, music, interviews, and other elements. They allow time for insertion of commercial messages by the local stations.)

The noncommercial sector includes college and university stations, National Public Radio (NPR) affiliates, regional networks (such as Minnesota Public Radio and Peach State Public Radio), and other independent stations.

The marketer will be looking at the full range of broadcaster types for airplay opportunities. For the start-up record label or the independent artist, the best opportunities for breaking in to radio, generally speaking, will be found in the noncommercial sector.

Radio Markets and Programming Formats

Within the commercial and noncommercial radio sectors, there are approximately 12,000 stations in operation in the United States, programming in about 80 different formats.

What is a format?

A radio *format,* essentially, is the category of programming—whether classic rock, country music, easy listening, or some other category—chosen by the station owner to attract its targeted audience.

What governs such a decision? To get the answer to this, you have to look closely at what makes the radio industry tick. And that insight, in turn, will reveal much about why it can be so difficult to get airplay for an unknown artist.

In the commercial sector, the governing force essentially boils down to this: Radio stations are in business to *make a profit,* not necessarily to showcase the best records. Their money comes from advertisers, who pay the stations to run ads. Radio stations need to *attract advertisers.* To attract advertisers, they need to get *market share*—that is, a significant portion of the targeted audience. The larger the market share, the more money the station can charge for advertising.

Basically, then, commercial radio is in the business of providing advertisers with the largest possible number of ears to listen to their ads.

Advertisers, in turn, choose the stations that offer the best opportunity to reach the correct demographic for their products.

What's a demographic? A *demographic* is the set of statistical characteristics—such as age, sex, education, and economic status—defining a population segment. This should sound familiar; as discussed in Chapter 5, you, the marketer, are in the business of aiming your product at audiences with particular demographic characteristics.

Just like product marketers, radio has its targeted audiences. Through research, the radio industry has subdivided the human race into demographic markets—specific population segments that programs will attempt to attract.

The two primary markets that radio stations target are the youth market and the adult market. Stations further subdivide these according to a variety of demographic characteristics.

The radio person selling time to a potential advertiser has to convince them that at a certain time of day the station can deliver X number of listeners within a targeted demographic—listeners, say, between ages 18 and 24, who make between $20,000 and $45,000 a year, and who buy the potential advertiser's kind of products.

(Market or audience share of a particular station—that is, a station's portion of listeners who have their sets turned on at a given time—can be determined by outside firms, like the Arbitron Company, who collect data using controlled samples of listeners. Stations check their success in reaching targeted audiences by periodically checking their Arbitron rating—the radio equivalent of television's Nielsen ratings.)

To attract listeners within the chosen demographic, the station will choose the type of programming—the format—that will appeal to the largest segment of that demographic. For the youth market (late teens through mid-20s), for example, roughly 80 percent of programming is derived from commercially released records dominated by rock and its derivatives. Programs feature deejay "personalities." The tastes of the adult market, on the other hand, have been tougher to pinpoint. The general view has been that post-teens prefer "softer" music.

Within those broad guidelines, the following music formats have proven the most commercially viable:

- **Commercial Hit Radio (CHR)** (also known as Contemporary Hit Radio and Top 40): Current mainstream pop hits.

- **Mainstream Rock:** New music by such straight-ahead rock artists as the Rolling Stones, Aerosmith, Fleetwood Mac, and John Fogerty.

- **Classic Rock:** Old music by such "classic" favorites as the Who, the Beatles, and the Rolling Stones.

- **Alternative Rock** (also called Modern Rock and New Rock): New rock artists and performers whose music is characterized as non-mainstream. Aimed at young audiences.

- **Adult Contemporary (AC):** Smooth, mellow rock and oldies—artists such as Celine Dion, Michael Bolton, Eric Clapton, Linda Ronstadt, Barry Manilow, and Stevie Wonder. For ages 25 to 54.

- **Adult Top 40** (otherwise known as Hot AC, Adult Standard, and Adult Hits): Hits by artists who appeal to more "mature" listeners than artists in the Alternative or Modern Rock category; examples are Sheryl Crow, Jewel, and the Dave Matthews Band.

- **Adult Album Alternative (AAA)** (also known as Adult Alternative): Music aimed at maturing audiences who retain their interest in rock (an audience termed the "gray-haired ponytail set" by one radio station); examples of artists in this category are Van Morrison, Eric Clapton, Dire Straits, and other rock middle-of-the-roaders.

- **Soft AC and Easy Listening** (sometimes considered two different categories): Even mellower music for the adult market (the Carpenters, Johnny Mathis). Includes pop instrumental music, sometimes called "beautiful music." For those age 55 and older.

- **New AC and Smooth Jazz:** Includes such "light" jazz artists as Kenny G and Pat Metheny.

- **Country:** A range of styles subdivided into such categories as Country Rock and Pop Country. There are about 2,000 country-oriented stations in the U.S., mostly in the South Atlantic and West South Central states. It's the "second most likely to succeed format," according to one survey.

- **Urban** (also known as Rhythm and Blues, R&B, and Black Music): Includes new rap, hip-hop, R&B, and dance tracks. Examples in 1998 included Puff Daddy, DMX, and Big Punisher.

- **Urban Adult Contemporary** (also known as R&B Adult): Includes soul music and other sounds aimed at the maturing "urban music" audience. Boyz II Men, Jodeci, and Keith Sweat are some artists who have been placed in this category.

There are numerous other radio formats. Here are some of them:

- Classical
- Gospel
- Jazz
- Big Band

- Oldies
- Nostalgia
- Asian
- Spanish

- International
- Religious
- Contemporary Christian

Radio stations change format frequently—sometimes as much as once a year—depending on changing market trends, the amount of competition from other stations, and the preferences of new owners.

Bear in mind, too, that the names of formats change over time. What is now called Easy Listening was once called Middle of the Road (MOR). What is now called Urban was at one time called Rhythm and Blues. It's a good idea to keep an eye on *Billboard, Radio and Records*, Radio on the Web (www.gebbieinc.com/radintro.html), and other trade information sources so that you stay up-to-date on the latest terminology.

One indicator of the importance of listener preferences in station programming is the practice of employing what is called reverse programming. Research has shown that many people will tend to listen to a radio station—let it drone on—until they hear something they *don't* like. Consequently, some stations attempt to determine not so much what their listeners will like, but what they won't like, and then avoid it. Such reverse programming is used when a station wants to maintain current audience share, rather than build new audiences.

So that's the backdrop to the music decision-making process that occurs in the commercial radio sector. The station formats and demographics will be your guide in choosing target stations for your promotion effort.

How Do Stations Choose Records?

Now let's look at the day-to-day, week-to-week factors influencing the choice of whether to give airplay to a particular record, assuming that it conforms to a station's format.

Stations like to play it safe—which is why they're unlikely to experiment with an untested record. They like to play records that have already begun to build some momentum, or that have a good chance of making it. Evidence of this comes in the following forms:

- The record is already successful on other stations.
- The record is by an established artist with a track record of hits.
- The record is already on sales and airplay charts in trade magazines and tip sheets.

- The record is currently generating sales in record stores.

- Listeners are calling the station to request the song.

- Market tests indicate that listeners like—or do not dislike—the recording.

- The record is being recommended by a promoter—a record company representative who shows up weekly at the radio station to push new records.

Once stations have determined that a song is worth adding, they create their own weekly charts—or *playlists*—with indications of how often a record should be played. Those near the top are considered in *heavy rotation*. Those in the middle are *medium rotation*. There are usually about 20 to 30 records on a station's playlist at any given time.

Needless to say, it is extremely difficult to break into that list. The way to start is to learn who makes the decisions.

Who Chooses the Music to Play?

In stations that choose their own music, the person responsible for making up the weekly playlist is the station's program director (PD). The PD oversees a music director (MD). It is the MD's responsibility to deal with programming details—that is, keep abreast of current releases, read the trades, and meet with record promoters. The MD then makes recommendations of records for the PD to add to the playlist.

In smaller stations, a single person may serve as both program director and music director.

Music directors generally set aside one day a week to meet with record promoters.

But know this: Decisions about playlists are increasingly being made by corporate owners of networks of stations—owners who choose the music to be played on all their stations. Obviously, this represents a contraction of the broadcast distribution channel, making it more difficult for makers of unusual or innovative music to get their records played on the radio.

Independent Promoters

At the beginning, you may be handling radio promotion yourself. But at some point in your campaign you'll find it necessary to hire an independent promotion firm to take over the tasks of meeting with MDs, making follow-up calls, and handling other promotional details. The need usually arises when your campaign has already generated some success and begun to move from regional to national.

Independent promoters work regionally. They know the stations and the music directors in their markets, and usually have longstanding relationships with these entities. This is helpful because the record will have a better chance of acceptance coming from a trusted supplier than from an unknown source (such as you when you're just starting out). But because promoters rest their success on positive relationships with MDs, they tend to take on only those projects that they think have some chance of success. So to some extent you'll have to sell the prospective promoter on the commercial potential of your record before they'll agree to work on it.

Costs for independent promotion vary widely. You might hire a firm for a month for a fee of $1,500. On the high end, indie promoters may charge major labels as much as $50,000 for each single that they promote.

To find a promotion firm, ask around. Get recommendations from managers of successful artists involved in music similar to yours. Look on the Internet using the keywords *record promotion.* And hunt through directories such as the *Recording Industry Sourcebook,* the *Gavin Radio and Record Industry A to Z,* and the *Radio Power Book of Music Radio and Record Promotion* (published by Billboard).

Again, you might want to hold off on hiring an independent promoter until you've laid the initial promotional groundwork yourself.

How to Promote to Radio

Given the fierce competition for radio time, how should you approach the job of promoting a record to radio? Apart from adhering to standard industry protocol, there are some guidelines to follow that will increase your chances of success. Among them are these: start small, target the right stations, coordinate radio promotion with the other parts of the marketing campaign, present a convincing promotion package, and establish positive relationships with people in radio.

The Basic Process. Before approaching a station with product, it's important to find out the name of the person to contact at the station and the best time to make that contact.

Ideally, you'll be telephoning this person before doing anything else. (In the case of mass radio promotion, the first step may be to mail a promotion package.) In the telephone call, briefly describe who you are and the record you're representing, and then ask if you can make an appointment to meet with the music director. If the answer is negative (possibly because the MD's time is all booked up), ask if they would like you to mail them a promotion package and a copy of the record.

If you're ultimately able to set up an appointment, bring promotion materials along with copies of the recording. At the meeting you'll be discussing the recording with the music director, the goal being to make the MD want to add the song to the station's playlist. Listen to the music with the MD, and go through the promotion material, emphasizing information that will convince the MD of the disc's potential for popularity. Points to mention include radio play on other stations, touring dates or live performances in the region of the station, press and media coverage and advertising, and sales activity in local stores.

That's the general order of events. Now here are some tips for improving your chances.

Start Small. Your best bet, if you're not an established label, is to start locally. Aim first at stations in the artist's home region—the area where the artist performs regularly. That way you'll have a built-in promotional angle to present to music directors. ("The artist has been performing here for years—has regular dates lined up for the next month, in fact—and has a large local following.") Starting small will have the additional benefit of ensuring that local radio play and live performances will have a reciprocal promotional benefit.

While you're at it, it wouldn't hurt to encourage audiences at live performances to call local radio stations to request airplay of the single.

As touring expands to new regions, expand radio promotion to stations in those regions. (Keep in mind that with expansion will eventually come the need to employ regional promoters—unless you, the marketer, can clone yourself to handle several regions simultaneously.)

Target the Right Stations. As with publicity, it's important to aim for outlets that reach your targeted audience. (After all, it wouldn't make much sense to promote an electronic noise band to a mainstream country music station.)

The way to ensure an appropriate match is to do some preliminary research. Check radio station directories that list stations by region, by format, by audience, and by market share. There are books that serve this purpose, including the *Radio Power Book,* the *Broadcasting and Cable Yearbook,* and Gebbie Press's *All-in-One Media Directory.* Also, the World Wide Web has several media lists that sort stations by various criteria. They include the BRS Radio Directory (www.radio-directory.com), Radio on the Web (www.gebbieinc.com/radintro.htm), and the MIT List of Radio Stations on the Internet (wmbr.mit.edu/stations/list.html), which includes a list titled "Local Stations in Your Area."

Make a list of the stations most likely to accept your product and add them to your media list.

Coordinate with Other Parts of the Marketing Campaign. The most effective radio play occurs in synchronization with live performances and other types of promotion. All components of the campaign then work together to create a kind of media blitz. Audiences see ads for concerts, hear the music on the radio, read reviews of the record, watch an interview on local cable TV, and soon become hyper-aware of the presence of this music entity.

When you undertake a promotion to radio, time it so that any radio play will occur simultaneously with a live performance in the station's region. And make sure the music director is aware of the upcoming performances—it'll make the MD more likely to want to play the record.

Present a Convincing Promo Package. The promotion kit presented to radio stations—either in person or by mail—consists of essentially the same material used for the publicity campaign. That would be a press kit, including a fact sheet, a bio, some press clips, some publicity photos, a cover letter, and some additional promo items like T-shirts and buttons. (See page 152 for more about press kits.)

It's extremely important that these materials present a convincing picture of the act's previous successes and potential for continuing growth in popularity. The cover letter, fact sheet, and bio should clearly illuminate the points that will be of key interest to station music directors, such as previous radio play, distribution strategy, current tour plans, and track record of media coverage.

Marketers often try to make the promo package more memorable by including a gimmick—a trinket of some kind that has a conceptual connection with the artist or record. Often these gimmicks lean toward the ridiculous, earning an immediate toss into the station garbage can and prompting an emotional backlash against the record and its promoters. To avoid this, make sure the item has usefulness, some degree of aesthetic value, or at least genuine humor.

Marketer Tim Sweeney, author of *Tim Sweeney's Guide to Releasing Independent Records,* describes mailing a miniature garden starter kit to radio stations as part of the promo package for a band called Weeds Peterson. "When we called the stations to ask if they'd received the package 'with the flower bulbs,'" recalls Sweeney, "every music director knew exactly what we were talking about, and several had already planted the bulbs."

Establish Positive Relationships with People in Radio. Music directors at radio stations are besieged with people promoting records. Chances are they'll give preference to those whom they trust, or with whom they have established good relationships. You should aim to be among that group.

Building trust means consistently demonstrating professionalism in your interactions with station personnel: following up on mailings, being proactive without being pushy, knowing the station's format and demographics, knowing your product inside and out so that you can answer questions, being knowledgeable about the music business and current musical trends, and generally showing that you know what you're doing.

Building a relationship has more to do with the "people" side of the equation. The introverts among us may bemoan the fact that "it ain't what you can do, it's who you know," but the fact remains that in the music business—as in many other businesses—"who you know" goes a long way toward getting the job done. In radio promotion, you need to be outgoing, sociable—the kind of person to whom someone would be happy to extend an invitation to meet again a week later, or the week after that. Because if you ever get to the point of having batches of records to promote, you'll be calling on certain music directors on a fairly regular basis. And it's nice to feel wanted when you make those calls.

Much has been made about payola in the music business—essentially, bribes funneled to radio personnel by record labels through independent promoters in order to get records added to playlists. The word is that that kind of thing doesn't go on anymore. What do go on are dining, socializing, gift giving, favor providing, and all the other types of unofficial "incentives" that tend to grease the rusty wheels of business and commerce the world over—whatever the industry. Like it or not, you the promoter-marketer-salesperson will have to put on your party clothes (figuratively speaking, of course) and become a glad-hander. A people person. And you'll have to do it in a relaxed and sincere way. Because the only things more off-putting to some people than aloofness are see-through phoniness and obsequiousness.

Take the music director to the occasional lunch. But don't forget to enjoy yourself in the process. This is the music business, after all. It's supposed to be fun.

Handling Rejection. What if you can't generate any radio interest? Keep in mind that even if radio stations reject a record initially, it's not necessarily the end of the road. They might add the record to their playlists sometime later, if they see that live dates and press are generating growing audience demand. For example, the Gin Blossoms' single "Hey Jealousy" was initially rejected by alternative radio. The band continued to tour and generate word-of-mouth interest. Months later the song was picked up by a Los Angeles rock station. The airplay translated into growing record sales, which caused the song to be added by several more stations. More touring success combined with more radio attention and more record sales, all adding up to a successful—if slow to pick up steam—marketing effort.

So don't treat an initial lack of radio enthusiasm as a rejection. View it as an impetus to work on building an audience, gathering press coverage, and marketing locally until you generate so much grassroots excitement that radio stations will be compelled to take a second look.

College Radio as Career Launching Pad

For both the fledgling record peddler and the more established marketer, college radio is often where all radio promotion begins. Where national commercial radio is largely inaccessible to those not affiliated with major labels, college radio can be approached successfully. Where commercial radio is singles oriented, college radio is more freewheeling in its programming, offering a wider selection of music than commercial radio and thus providing better opportunities for smaller acts to get airplay. Often, success at the college radio level will snowball into acceptance by commercial radio.

College radio is also used by major labels to test-market their acts before promoting at the national commercial level. The artist Jewel, for example, was intentionally promoted first at the college radio level by her label, Atlantic, to drum up grassroots support among college-age listeners. The songs that college radio chose to play, and the geographical locations of listener interest, helped guide subsequent marketing and promotion decisions by the Jewel marketing team.

Stephanie LeBeau, head of a San Francisco-based independent promotion company called Vision Trust, specializes in college radio, and she emphasizes its importance to the careers of developing artists:

> "[In the case of more-established labels] college radio is the first market all artists/bands are sent to. Some call it a test market. The reason this is the first market is that it is a *free* format and can play whatever tracks they wish. The stations are supplied with records, and it is up to the volunteering music director to pick and choose what music will best suit his or her market.
>
> The end result [of college radio promotion] is to create a buzz, build awareness, and build a solid foundation from which the artists/ bands can grow. For some majors it's not only to create a buzz but also to help sort out [identify] the commercial hit track. The label will usually have the single chosen, but then the information coming back from the college market could change the track or confirm it.

The better the artist does at college radio, the more ammo, if you will, the label will have at getting national commercial [radio] interest.

[In the case of small-label and indie promotion efforts, college radio] informs the artists/bands of where their markets are, what the popular tracks are, and indeed if they have a market. They can use the information collected and schedule a tour, get consignment with retail stores (because now they know where a buying market is), or even get a distribution deal. The [college radio play] information also shows a buyer/investor that the artist/band is worthy of further investing with the potential of making their money back.

A band that is struggling and gets enough money together to produce a CD should definitely do their research before they send it out to college radio stations. There are books available. I have found that *Getting Radio Airplay,* by Gary Hustwit, and *The Musician's Guide to Touring and Promotion* are the most useful. [The latter] lists radio stations across the country and gives you a heads up to the lingo needed to best express [your promotional pitch].

Our job [as college radio promoters] is to make sure the music director—who is a volunteer in most cases—doesn't let the release we are representing slip through the cracks, the black hole, which could mean [being used as] a coffee coaster in the lobby or sold to the nearest used-record-store bin. The average college radio station receives anywhere from 50 to 100 CDs per week. That is one reason the life of records in this market is so short. The other reason is that the deejays can play whatever tracks they fancy. Which means the record will burn out at a faster rate. Every week is crucial. The life ["impact time"] of a record in this market is 10 weeks. At the end of the promotion the label or artist will still continue to get played, but the impact time is gone.

If the band can afford to hire a college independent radio promotion company, it may prove money well spent, especially when you consider the long-distance calls and the impact/life of your record at the stations. The music director will also take your CD more seriously coming from a person they trust. Most music directors don't like talking to band members, because they are not objective and usually do not know what the radio station is currently playing or when the MD holds their office hours. They would have to do weeks of research just to obtain that information. But of course, if there is a dedicated band member who will take the time to do all the grassroots work, like readers of this book, they may be able to accomplish a lot on their own. **"**

VIDEO AND TELEVISION
AS PROMOTIONAL TOOLS

How do videos and television fit into the music marketing and promotion picture? What impact do they have on the distribution and consumption of popular music?

Like radio, they provide outlets for getting music to the ears of consumers. Unlike radio, they provide the added promotional power of visual information, filling out the consumer's mental picture of the artist.

Performers for whom visual exposure has been vital—or extremely valuable—including the following:

- The Beatles, whose appearance on "The Ed Sullivan Show" in 1964 made them household names in the United States
- Madonna, whose music videos were essential in establishing her image and persona
- Duran Duran and other "new romantic" pop groups of the early 1980s, whose videos helped make visual image an important part of music marketing and promotion
- Tina Turner, who staged a comeback with the help of video in the mid-1980s

Overall, videos and television exposure are extremely potent promotional tools. Handled intelligently, they can make the difference between relegation to the commercial fringe and acceptance by mass audiences.

Video Promotion

Since the launch of Music Television (MTV) in the early 1980s, the music video has become a staple of the music business. Videos—while they won't necessarily "break" an artist or directly affect record sales—are generally thought to have an important indirect impact on solidifying and increasing sales. They are indispensable for increasing name recognition and shaping an artist's public image and personality.

With the introduction of music video, a new weight was added to the shoulder of the musical performer: it was no longer enough to be musically proficient; the artist now also had to develop a visual image that would permit exposure in a variety of visual as well as audio media. The dawn of the music video was also the dawn of the cross-media marketing vision that now dominates the entertainment industry. For example, Madonna—one artist—is marketed through recordings, videos, movies, television guest appearances, magazine articles, and books.

For the beginning act, a video is not essential. Again, the story of the Gin Blossoms carries a pertinent lesson. As label executive Jim Guerinot told writer Bud Scoppa, the band initially "had no need whatsoever for a video other than it's occasionally useful, whether it's a sales presentation or in some remote local show. We didn't think MTV for a second."

Only after the marketing-promotion machine has been in motion for a while—generating radio airplay, press coverage, and the rest—will it be time to approach the video programming giants for a shot at adding a clip to their rotation schedules.

When it comes time to prepare a video, follow all the guidelines you applied to other promotional materials. Make sure the style and mood of the clip match the image and personality you are trying to convey. Visuals of the video must reflect the nature of the artist and music—just like CD packaging and print ads.

Television Promotion

Now for television itself. How important is it? Let's put it this way: if an artist performs on "The Late Show with David Letterman," "The Tonight Show," or "Saturday Night Live," it means one of two things: (1) either it's a new artist who, through the appearance, will instantly become known to millions, or (2) it's an already famous artist who, through the appearance, will promote a new record to millions. TV is one powerful promotion tool.

Promoting to Television

To promote to television, you'll follow the general approach used for both publicity and radio promotion.

Contacting programs will involve sending press kits and video clips to individual TV producers. As with publicity and radio promotion, the press kits should provide convincing information about sales success, media coverage, popularity, and so on. (The producers want to know that an audience exists for the clip they are being asked to broadcast.) After mailing, you'll use follow-up telephone calls to verify receipt and determine the degree of interest.

As with radio, start small, mainly because you'll have to; the national programs won't consider you unless you've established a track record. At initial stages, think in terms of local cable programs—any type that broadcasts video clips or includes musical guests.

Target appropriate programs. Channel-surf until you're familiar with all the relevant programs on the dial. (For categories of shows, refer to the list in "Broadcast Media" on page 149.) Then add them to your media list. Find out the name of the producer of each show, so that when you establish contact you're able to do it person-to-person rather than send your material to "whom it may concern."

When producers indicate interest, work with them to ensure that the video programming or the on-air performance occurs on a date (or dates) around the same time that a recording is available in stores and tracks are getting played on the radio. When this works well, as mentioned earlier in the chapter, you'll achieve a bona fide media blitz.

SALES PROMOTION

Other types of promotion are designed to directly encourage sales, provide incentives to keep prices down, or draw attention to the product via methods other than publicity and advertising. Such programs fall in to the category of sales promotion.

Sales promotions are generally of two types: (1) programs aimed at members of the distribution channel, such as wholesale distributors and retail outlets, and (2) programs aimed directly at consumers.

Distribution Channel Promotions

As mentioned in Chapter 9, ideally you'll want to have your CD prominently displayed in stores that stock it. In other words, you'll want the stores to give your product special treatment. But stores have no vested interest in doing this; all they care about is that products are selling, *whatever* they are. Add to this the heavy label competition for limited display space and you might quickly conclude that you'll have to give stores some kind of incentive to specially promote your product. You'd be right.

What kinds of benefits can you provide to retail so that they will agree to give you prominent display space? There are several that are standard.

One is a reduction in price for an order of recordings (passed from you through the distributor to the retailer) in return for prominent display in the store. This can run you anywhere from several hundred dollars for a CD promotion in a single store to many thousands of dollars for a promotion in multiple outlets of a national chain. It would buy you space in window displays, wall displays, end caps, and tables for a period of several days to a week.

In addition, you can promote your album through the record store using what is called co-op advertising. Here's how it works: The retailer places a newspaper ad that plugs both the store and several new (or old) albums being sold in the store. (You've undoubtedly seen newspaper ads for stores such as Sam Goody, including blurbs on a handful of albums.) You pay for the portion of the ad that features your product. The retailer pays for the entire ad and then deducts your share of the cost from its account with your distributor. The distributor, in turn, deducts this amount from what it owes you. The retailer often backs up the ad with prominent in-store display and discounting of your product for a specified time period.

Several of the larger record store chains now publish magazines to promote new music that they sell. For example, Tower Records puts out *Pulse*. Musicland publishes *Request*. Part of retail promotion is getting the stores to cover your product in their magazines. Your incentive package can include a request that the store provide such coverage.

Consumer Sales Promotions

Sales promotion programs can be aimed directly at consumers. Giving prospective buyers an extra "push" is often what's needed to get them to make a purchase. There are any number of ways to do this, and marketers are constantly coming up with new ones. Here are some incentives that are fairly common:

- Tear-out coupons, printed in newspapers or other media, that offer money off the "suggested retail price" of products purchased within a specified time period.
- Direct discounts off the retail price, indicated with stickers on the products themselves. (A common tactic is to give retailers a discount on product so that they will pass on a discount to customers.)
- More product (such as extra tracks on a compact disc or cassette) without an increase in price.
- A premium (such as a poster) included with the product at no extra charge.
- Two products (such as a full-length CD plus a CD single) for the price of one.
- Merchandise (such as T-shirts, coffee mugs, and cigarette lighters) either given away or sold.
- CD sampler giveaways at retail stores, timed to coincide with radio play.
- CD sampler giveaways at concerts.
- Contests, coordinated with local radio stations and retail stores.

LIVE PERFORMING AS PROMOTION

One of the most effective forms of promotion is live performance. Tours and concerts result in an artist's direct contact with the audience and in increased media coverage due to reviews and personality profiles in the press.

It is common for an artist to go on tour in support of a new album release. Because of the promotional value of touring, record labels often provide financial tour support (repayable by the artist out of record royalties). The investment pays off in the form of a steadily growing audience base, which eventually translates into record sales. This process worked for the Gin Blossoms, as explained by Jerry Weintraub, A&M Records Vice President of Artist Development, to writer Bud Scoppa:

> "I was into that band hundreds of thousands of dollars in tour support...they were our road dogs. The Gin Blossoms could play anywhere, at any time. Some of those shows they had to do I wouldn't wish on anybody. But it paid off....
>
> The band was really super—they did it in a van; they worked. It was a healthy commitment of cash because it took so long; relatively, on a per-week basis, it was modest. But when you have a band that's willing to go through that kind of ordeal for as long as they were willing to go through it, the cash added up....
>
> The thing that kept happening, though, that made it worthwhile, where it became clear to us that we needed to keep doing this, is there was growth. We were getting growth in terms of, oh, 200 people at a show is now 320 the next time they show up. Then they'd go support someone, go back in that market again and it'd be 500 people, support someone, come back and it would be a sell-out....It was truly artist development at that point—the band growing and developing an audience. Same thing with Blues Traveler, same thing with Soundgarden....Develop an audience base and the record sales will follow....
>
> We hung out long enough to get the lucky break that you eventually need to break a band. It was all about the touring. It was keeping the band on the road until the radio climate started to change. The marketplace shifted a little bit in our direction, and we were still around. We hadn't abandoned hope."

The media value of touring is that it functions as a news event, which can serve as the basis for a publicity campaign. An upcoming live appearance in a region or locale is an ideal "story" for a publicist to pitch to editors and producers of local newspapers and electronic media.

To more directly promote a new recording via live performance, you can use the appearance as an opportunity to distribute copies of the CD as well as posters, bumper stickers, and any other collateral material. Having the venue play tracks from the recording before and after the stage act wouldn't hurt, either.

CROSS-PROMOTION

In the business realm, the years near the turn of the millenium have been a time of corporate partnerships—separate companies sharing certain resources for mutual benefit, each helping to extend the other's marketing reach.

Here's how this applies to you: One of the more imaginative, and increasingly prevalent, promotional techniques is *cross-promotion*. It involves partnering with another business entity to simultaneously promote each other's products. The beauty of it is that costs are shared by both partners, and each benefits from access to the other's customer base.

An example you've probably noticed is the promotion of a new movie via linkage with a fast-food chain, such as McDonald's. Television ads tout movie-related toys, mugs, and other merchandise to be given away with certain meals (for a limited time encompassing the opening of the movie); the fast-food outlets feature in-store point-of-purchase promotional items, posters, and other attention-getting devices. The benefit to the foodery is that the number of customers increases because families are attracted by the gifts. The benefit to the movie is that promotion of the flick is extended to customers who might not otherwise be aware of it.

Another example of cross-promotion is a coupon for computer software on a box of breakfast cereal. The customer is offered a cheap price for the software if he or she mails in the coupon along with, say, three cereal boxtops. The cereal manufacturer benefits from increased sales due to the special deal; the software manufacturer benefits from access to cereal consumers who are outside the usual software-consumer base.

One music-related cross-promotion involved Windham Hill Records, Macy's department store, and Tower Records. The three set up a deal in which any customer buying a CD player from Macy's (involving 23 stores in California) would get a free Windham Hill sampler CD plus coupons from Tower Records for discounts off Windham Hill CDs and videos. To draw attention to the promotion, Macy's sponsored an in-store concert by a Windham Hill artist, included the label in its print ad campaign, and used in-store display advertising. Tower also set up special in-store Windham Hill promotional displays.

All three businesses stood to gain from this deal: For Macy's, there was the potential for selling more CD players thanks to the giveaway CD and coupons. For Windham Hill, there was exposure to Macy's huge customer base and increased sales due to the coupons given away by Macy's. For Tower Records there was the chance to sell more of its Windham Hill product.

A successful cross-promotion is one where the partners cater to the same *demographic* but reach different segments. That way, each gains access to the other's segment and thus increases the size of its customer base. As Windham Hill marketer Roy Gattinella told *Billboard:* "[Macy's] wanted to tie in a label, and Windham Hill is fairly obvious because you figure the Windham Hill buyer and Macy's customers are demographically similar."

When considering cross-promotion, think in terms of businesses outside your usual distribution channel. And think of ones that cater to the types of people who would like your music. Then envision ways in which both your business and the other would benefit from cross-promotion. Use that concept as the basis for a proposal to the other business.

Another Windham Hill cross-promotion (and we keep referring to this label because its programs have been consistently creative and successful) was with a Napa Valley winery, Sterling Vineyards. Sterling, recognizing the demographic similarity of Windham's customers and its own, sponsored a tour by Windham Hill musicians to benefit tree-planting groups across the United States. It then co-sponsored a Windham Hill CD featuring music from the tour. (For more information about CD "partnerships," see "Custom Albums" on page 211.) Each partner's visibility was extended to the other's core customers, and both benefited from association with an environmental cause.

ADVERTISING

In music promotion, paid advertising is used as a supplement to publicity, radio promotion, and all other programs aimed at drawing attention to the product.

There are two major downsides to advertising. One is that it is relatively expensive. Another is that it can be perceived by customers as "hype" (in other words, not as objective as, say, a review in a newspaper—a problem that can, however, be solved by using endorsement quotes in the ad).

The basic purpose of advertising is to assist in the sale of the product by increasing awareness of it and by making it attractive to a targeted audience.

Types and Cost of Advertisements

There's a long list of possible ways to advertise your music, all of which boil down to these categories: display ads in newspapers and other print media; direct mail pieces such as brochures (see Chapter 10 for more information); flyers for placement in cafés and other public places; outdoor billboards and signage; transit ads (in buses, taxis, trains, and subways); Internet ads (see Part 3); and commercials on radio and television.

Ad costs vary tremendously and are affected by a number of factors.

In print media, factors affecting cost include the size of the publication's audience (circulation), the size of the ad, whether the ad is black and white or color, the number of times the ad is run (frequency discounts apply), and the position in the publication (back and inside covers are more expensive, for example; and when there's competition for prime space, publications usually give preference to repeat customers).

Factors affecting cost in broadcast media include the size of the outlet's audience, the length of the commercial, the number of times the commercial is broadcast (frequency discounts apply), and the time of day of the broadcast (for example, in radio, "morning drive" time is more expensive, and in TV, "prime time" is more expensive).

The following charts provide sample ad rates in various media.

TYPICAL PRINT MEDIA AD RATES (1998)*

Media Type	Smallest Ad	Largest Ad
Newspaper		
College	$10†	$1,260‡
Community	$24†	$3,024‡
Small Daily	$60†	$7,560‡
Major Daily	$300†	$37,800‡
Magazine		
Specialty (50,000 circulation)	$500	$3,000
Regional Consumer (150,000 circulation)	$2,500	$10,000
National Consumer (500,000 circulation)	$6,000	$27,000

* Black-and-white ad, one time only

† Per standard advertising unit (SAU), a.k.a. standard column inch, which measures $2\frac{1}{16}$ inches (one column) by one inch deep

‡ Full page (broadsheet size), or 126 SAUs

TYPICAL BROADCAST MEDIA AD RATES (1998)

Media Type	Least Expensive (per 1,000 customers)*	Most Expensive (per 1,000 customers)*
Television (30-second ad[†])		
Network	$3.00 (daytime)	$25.00 (prime-time)
Cable	$3.00 (most programming)	$20.00 (national network)
Radio (60-second ad[†])	$2.00[‡] (local)	$5.00[‡] (national network)

* All dollar values represent cost per 1,000 consumers reached.

[†] Timings are those most commonly used in the given media type, although other timings are sometimes used.

[‡] Price variances depend additionally on the time of day of the broadcast.

Placement

It's essential for the effectiveness of advertising that the ad be placed in media that are known to reach the target audience or potential new audience members.

One group of music publications, collectively known as the BAM Network, seeks to attract music advertisers by emphasizing its ability to reach targeted music consumers. "Our guarantee," claims the Network on its Web site, "is that these publications will deliver a specific audience, defined by its love of music, which resides in major markets across the United States." The Network also claims to reach consumers "where they live, shop, and hang out...in record and retail stores, clubs and cafés in markets that matter most." For target advertising, you'll want to deal with media that deliver this kind of audience.

An alternative to target advertising is high-dispersion advertising, where you seek to build audiences by aiming for the maximum number of different consumers. The best media for this are network television and large-circulation consumer magazines. Not surprisingly, the costs of placing ads in these media are high.

Message

In fashioning the message to be delivered in the ad, keep in mind that the overall purpose is to spark interest and create positive feeling about the product, and to provide the impetus to buy it.

The central message of an ad is often referred to as the Unique Selling Proposition—the notion that the product has something appealing that makes it different from other products. In the product development phase of your marketing effort (discussed in Chapter 5), you identified your music's selling points and the characteristics that made it different from other products. In an ad, you'll have to boil those characteristics down to one simple, powerful, and convincing message.

Ideally, the message will speak—directly or indirectly—to the self-image and preferences of the target consumer group. (Remember Apple Computers' ad line, "Here's to the crazy ones"?)

For more discussion of ad copy and content, see page 141.

Other Advertising Approaches

There are various ways to advertise without breaking the bank. One is to use co-op advertising, where a retailer places an ad that includes your product and charges you for that portion of the ad (see the discussion on page 175). Another is per-inquiry advertising—an arrangement where you place an ad in a magazine without paying an up-front fee. Instead, the magazine takes payment only when a sale comes directly from the ad. Payment is in the form of a percentage of the retail price of the product.

TRADE SHOWS AND CONFERENCES

Trade shows like South by Southwest, CMJ, NAMM (the National Association of Music Merchants), NARM (the National Association of Recording Merchandisers), and AFIM (the Association for Independent Music) offer a different kind of promotional opportunity. They are music industry conventions, so they are not much good for promoting to the final consumer. They are better for promoting to potential members of your distribution channel, like wholesalers and retailers, and for increasing your (or your product's) visibility within the music industry.

South by Southwest, for example, provides new musical acts with the opportunity to be heard by, and network with, record companies, producers, and managers who might be able to provide career assistance.

SAMPLE PROMOTION STRATEGIES

Creative, imaginative promotion professionals draw from all of the methods discussed thus far to develop campaigns carefully tailored for the specific product. And, as also pointed out previously (several times, because it's important for you to grasp), successful architects of promotion campaigns often look beyond the standard approaches to find innovative ways to gain exposure to new audiences and places where commercial transactions occur.

CONVENTIONAL WISDOM

Succeed by attracting as large as possible a share of the existing market.

Many marketers aim primarily at typical record buyers, competing with other marketers for their attention in mainstream music outlets.

UNCONVENTIONAL WISDOM

Go where other haven't gone, and find new audiences; create new markets.

Windham Hill, for example, found new markets for their records by promoting in bookstores, health-food stores, and other non-music outlets. As Silicon Valley marketing expert Regis McKenna put it: "Marketing should focus on market creation, not market sharing.... Rather than taking a bigger slice of the pie, [marketers] must try to create a bigger pie" (*On Achieving Excellence,* February 1988).

Two independent music marketers who think creatively are Luann Sullivan Myers and Eva Dickenson-Post, partners doing business under the name EvaLuTion Entertainment Marketing. They describe themselves as being "in the idea business....What we try to do as a specialty is to create means of exposing music without necessarily having to get it on the radio. And sometimes even bypassing the traditional music retailer."

Here are a few examples of imaginative campaigns—they call them "awareness campaigns"—that Myers and Dickenson-Post conducted for several clients.

FOR A NEW BLUES RECORD RELEASE:

- Sent CD mailings to national blues societies, with mail-back surveys that supplied information on local blues retail outlets, newsletters, and radio. Used the information to create a custom marketing database.

- Set up links with several blues-oriented Web sites.

- Sent CDs to nationally syndicated blues radio shows.

- Sent a two-song CD sampler to blues radio stations and blues clubs in 13 focus markets.

- Set up CD sampler giveaway to visitors at Riverwalk Blues Festival in Fort Lauderdale and to "blues cruise" patrons.

FOR THE RELEASE OF AN ALBUM BY I MOTHER EARTH:

- Acted as Florida regional sales director and local promotion manager.

- Worked Florida stations on the song "One More Astronaut," sending out powdered eggs and Tang and following up with faxes and phone calls.

- Coordinated July 4th radio performance with an autograph session following at a Blockbuster Music tent that included a portable listening station featuring the new release.

- Set up a fund-raising event (cross-promoting the album *Scenery and Fish*) with the organization Save Our Everglades, involving retail, radio, the press, and the local I Mother Earth fan club. (See the flyer at right.)

- Set up an opportunity for the public to e-mail an astronaut on the Mir space station via I Mother Earth's Web site. Notified radio stations to participate. Listed the opportunity with all available Internet search engines.

Flyer cross-promoting an album and a fund-raising event.

FOR ANOTHER ALBUM RELEASE:

- Set up cassette sampler giveaways with retail in the radio airplay markets to promote current focus track.

- Set up cross-promotions with coffeehouses and restaurants in several markets, using specially produced samplers and coasters.

- Booked listening booths at most of the stores affiliated with the Coalition of Independent Music Stores to ensure visibility during the holiday buying season.

FOR ANOTHER ALBUM RELEASE:

- Aimed to increase exposure in focus tour and radio airplay markets.

- Emphasized getting music played in coffeehouses, health-food stores, clothing stores, clubs, cafés, and bed and breakfasts.

So use your imagination. Start with the ideas explored above and use them as springboards to your own promotional planning. Think beyond the traditional channels through which music flows. Think of all the ways music gets to people's ears: on airlines, in supermarkets, in boutiques and other clothing stores, on obscure cable TV shows, on Web sites, in hip hotels, in coffee bars, in movie theaters—wherever people congregate in public or receive information. Then find ways to get your music into those environments. (Think of yourself as a new-millenium version of the early-1900s song pluggers described in Chapter 1.)

The idea is to create new markets. Let the other music enterprises battle each other only for the small remaining portions of the existing music consumer base. With innovation, hard work, and luck, you'll have a whole new market all to yourself.

CHAPTER
12
Working the Live Performance Market

Playing live is the most basic way to get music to the marketplace.

The nightclub or concert stage is where the initial "sales pitch" is made, for most musical artists (the exceptions being media personalities like Madonna, who are sold first on disc and video). The stage is an ideal site for test marketing: The music is played and the audience either likes it or not. The audience also accepts or rejects the *way* the music is presented—that is, the artist's stage presence, visual image, and personality.

Traditionally, it all starts here. If the music proves saleable at a given venue, other live performances follow. If the artist builds an audience, sales of recordings follow. If the recording is successful, more recordings and higher-level concerts follow. And on it goes, until the continually successful artist becomes an established headliner, marketable in all sectors of the music marketplace, from large performance venues to new media to broadcasting.

As a tool in the total marketing program, live performance serves two purposes: it earns money directly and it promotes other products the artist has on the market. (See page 177 for more on the promotional value of live performances.)

As a direct source of income, live performing—even if only on the local level—can keep a music career afloat for years. It's a major part of the musician's financial pie.

As promotion, it's especially valuable for up-and-coming artists who don't yet have extensive radio play, where it can provide the spark needed to ignite record sales. Such was the case with singer-songwriter Jewel: "When she was on the road she was selling records," said A&R rep Jenny Price to ASCAP's Bud Scoppa. "She was getting very little radio airplay....she was selling at least 1,000 records a month from basically just live shows."

CONVENTIONAL WISDOM

Before issuing a CD, a performer has to build a following by performing live.

In the past, musicians began by working steadily in clubs, building popularity at the local and regional levels in the hope that a record company would eventually take notice and sign them to a recording contract.

ALTERNATE REALITY

Today, a musical act may release a CD—independently or through a major label—prior to embarking on a steady live performance schedule. Some clubs, in fact, won't book an act that doesn't have a CD on the market. (The practice of releasing a record first has roots in the distant past: The 1967 Summer of Love song "A Whiter Shade of Pale" was recorded before the artist, Procol Harum, was a complete band. Only *after* the song became a hit did singer Gary Brooker assemble musicians and take them on the road.)

There are several levels of live activity. The first is that of the start-up or local act. The next step up the success ladder involves performing regionally in concerts and large showcase clubs. The third level is that of the headlining recording artist, involving large-scale touring.

While there is not always a strict separation between these levels (for example, a regional act may also open for a major artist on a national tour), each move up the ladder requires some adjustment in business strategy.

For purposes of the following discussion, let's assume that the "product" has already been developed—that is, the musician has already achieved a performance-ready level of competence, complete with a repertoire, a set list, the needed personnel, a sense of how to "put on a show," and all the necessary instruments and sound equipment.

NEW OR LOCAL ARTISTS AND LIVE PERFORMING

Many successful music careers start out at the level of playing at nightclubs, hotel lounges, restaurants, weddings, office parties, and private get-togethers in areas immediately surrounding home locales. Other careers both start and end at this level. Either way, nearly every musician deals with it at some point along the career trajectory.

Booking Performances at the Start-Up or Local Level

Getting the job for the local or beginning artist is most often a do-it-yourself process.

Friends and acquaintances are the first source of work. Musicians can put out the word that they're available and thereby line up bookings at private parties, school dances, and other types of local functions.

Booking work in commercial venues like nightclubs requires a more professional approach. It includes the following steps:

- Create a demo tape, using three or four representative recordings and putting the best first. (Be prepared to program different demo tapes for different prospective employers, depending on their music preferences.)

- Create a basic promotion kit, which should include the demo tape plus an 8-by-10-inch photograph, a fact sheet describing the artist and listing past engagements, several press clips if available, and a folder to put it all in. (See page 152 for detailed information on professional press kits.)

- Identify the target audience and the clubs, cafés, and other venues that cater to it.

- Telephone or visit each venue to get the name of the person who does the booking.

- Mail press kits to those individuals or deliver the kits in person.

- Follow up by telephone several days later. Offer to provide additional information, if needed, including professional references. If no bookings are offered, ask if a future callback would be advisable. Make note of the answer, and follow up at the appropriate time.

Pricing and Payment at the Start-Up or Local Level

The amount of money that can be earned at the start-up or local level varies considerably. On the low end, a member of a performing group might leave a local club gig at 3 a.m. with a total of $15 in the pocket. On the high end, a corporate party might pay several thousand dollars for a small group. Here are some ballpark examples:

- Subway platform or business-district street during rush hour: $75
- Small restaurant, Sunday brunch: $100 for a duo, several sets
- Folk music or jazz club/café, evening performance: $200 for a single or small group, one to three sets
- Rock club: $200 for a small group, one to three sets
- Wedding: $2,000 for a quartet or quintet, two to three sets
- Corporate event: $2,000 for a quartet or quintet, two to three sets

Parties, weddings, and restaurants generally pay a flat fee. When you get into the realm of nightclubs, however, there are numerous possible approaches to handling payment, as follows:

- Flat fee.
- Percentage of the door. The performer gets paid only from ticket sales or the cover charge, at a rate typically somewhere between 15 and 50 percent, negotiable. (For example, if 25 people show up, the cover charge is $10, and you're getting paid 50 percent of the door, you'll be paid $125.) If the club expects to make most of its money from alcohol and food sales, you may be able to negotiate a higher percentage.
- Flat fee or a percentage of the door, whichever is greater.
- Flat fee *plus* a percentage of the door.
- One hundred percent of the door, after deducting a "house fee." The club would require a specified dollar guarantee, to be recouped from ticket or cover charge receipts. After recoupment, all "door" money would go to the performer.

There are many, many variations on these methods of payment. Generally, avoid paying the house to let you use their facilities. And if payment is a percentage of the door, go all out to get as many people as possible to show up.

When you book an appearance, make sure to have a contract written up. It should specify—at the very least—the location and date of the engagement, the schedule and hours of the performance, the amount of compensation, the method and timing of compensation, and the names, addresses, and signatures of both purchaser and performer.

Promoting Performances at the Start-Up or Local Level

In club work, attracting customers is vital not only when the performer is paid a percentage of the door (where earnings depend on attendance) but also because a booker's willingness to rehire the performer may depend on it.

To promote a performance, prepare informational flyers with the gig's place, date, time, and door charge and mail them to friends, family, acquaintances, and anyone else who might be remotely interested.

Post flyers in windows and bulletin boards of record stores, cafés, and any other appropriate commercial and public spaces that will allow them.

Get the performance listed in entertainment calendar sections of local media. Do this by sending newspapers and local magazines a simple notice showing the name of the act, the venue, and the date and time. Include a publicity photo if there are enough extras. For radio do the same, but add a copy of the artist fact sheet.

Encourage coverage in the local media by sending simple promotion kits to local music writers. Follow up by telephone and offer them press passes to the performance. After the gig, call them to thank them for showing up (if they did) and offer additional information if they'd like it. Demonstrating professionalism and concern just might nudge the writer toward deciding to write a review.

Onstage Marketing

The task of marketing doesn't stop when the performer hits the stage. Any attempt to win over the crowd is, in fact, a form of marketing. The performer should use all the skills at his command to "close the sale" onstage in a manner appropriate to the setting and in keeping with his artistic vision and musical style.

CONVENTIONAL WISDOM

Job One for the club musician is to keep the crowd happy.

The club musician is in partnership with the club owner. If the band holds the crowd and the crowd buys drinks, the club owner makes money, is happy, and rehires the band.

BREAKING THE RULE

The seventies proto-punk band Suicide routinely shocked its audiences with its confrontational stage show, often driving people away from the club. Silver lining: though rarely hired, Suicide eventually became regarded as art-rock innovators and performance pioneers.

MIDDLE-LEVEL ARTISTS AND LIVE PERFORMING

Let's define a middle-level artist as one who has prior experience at the start-up level, has developed an original approach to music, and has a recording on the market, but hasn't yet reached the national headliner level.

Such artists are usually attempting to expand their market to include new geographic areas. Instead of staying close to home they travel in cars and vans to club dates and concerts booked in a multi-state region. Their goal may be to "break out" and get known on a national level.

Venues include large nightclubs, midsize concert halls, and college gyms and auditoriums.

With luck and the right connections, the middle-level performer can end up as an opening act on a major tour or as one of numerous artists on a national package tour, gaining impetus for a step to the next level of success.

Booking Performances for the Middle-Level Artist

While artists may handle bookings themselves at this level, it's more common to get work through a personal manager or a booking agent. An agent lines up engagements, handles the contracts, collects the money, and pays the musicians after subtracting a commission that is usually in the range of 10 to 15 percent of gross earnings.

When booking shows, the agent or manager will make sure that the venues (or headlining acts on a major tour) are appropriate for the performer. For example, no hard-core country music roadhouses for a high-tech dream-pop band.

The agent will also strive to set up an itinerary that won't saddle the performer with unreasonable travel demands.

To find a booking agent, consult such directories as the *Billboard International Talent and Touring Directory*, the *Musician's Guide to Touring and Promotion*, and the *Recording Studio Sourcebook*. You can also check the American Federation of Musicians (AFM) Web site at www.afm.org to find regional listings of AFM-approved agents.

Pricing and Payment for the Middle-Level Artist

With extensive road work comes extensive spending—for hotels, food, gasoline, and a full-time road manager at the very least. On a bare-bones budget, one week's worth of expenses for five people could total

$2,250 ($500 for food, $1,000 for hotel rooms, $250 for gas, and $500 for the road manager's salary). An artist's record company will sometimes provide tour support—in other words, foot the aforementioned bills—and recoup the costs from the artist's record royalties.

For the musicians to earn even minimal pay over and above costs—even when traveling on the above shoestring budget—performances would have to bring in at least $500 to $600 a night, six nights a week.

The types of payment typical at this level are the same as listed in the start-up act section: a flat fee, a share of the gate, a guarantee against a share of the gate, or a guarantee plus a share of the gate.

Unless a CD is getting noticed and beginning to sell, the amounts of money earned won't be significantly more than for a start-up or local act. It's not unusual for a traveling performer, lacking CD sales, to play in a remote club to an audience of five.

The moral is: don't expect to make much money on the road unless your CD is selling. If it isn't, treat the road work as necessary promotion to make sure the CD eventually does sell. (Many are the bands who have paid dues on the road and reaped the benefits years later.)

For an act whose recording is selling well, the financial picture is quite a bit different. The act will be able to play large clubs and amphitheaters and gross several thousand dollars per night.

Pricing of tickets for concerts depends on going rates, what the customer is willing to pay, and the preference of the performer. Some performers prefer to keep ticket prices low, to make access affordable to as many customers as possible.

Payment is generally made in advance—usually 50 percent up front—with the balance paid at the time of the performance.

THE AMERICAN FEDERATION OF MUSICIANS

The American Federation of Musicians (AFM), also known as the musicians' union, sets standard minimum hourly pay rates (called *union scale*) for its members for live performances, recording, and work in various media. The union also provides standard employment contracts, and it franchises booking agents "who meet the highest levels of professional service."

Membership in the union becomes important at the large nightclub and concert hall level of performing. But even non-union members working in situations outside the union's jurisdiction (private parties, small coffeehouses, and so forth) can get a sense of what to charge and how to do business by referring to the union's pay and contract guidelines.

For more information, call 212-869-1330, or check www.afm.org.

Promoting Performances
for the Middle-Level Artist

Promoting on the road involves a lot of advance planning. Press kits should be sent, entertainment calendar notices mailed, and ads placed well in advance of each and every personal appearance. If possible, an advance person should be working ahead of the tour to put up posters and flyers and contact the local media in towns soon to be reached. Radio interviews and record store appearances should be set up, if the act's CD success warrants it.

Those invited to appearances should include—in addition to press people—local record store owners, key personnel from the distributor, and radio deejays.

NATIONAL HEADLINERS
AND LIVE PERFORMING

With national recognition, substantial radio play, and unit CD sales in the hundreds of thousands, the performer has graduated to the level of national headliner. Tours at this level generally cover midsize venues (anywhere from 1,500 to 5,000 seats) and larger.

With CD sales at the platinum (one million copies) or multiplatinum levels, the headliner is operating at the "superstar" level, able to fill arenas and stadiums that can seat many thousands of customers.

CONVENTIONAL WISDOM

Tours are set up mainly to promote a recently released album.

Bruce Springsteen's Born in the U.S.A. Tour, for example, was set up to promote his album of the same name. The tour helped to boost him to superstar status and lift sales of the Born in the U.S.A. album to the multiplatinum level.

BREAKING THE RULE

The Grateful Dead toured constantly, whether or not they had a new record out. Their success, in fact, rested more on live shows than on recorded music. With only a single mainstream radio hit in their 30-year career, they routinely ranked among the world's highest-paid entertainers.

At this level, a tour is a complex and expensive operation. In addition to the performers, numerous personnel are involved, including management, road manager, road crew, sound and lighting technicians, advance person, and possibly a full-time tour publicist. For top-level acts, there may be additional participants, such as a tour photographer, a writer assigned to cover the tour for a national magazine, a video or film crew shooting a documentary, and so on. The logistics of running such an operation involve coordination of air or land travel, hotel bookings, local press coverage and advertising, rehearsals and sound checks, and payments.

Booking Performances at the National Headliner Level

A certain amount of strategizing goes into choosing venues to book and markets to cover in a tour. There are several key issues involved:

1. The cachet of the venue. A beautifully remodeled state-of-the-art concert hall will reflect better on the artist than a seedy, dilapidated amphitheater.

2. The venue's proximity to the site of another concert on the tour. Multiple appearances in the same geographic area could split the audience, resulting in empty seats.

3. The amount of time since the artist last performed in the geographic area. If the last appearance was too recent, there may not yet be enough demand for another concert (a problem called *market saturation*, as is the problem cited in item 2).

Performances at the headlining artist level are booked through local, regional, or national concert promoters. Promoters are essentially concert *producers*: they book the venue, handle associated costs, and take the financial risk. Their profit comes from a percentage of ticket sales after expenses have been recouped.

Bill Graham Presents (BGP) is an example of a concert promoter that operates regionally—primarily in Northern California.

Costs for the concert promoter include renting the hall; paying personnel (stage crew, security, box office); renting equipment (lights, sound, instruments); and additional payments for advertising, ticket printing, ticket agency fees, catering, insurance, and ASCAP/BMI licenses for public performance of the music. (See page 220 for more about performance licenses.)

Concert promoters deal with the artist's representatives—the booking agency or personal management—when putting a concert together.

Pricing and Payment
at the National Headliner Level

The standard payment arrangement for a performer at this level is a guarantee against a percentage of net profits (net profits being ticket receipts after the promoter's expenses have been deducted). (Acts with clout can sometimes get payment on gross income.) Such guarantees can run in the range of $20,000 to $100,000 per concert, depending on ticket prices, which can range from $10 to $100. A typical split of profits is 85 percent to the artist and 15 percent to the promoter. If final sales are less than the guarantee, the artist gets to keep the entire guarantee. (That's why it's called a guarantee.) If final sales are greater than the guarantee, the artist gets additional money to make up the difference between the guarantee and the total percentage of profits due the artist.

The promoter pays the booking agent a deposit of 50 percent of the guarantee, usually one month before the concert date. The balance is payable—in cash or by cashier's check—after the performance.

Personal appearance contracts at music's upper levels can get complex. In addition to covering the basics, a contract will often include a lengthy rider or addendum addressing such issues as rehearsal times and locations, accommodations and dressing rooms, compensation for travel and cartage, additional music equipment, other technical requirements, and provisions for cancellation due to weather or *force majeure*. Generally, no stone should be left unturned in detailing the artist's and promoter's requirements in the contract.

Promoting Performances
at the National Headliner Level

Because concert tours can have such a profound beneficial effect on record sales, promoting each appearance effectively is of key importance.

The steps to take are much the same as for the middle-level artist (see page 193). In the case of national headliners, however, promotion at different legs of the tour is often handled by different offices or individuals, coordinating their efforts to do the following:

- Book television appearances and radio interviews on both national programs and those in local markets (timed to coordinate with local concerts, of course).

- Set up special promotions with record stores, radio stations, and other related businesses (not limited to those focused on music— see pages 182–185 for some ideas).

- Set up feature stories with entertainment editors in the local press. The goal is to have artist profiles appear in newspapers a week or so before the live appearance. The goal is also to have reviews appear after the performance.

- Take care of all of the above well in advance. Press kits to local radio and TV should be mailed four to six weeks in advance of the local appearance. Kits to newspapers should go out three to four weeks in advance. National television and magazines should be contacted months before the tour begins, because of the booking and production lead time they need.

MERCHANDISE SALES AT PERFORMANCES

A significant amount of money can be earned through the sale of tour-related merchandise bearing the name and/or likeness of the performer. This includes material like posters, sweatshirts, program booklets, and just about anything else deemed saleable to a fan hyped up on concert excitement. (Separate merchandise can also be sold in retail outlets, but that's a separate topic, discussed on page 212.)

The artist licenses the right to use his or her name and likeness to a merchandiser. The merchandiser handles manufacturing and sale of the items at concert halls and pays the artist an advance against a royalty in the area of 25 to 40 percent of gross sales.

Such agreements tend to run for a term of one year or until the advance is recouped, whichever is longer.

One of the dangers of a merchandising agreement is that the final product may conflict, in design or quality, with the kind of image the artist is trying to project. For this reason it's wise to retain some degree of creative control over the product and to stipulate as much in the merchandising contract.

Another pitfall is that some merchandisers require exclusivity, meaning you're prohibited from selling similar products in the vicinity of their merchandise stands for a given period of time (which could, of course, cut into their sales). But what if you already have merchandise on the market, which you're selling through stores in a nearby town? If so, it's important that this merchandise be excluded from any exclusivity agreement with the tour merchandiser.

How much money can be made? If 10,000 sweatshirts sell for $15 each over the course of an entire tour, and the royalty is a middling 30 percent of gross sales, you'd receive $45,000. ($150,000 × 30% = $45,000.)

And that's just for sweatshirts. Don't forget the T-shirts, caps, mugs, brandy snifters, cigarette lighters, wall posters, refrigerator magnets, buttons, mittens—whatever.

It's something to aim for, isn't it?

CORPORATE SPONSORSHIPS

Mention was made earlier of the high cost of touring. One way some artists have cut these costs is by gaining the sponsorship of a corporation. The sponsor underwrites some of the costs of the tour in return for plugging the corporation's product via onstage banners or displays, inclusion of the company logo on tour posters and in ads, and other artist-corporation tie-in strategies.

13

Expanding the Marketing Program

After you've dealt with the basics of the music marketing program—product development, packaging, pricing, distribution, and promotion—you have the option of expanding the program. This means finding additional ways for your basic product—in this case, the recorded music and the artist who made it—to bring in money.

Keep in mind a point made earlier: recorded music is a piece of raw "content" that can be packaged, repackaged, and delivered to customers in any number of ways. We have already taken a look at the different *formats* in which a recording can be presented, from CDs to laserdiscs to DVDs (see Chapters 5 and 8 for details). Now the focus will be on the different *sources of money* for the use or sale of a piece of musical content—beyond the primary sources discussed in preceding chapters.

The current world of entertainment is exploding with multiple media and varied means of delivering content to consumers. There are movies and movie soundtracks, television, video outlets, compilation albums, custom records, and more. Each of these makes use of music. That means each is a potential source of money for the sellers of music.

And beyond the music itself is the potential for making money from the likeness of the performer, on T-shirts, mugs, posters, buttons, calendars, and other retail merchandise.

Since a complete marketing program means wringing every conceivable dollar from your basic product, let's take a closer look at the different sources of those dollars and what can be done to tap them.

These discussions are intended as introductory overviews. Some of the sources—especially television and movies—involve business complexities that can't be fully covered in a single chapter. We suggest that you consult more-detailed information sources before starting to do business in these areas. The books *This Business of Music* and *This Business of Television*, both published by Billboard, are good places to start.

Another note: As you read through this chapter, keep in mind that the revenues discussed represent only one kind of earnings—those for recordings and recording artists. The other kinds are writer and publisher earnings, which are discussed in Chapter 14. We'll remind you of this every few pages or so, just so you don't get confused.

NEW MEDIA

The term *new media* has come to mean any new-to-the-marketplace digital communication format or channel. Some types of new media—whether digital or analog—may not catch on or last for long. (Remember the Betamax video format, eight-track cassettes, and consumer DATs?) Others, such as compact discs, eventually become widely accepted, making them no longer "new" media.

Current leading examples of new media (as discussed in Chapter 8) are digital versatile discs (DVDs) and CD-ROMs. Undoubtedly others will be available within months of this writing.

New-Media Revenue Potential

By definition, new-media formats are not yet widely accepted and thus won't necessarily sell in large numbers. That makes them a poor financial risk, especially considering the high cost of producing them. Generally speaking, sellers move into the new-media arena only after their products have proven successful in traditional formats, thus minimizing risk by capitalizing on name recognition.

To make up for their high cost and narrow customer base, new-media products sell at higher prices than "old" media formats. For example, as of this writing, retail prices of CD-ROMs range from $19.95 to $50. DVDs sell at prices between $24.95 and $30.

Bearing in mind that you'll actually be selling at a wholesale price of around 50 percent of retail, the monies you'd be receiving would be in the following ballpark: for CD-ROMs, $10.00 to $25.00; for DVDs, $12.50 to $15.00.

Here's a reality check: In the case of a CD-ROM, manufacturing cost alone is in the area of $3.50 per unit. The cost of development, which may include graphics, animation, writing, computer programming, video photography, still photography, and licensing, can add up to a minimum of $100,000. (Know this: a computer game, with animation, sound, and all the works, typically costs around $1 million to develop.) If you do the math, you find that you'd have to sell around 7,500 copies of that CD-ROM at a retail price of $30 *just to break even.*

Another, less risky way to make money through new media is to license your recording for use in a new-media product being produced by someone else. (In other words, they take the risk.) In this case, there are several types of deals that can be set up. One is a royalty arrangement, where the owner of the master recording receives 10 to 20 percent of the wholesale price, prorated. (*Prorated* means reduced proportionate to the total number of songs included in the new-media product. For example, if there are nine songs other than yours, you'll receive one-tenth of the total royalty—in this case, 1 to 2 percent of the wholesale price. Another, less common, method of prorating is to provide a reduced royalty proportionate to the duration of your song relative to the total time taken up by all songs.) Another type of deal is a 50-50 split of profits (split between the product maker and the owner of the master recording). Overall, the licensing arrangement is negotiable, and depends on how important the recording is to the new-media product.

How to Generate New-Media Revenues

Since new-media products are sold in many of the same stores that sell CDs and tapes, use the distribution guidelines offered in Chapter 9. Make sure not to overlook non-music stores that sell new media: computer hardware and software outlets, certain bookstores, and retailers that cater to some other interest of your target audience.

For non-store sales, use the techniques described in Chapter 10.

To set up deals to license your recordings to separate new-media production entities, the situation is a little more complicated. The way it usually works is a producer—of a CD-ROM, say—comes to you with the idea, because he or she is familiar with your work. That means that you have to be known to the public before hungry new-media producers come knocking at your door.

Still, you can take a stab at promoting your music to new media by targeting companies that do the kind of work you think your music would match, and then sending them press kits and sonic samples.

VIDEO

As discussed in Chapter 11 (page 173), videos can provide substantial promotional benefits. However, they can also serve as sources of income. Be advised, though, that it's the rare artist who earns back the cost of video production through video sales. (And video production costs are charged back to the artist in the mainstream music biz, recouped from royalties—sometimes from both video *and* album royalties.)

Video Revenue Potential

There are three main ways to make money with video:

- You are the producer and seller of the video (in other words, it's issued under your label) and your money comes directly from product sales.
- You sell someone else the right to manufacture and distribute your video, and your money comes from a licensing fee or royalty.
- Your master audio recording is used in someone else's video and your money comes from licensing fees or royalties.

Sales of Your Own Video. If you're the owner (that is, the maker and seller) of the video, you'll be dealing either with short-form video (which will be a one-song video clip) or long-form video (which will usually be a full-length concert video, a documentary about the artist, or a compilation of short video clips).

Long-form video revenues will come mostly from retail sales to record/entertainment chains (like Tower Video and Virgin Megastores), video stores, supermarkets, and specialty stores. Through these outlets, videocassettes will be sold or rented to customers for home play on video-cassette recorders (VCRs).

A typical long-form music video retails for $19.95 (as of this writing). Subtracting discounts for retail outlet and distributor may yield around $10.00 to the video maker. Subtracting a recording artist royalty of, say, 20 percent of wholesale ($2.00) leaves $8.00. Say the video is a compilation of 10 songs. The publishers of those songs must be paid royalties—let's say 8¢ a song (for each video distributed). That's 80¢ total, leaving you $7.20. Out of that, you'll need to subtract the cost of production, and here's where the fun begins: It's not unusual to accrue $100,000 in production costs for a single-song video. A compilation of 10 songs, then, might involve $1 million in combined production costs. To break even, you would have to sell a very large number of copies (even given the fact that production costs are earned back before you pay out royalties to the recording artist).

Other sources of income for both long- and short-form videos include broadcast on network, local, public, and cable television and exhibition in nightclubs. Note that, in general, play of video clips on local TV generates no payment to the record company; such uses are considered promotional.

Short-form videos are the lifeblood of such cable music channels as MTV and VH-1. MTV has been known to pay millions of dollars to a major record label for the exclusive right to broadcast a specified number of videos for a specified period of time. For the most part, however, labels provide clips to these channels—and to other broadcasters of short-form videos—for free.

Licensing Fees from a Separate Manufacturer-Distributor. If you're granting a license for someone else to manufacture and distribute the video, your receipts will be a royalty, from which you will pay the recording artist 50 percent of your net receipts (*net receipts* meaning the money you receive minus your expenses).

Use of Your Recording on Someone Else's Video. If you're simply licensing a master recording of a piece of music for someone else's use in a video (usually a video version of a television show or movie), the money could come in a couple of different ways. If the original source was a motion picture, the video licensing fee would most often have been included in the single "buyout" license granted to the movie company. (For more about licenses for movie use, see "Movie Revenue Potential" on page 205.) If the original source was a television program, the home video rights might bring you a licensing fee of between $3,000 and $7,000.

How to Generate Video Revenues

For retail sales of videocassettes, the marketing methods used are much the same as those discussed in Chapters 9 and 10. To find distributors that specialize in video, ask at local video outlets, look in directories such as *The Video Distributors Directory* (Corbell Publishing), and look on the Internet using the keywords *video distributors* or *video distribution;* on the Net you can also go to Yahoo: Business and Economy: Companies: Entertainment: Video: Distribution.

Another option is to try to license your video to one of the major-studio video labels (an arrangement not unlike the pressing-and-distribution deals mentioned on page 128). Find these studios by investigating the sources cited above.

To get a video on MTV and other music television channels usually requires prior success in record sales—as do most other types of video success. You can take a long shot and mail press kits and video clips to producers of programs on these channels, but before establishing a sales track record your best shot for video play is on local cable stations.

In the case of licensing an existing recording to other video producers, the normal way this happens is someone comes to you with a request to use your recording. For details, see the "Television" and "Movie" sections that follow.

TELEVISION

Like videos, television can be a tool not only for promotion but also for generating money.

Television Revenue Potential

Television uses of your basic musical product generally fall into the following categories:

- Use of an existing master recording in a television program either as a theme (for example, the Frank Sinatra version of "Love and Marriage" used in the show "Married...With Children") or as background during a scene
- Use of a recording in a soundtrack album for a TV show (rare, but it happens)
- An appearance by a performer as a guest on a television program
- Use of a video clip on a television program, or a full-length video as the main content of a program

Television Use of an Existing Recording. If your recording is chosen for use in a television program, you will charge a licensing fee. This will range from $500 to $10,000, depending upon the term of use (typically five years); type of use (main theme or background); the popularity of your recording; the frequency of use (every episode of a series, or once only); the duration of the use (that is, how many minutes or seconds the music will be played); and the success of the television show itself (if the show has already proven it has "legs," you may be able to charge more). Additional uses, such as in a home video release of the show, a foreign theatrical release (such as of a made-for-TV movie), a pay-TV broadcast, or a cable TV showing, will bring you additional fees. (Here's the reminder we promised: Note that we're talking here only about fees for a master recording. Songwriter and publisher fees are separate. See Chapter 14 for information about these types of payments.)

Television Soundtrack Albums. Occasionally a successful TV series will issue a soundtrack album. ("Miami Vice" was one that did, quite successfully.) If your recording was used on the show, it could end up on the album. In this case, you the recording owner would be paid a licensing royalty (negotiable, but often 11 to 13 percent of the retail price) prorated according to either the total number of songs on the album or the percentage of total album playing time used by your song. (From this amount you would subtract expenses and then pay 50 percent of the remainder to the recording artist—who could, in fact, be you.)

Artist Appearances on Television. What if the recording artist gets hired to appear on a television program—say, to perform a song on a late-night talk show, a series, a variety special, or a made-for-TV movie? Unless the recording artist is a celebrity, payment will be the standard "scale" hourly rate of one of the following three unions: the American Federation of Musicians (AFM), the American Federation of Television and Radio Artists (AFTRA), or the Screen Actors Guild (SAG). (Celebrities are paid more than union scale.)

The question of which union governs a TV performance is a little complicated, but here's how it works: If the featured performer is a singer, he or she is paid through AFTRA. If the performer is an instrumentalist only, the payment is through the AFM. If the performer is a singer *and* instrumentalist, he or she is paid though whichever of the two unions pays the higher rate. (The unions have a reciprocal agreement that permits this to happen.) Another complication is that AFTRA only covers videotaped performances—which applies to most TV appearances, like talk shows. If, on the other hand, the performance is shot using film (as in a made-for-TV movie), the governing union for a featured singer is SAG. Got all that? If not (and if you want information about the unions' standard pay rates), consult the main offices of these three unions, telephone numbers for which are listed in the Appendix.

Television Use of Music Videos. As mentioned previously, prerecorded video clips played on one of the cable music channels such as MTV or on other TV broadcasts will generally yield no income, unless it is part of a blanket fee paid by a music channel for the use of many videos for a specified time period (an arrangement not normally available to small record companies).

How to Generate Television Revenues

Generally, television uses of recordings and performers are generated by television producers based on their familiarity with a particular recording or artist and their desire to license a particular song or book an appearance. That is, television uses generally don't happen unless the musical product is already on the market and has attracted some attention, so that producers know it's out there.

You can, however, take some steps to generate interest in a performer as a potential TV show guest. Do this by sending press kits and video clips to producers of appropriately targeted programs, concentrating on local cable programs if the act is new. (See page 174 for more information on getting media exposure.)

Representation of the artist by a well-known, full-service talent agency such as the William Morris Agency, International Creative Management (ICM), and Creative Artists Agency (CAA) can be very helpful in getting television work. These agencies have ties to all entertainment media, and offer their clients the inside track to activity in these areas.

To encourage the use of a recording in a television show, start by staying up to date on the kinds of programming that production companies and studios have in preproduction. (Do this by consulting such sources as *Variety* and the *Hollywood Reporter.*) If you have a recording that would be ideal for a show, contact the production office to let them know. (*Don't* contact them just to promote a scattershot of random tracks; only do it for a track or tracks that you strongly feel are appropriate.)

To promote the use of a video on programs that regularly feature them (such as those on cable music channels like MTV), mail press kits and video clips to the producers of targeted programs.

MOVIES

Film companies often use existing recordings, in addition to background scores, to serve as a main theme or to add flavor to particular scenes. And more and more, movie companies are boosting their revenues by releasing soundtrack albums of featured songs and music. For the owner of a recording, use of it in a movie and subsequently on the movie soundtrack album can be a very substantial source of income. Movie soundtrack albums often reach the top of the sales charts. (*The Bodyguard, Pulp Fiction, Purple Rain, Dirty Dancing,* and *Titanic* are some examples.) Even minor songs in a film are potential moneymakers if included on a hit soundtrack album.

Movie Revenue Potential

Typical money-generating movie sources include the following:
- Use of an existing recording as a theme or in the background (for example, "Can't Take My Eyes Off You" in 1997's *Conspiracy Theory* and "I Say a Little Prayer" in 1997's *My Best Friend's Wedding*).
- Use of an existing recording on a movie soundtrack album
- Use of a performer in a movie

Movie Use of an Existing Recording. For the use of an existing recording in a movie, the license fee may be anywhere between $5,000 (or much less for a low-budget movie) and $250,000 depending on whether the song is well known, whether it is used as a theme or in the background, how long it is played, and how many times it is heard—and depending, of course, on the overall budget of the film project. Additionally, the per-song amount may be less if a movie studio agrees to use several of a record company's songs in a single film.

Unlike most television licenses, the movie license has no time restriction (it's "in perpetuity"), and movie license fees tend to be buyout fees—that is, they cover all other uses the movie studio might want to exploit, including home video and television broadcast. From the licensing fee, the recording owner pays a royalty—generally 50 percent—to the recording artist (which, of course, is not an issue if the owner is also the artist).

Keep in mind that, as in television, the movie production company will also have to get permission from the writers and publishers to use the music, and will have to work out separate licensing deals with those entities (who could also be you). You'll find more about this topic in Chapter 14.

Movie Soundtrack Albums. For the use of an existing recording on a movie soundtrack album, the owner of the recording will be paid a royalty. The amount will be prorated according to either how many tracks are on the album or the percentage of total album playing time taken up by the individual track. For example, using the first method, if the total royalty is 12 percent of the retail price and your track is one of 10 on the album, your royalty would be 1.2 percent of the retail price. Now let's fantasize that the album is as successful as 1987's *Dirty Dancing* soundtrack, which sold 10 million copies. At a $17.99 retail price (for the CD), you'd earn $2,158,800 for that single song.

Artist Performances in Movies and on Soundtrack Albums. What if the movie studio wants the artist to perform onscreen in the movie? This, essentially, is a deal that does not include the record company, since it's for the performer rather than a recording. The artist's fee for such an onscreen appearance can range from union scale (the appropriate union being the Screen Actors Guild) to upward of $100,000 for a superstar performer.

The movie company may want to include the audio of this new performance on a soundtrack album. The artist royalty for this use would generally range from 10 to 18 percent of the retail price, depending on the artist's level of popularity (translation: clout), and the royalty would be prorated. (In addition, the artist will have to consult with his or her label for permission to be included on this soundtrack if it is being released by a different label. And the royalties may be sent to the artist's own record label, who may take a cut.)

How to Generate Movie Revenues

It's usually the movie production company, rather than the owner of the recording, that initiates a deal to use a recording or a performer in a movie. For that reason, having the product out in the market where people will hear it is a near prerequisite for getting movie play.

To take an active role in promoting the product to movie makers, try to keep abreast of current films in preproduction by referring to the *Hollywood Reporter, Variety,* and other trade information sources. Contact a film production office only if you feel strongly that your recording would be appropriate for their film.

An additional tactic is to keep a list of music supervisors—the invaluable professionals whose job is to plan the program of songs to be used in a movie and to acquire the rights to use those songs. Music supervisors tend to move from movie to movie, and keeping tabs on them—and promoting your music to them—is one way to increase the chances of getting your music chosen.

Just so you know, it's not uncommon these days for a music supervisor to subcontract a single record label to provide all the songs to be used in a movie and on a soundtrack album. This makes the music supervisor's life easier: there's only one deal with one label rather than a lot of complicated little deals with separate labels for different songs. It's good for the label, too: the label has the potential opportunity to include songs by some of its lesser-known artists, thus giving them a promotional boost. The label can offer an "all-in" deal of reduced per-song licensing fees if the music supervisor agrees to use several of its songs in a single movie.

Because movie music deals are so complex—requiring, at the very least, the approval of record label, artist, music publisher, and songwriter—movie producers are more likely to work with music suppliers who know how to smooth out the process and who are easy to deal with. You should aim to be that kind of person.

There is no hard and fast rule about how songs get chosen for movies. In the case of writer-director Quentin Tarantino, who places a lot of importance on the choice of music, "a good half of the songs are usually ones in my collection," as he told Neil Strauss of the *New York Times.* Director Gus Van Sant, on the other hand, tends to choose music as an afterthought; in one case he reportedly picked a song by taking the top tape from a pile of music being considered for a movie.

The moral is: Serendipity sometimes does play a role. And all you can do is make sure your music is in the right place when the serendipity starts kicking in.

(A point to bear in mind here: In these days of corporate vertical and horizontal integration, it's not uncommon for a movie studio and a record label to be owned by the same umbrella corporation. In such a case, music may be chosen in part because it is owned by a music subsidiary of the corporation.)

To arrange for performer appearances in movies, either send press kits directly to production companies or go through a talent agency or entertainment attorney with strong ties to the film industry. Ideally, the performer's talent agency is one of the full-service firms such as those mentioned in the preceding section on television. These agencies serve both the music and film industries and can easily make links between one and the other.

COMMERCIALS

You've undoubtedly heard hit songs revived as product themes on television commercials: Sly and the Family Stone's "Everyday People" for Toyota, Bob Seger's "Like a Rock" for Chevy Trucks, Canned Heat's "Going Up the Country" for Chevrolet—the list goes on. For the owners of those songs, such commercial uses can mean a jackpot of high earnings. A well-known recording used in a national TV and radio commercial can earn as much as $500,000 per year (in combined record company and music publishing fees).

Because of this expense, pre-existing songs are most often used by advertisers with large budgets. Which means they'll be on the lookout primarily for proven hits.

Ad Music Revenue Potential

When an agency requests the use of a pre-existing recording in a commercial, the owner of the recording issues a license (the fee for which can be anything from very little for a small-town radio ad to an astronomical figure for a national media campaign).

The license to use the song in an ad should provide specification of the following points: term of use (usually one year or less, with options to license for additional periods of time); the number and kind of commercials produced (for example, one 30-second TV ad, one 60-second radio spot, and so on); the kinds of media used (free TV, basic cable, pay cable, radio, print); the territory (a specific city, a state, a region, the entire United States, Canada, other countries, throughout the world); and exclusivity (which would involve prohibiting the use of the song in other ads, whether *all* other ads or just ads for competing products).

If you're fortunate enough to have an advertiser requesting the use of your recording, carefully consider the ramifications of having your song associated with the product. The target audience you have so carefully cultivated in your marketing program may be put off by the commercial, resulting in damage to the artist's public image. On the other hand, the amount of money offered for the ad use may outweigh all other considerations in deciding whether to go ahead.

How to Generate Ad Music Revenues

Don't plan on hearing from an ad agency unless your recording has already earned its rightful place in the mass public's collective memory—which is often where ad copywriters look first when hunting for musical ideas.

On the other hand, if you have a "reel" (a demo tape or CD) of recordings that sound catchy or gripping enough for the ad airwaves, there's little reason not to submit copies to creative directors at advertising agencies. This works best if the recordings sound appropriate for specific types of products—a propulsive techno groove for a car ad, an expansive orchestral sound for an airline—and you know which agencies handle those types of products. You can inform yourself about what's going on in the ad world by referring to such trade information sources as *Advertising Age* and the Internet's www.mediafinder.com.

It doesn't hurt if you know someone who works in an ad agency—someone such as a producer, copywriter, or creative director—who knows your work and will give your music a listen. On rare occasions, a prerecorded song that's unsolicited—even a song that's not a hit—will strike the powers-that-be as having just the right message for an upcoming ad campaign.

COMPILATION ALBUMS

Increasingly popular are albums and boxed sets that feature collections of recordings—sometimes by different artists—that share a common theme. These compilations have proven to be an effective means of making new money with old, or previously packaged, recordings. They cost less to create than new recordings, because they don't require spending money on new music production.

Compilation recordings are generally of the following types:

■ *Record label retrospectives.* Motown, Atlantic, Stax, and Chess are just a few of the labels that have repackaged their hits into historical collections.

- *Artist retrospectives.* Individual artists with extensive track records are often the subjects of multi-disc collections of their work. Bob Dylan, Miles Davis, Eric Clapton, and John Coltrane are examples of leading artists whose performances have been collected in new album packages. Record labels have occasionally sought profits by releasing retrospectives of songs by newer or less widely popular artists.
- *"Greatest Hits" collections.* The most common type of compilation is a repackaging of a single artist's past hit songs.
- *Style retrospectives.* Historic music styles have proven to be popular themes for compilation albums. Examples include garage rock of the 1960s, rhythm and blues hits of the 1950s, and big-band jazz of the 1930s.
- *Theme collections.* Compilations are sometimes created around musical themes, such as disco dance hits, cult rockers, popular television themes, and psychedelic surf music. There have also been instances of popular nightclubs releasing albums of tracks by artists who have performed on their stages.
- *Tribute albums.* Increasingly common are albums that feature songs of an influential artist, as recorded in new versions by other performers. Jimi Hendrix, Jimmie Rodgers, the Grateful Dead, and Richard Thompson are just a few of the artists who have been the subjects of tribute albums.

Compilation Album Revenue Potential

There are two main ways to make money from compilation albums: (1) you're the producer and seller of the entire compilation album, or (2) you're licensing one of your recordings for use on someone else's compilation album.

If you're creating a compilation album and you own the master recordings, your income per album will be the same as for a new recording plus the money you save by not having to pay for new music production. (You will, of course, have to pay royalties to the recording artists as well as mechanical royalties to the publishers of all the songs. See page 217 for more about mechanical royalties.) If you're creating a compilation album and you are licensing the tracks from other sources (Rhino Records is a company that specializes in this approach), you won't be paying for new music production but you will be paying licensing fees to the owners of the masters. That fee is generally a penny rate of 6¢ to 10¢ per CD and slightly less per cassette for each song on the album. (The rate depends on how many songs are on the album and whether the album will be sold at full price, mid-price, or budget price.) You will also have to pay mechanical royalties to the publishers.

If you are licensing your recording (one song, say) for use on someone else's compilation album, you will be the recipient of the licensing fee described above, half of which is payable to your recording artist.

How to Generate Compilation Album Revenues

The method of distributing and promoting compilation albums is essentially the same as for standard, new albums, as described in Chapters 9 through 11.

CUSTOM ALBUMS

A relatively rare but lucrative marketing avenue is the sale and creation of custom albums. This kind of marketing activity is often categorized as a "special sale," since it occurs outside standard music sales channels. A custom album is one that a record company specially produces for, and delivers to, another company or business entity, whose name goes on the product and who distributes it through the company's own channels. Such companies often have these albums created as a special supplement to their own product line, or as a premium to give to employees or customers.

Here's an example: The national home furnishings retailer the Pottery Barn sells a CD, under its own label, titled *Martini Lounge*. The CD is a collection of cocktail lounge-type songs by the likes of Dean Martin, Peggy Lee, Rosemary Clooney, and Esquivel. Pottery Barn displays the CD in baskets on a table alongside various martini-oriented products like glasses and trays. The idea is that the customer can purchase an entire martini "environment"—music included. *Martini Lounge* was prepared for the Pottery Barn by EMI-Capitol Music Special Markets.

Custom-Album Revenue Potential

Custom albums offer the record company the opportunity to make a clean profit. The label charges the corporate customer a fee that covers all manufacturing costs (including licenses, royalties, packaging, pressing, and whatever else) and includes a markup.

How to Generate Custom-Album Revenues

Start by making a list of high-profile companies and envisioning the kinds of music that would match their products or services. If you find a promising prospective customer, present them with a proposal for an album custom-programmed according to their specifications. Offer a list of potential tracks, and work with the customer to narrow the selection down to a list of primary and secondary choices (in case licenses are unobtainable for all the primary choices). Determine how many copies of the album the customer would like to order. Prepare a manufacturing budget that covers everything—including shipping to the customer's warehouse. Add your desired markup to the total manufacturing cost, and use this as the total fee for your service.

RETAIL MERCHANDISE

For well-established performing artists, an important supplementary type of income is licensing fees for merchandise that incorporates the artist's name or likeness. Such merchandise could include T-shirts, sweatshirts, jackets, mugs, posters, buttons, souvenir publications, and more.

Merchandise can be an important promotion tool and a source of some money even if the performing artist is not a national headliner.

Some merchandise sales occur in connection with live performances and tours (as discussed on page 196). Other sales occur through normal retail channels, including stores and mail order. It is the retail type that is the subject of this discussion.

Merchandise Revenue Potential

The seller of the artist's likeness and name—which could be the record label or the artist, depending on which one holds the rights—receives a licensing royalty from the retail merchandiser (the company that manufactures and distributes the merchandise). This royalty is generally in the realm of 10 to 20 percent of the wholesale price for retail store sales, and 25 percent for mail-order sales.

The retail merchandiser may sublicense merchandise rights to other manufacturers who specialize in making particular items. In such cases, the retail merchandiser keeps 20 to 30 percent of the sublicense royalty and pays the remainder to the original rights holder.

If the seller (the rights holder) is the record company, it pays the recording artist a royalty that is normally 50 percent of net receipts.

If the artist has retained the right to peddle his or her own name and likeness, the royalty will go directly from the merchandiser to the artist.

The seller usually receives an advance against royalties, the amount of which can range from very little for an unestablished act to hundreds of thousands of dollars for an established artist.

CHAPTER

14

Writing and Publishing Revenue Sources

In addition to making money from recordings, earnings can be generated from music writing and publishing.

Before examining some of their specific revenue sources, let's look at how writing and publishing fit into the overall marketing scheme.

In the music business, the product sold directly to the consumer is most often the musical performance, in whatever format chosen, from live presentation to audio CD to audiovisual software.

But a great deal of money-making goes on beneath the surface consumer world. It happens in the world of business-to-business commerce, where a product is sold by one business to another for further processing and resale. (Like lumber sold to a cabinetmaker, who will use it in building a cabinet and then sell the cabinet to the public.)

One of the primary music business-to-business products is the raw, unrecorded music composition, known in legal parlance as *intellectual property*. The owner of this property is said to hold the *copyright* to the property—that is, the right to reproduce, publish, and sell the work. The copyright holder is the original author or another entity to whom the author has assigned the copyright.

As owner, the copyright holder is entitled to make money from the property. This is done by selling the right to use the property in some way. The permission to use is called a *license*. The copyright holder grants a license to another business (say, a record company) to further process the product (to record a song, say) and then to sell it to the public or to another business.

The song "Yesterday," by Lennon and McCartney, is an intellectual property. It's been recorded hundreds of times by a variety of artists. Each one of those recordings represents a separate licensing of the song by one business (the owner) to another business (the record label), each license bringing new money into the coffers of the "Yesterday" owners.

In the marketing program discussed up to this point in the book, the assumption has been that you are marketing a musical product in the form of a recording or a musical performing artist. But what if you own a music composition, because you wrote it, co-wrote it, or at some point obtained the rights to it? In this case, you'll be able to draw earnings that are separate from those for recording or performing.

If you're a combination songwriter, recording artist, and performer, those writer earnings will be *in addition* to the recording and live-performance earnings.

If you're both the record label owner and the music composer-publisher, you get to keep the money that would otherwise be paid to an outside writer and publisher.

The main sources of income for music writing and publishing are summarized in the upcoming discussion, and diagrammed below. (Because the details are too complex to fully cover in a single chapter, you're advised to consult additional information sources that focus specifically on the individual topics.) But first let's briefly revisit a subject introduced back in Chapter 3—that is, music publishing.

Types of income-generating uses for a song.

WHAT IS MUSIC PUBLISHING?

Music publishing, in essence, is the set of business activities aimed at exploiting a music composition for profit. These activities usually include, but aren't necessarily limited to, marketing, promotion, publication of printed music, collecting fees and handling the money, and overall business administration.

Signing with a Music Publisher or Doing It Yourself

Many musicians decide to do their own music publishing rather than pay a portion of royalties to a separate publisher. This works best when the musician-songwriter isn't especially interested in trying to convince others to record new versions of the songs.

It's best to work with an established music publisher when you want active promotion of your songs in the music market but don't have the time, energy, industry contacts, knowledge of money sources, and business expertise offered by a professional publisher.

Types of businesses and organizations with which a music publisher interacts.

Standard Writer-Publisher Royalty Shares

The usual writer-publisher split of royalties is 50-50. That is, the publisher gets half and the writer gets half. If there are two writers, they would split the writer share, in whatever percentages they agree are reasonable.

Often, two writers of a song have their own separate publishers. In this case, the standard royalty shares would be

Publisher 1:	25%
Writer 1:	25%
Publisher 2:	25%
Writer 2:	25%

That is, the publisher percentages match the corresponding writer percentages.

Royalty division can get more complicated. If authorship of the song is divided between three writers, two of whom split half of the writer share and one of whom owns the other half—and each writer has her own publisher—the royalty division would be as follows:

Publisher 1:	12.5%
Writer 1:	12.5%
Publisher 2:	12.5%
Writer 2:	12.5%
Publisher 3:	25%
Writer 3:	25%

There are any number of variations of this royalty division, depending on the number of writers and publishers and the percentages of the song that they own.

Now let's go on to the various sources of revenue available to music publishers and writers.

Keep in mind that in nearly all cases the fees collected are shared by publishers and writers per the above guidelines.

MECHANICAL LICENSING FEES

Whenever an audio recording is created and distributed, the writer of the music (as opposed to the performer on the record, although they are sometimes the same person) is due some money. So is the publisher that represents the writer.

The license for this kind of use is called a *mechanical license*. More specifically, a mechanical license covers the incorporation of a copyrighted music composition into commercial records, tapes, and CDs to be distributed to the public for private use.

As an example, if Bonnie Raitt records a song by John Hiatt for her new album, her record company must obtain a license from, and pay fees to, Hiatt's publishing representatives.

When a record company wants to use your song on a record, it informs you, your publisher, or an organization called the Harry Fox Agency (see the description on the next page) of the intended use. (If you have previously recorded and distributed the song, you are *required* to grant a mechanical license to anyone else who wants to record it, as long as they pay the required fees. Underscoring this requirement, the license is called a *compulsory mechanical license*.)

The standard fee payable by a licensee to the copyright holder is currently 7.1¢ per composition or 1.35¢ a minute of playing time, whichever is greater, for every CD, tape, or record that is manufactured and distributed. This royalty rate is the statutory, or compulsory, rate established under the United States Copyright Act. It is adjusted every couple of years to reflect changes in the Consumer Price Index.

The licensee may negotiate with the copyright holder for a royalty rate lower than the statutory rate.

Mechanical royalty rates are generally set lower (usually 75 percent of the standard rate) for reduced-price records.

And note this important point about recording artists who write their own songs. (Such a song is called a *controlled composition,* in music business parlance.) When artist-written songs are included on an album, you'd think that a record company would pay the artist separate royalties covering recording (artist royalties) and songwriting (mechanical royalties). And they do. But it's common practice for record companies to include a "controlled composition clause" in the recording agreement, setting the mechanical royalty at a reduced rate—usually 75 percent of the minimum statutory rate, with a total album limit of 10 times the per-song royalty (even if the artist includes more than 10 original songs on the album). Artists with clout can sometimes negotiate a higher percentage.

THE HARRY FOX AGENCY

To facilitate the licensing of their compositions for certain uses, music publishers may engage the services of the Harry Fox Agency, a subsidiary of the National Music Publishers' Association (NMPA). The Harry Fox Agency serves as a clearinghouse representing thousands of music publishers, and its service is useful to both music customers and music copyright holders: For customers, it provides a single place to go to obtain licenses and offers a standardized procedure for requesting licenses and paying fees. For copyright holders, the Agency does all the paperwork related to licensing, collects and distributes the royalties, and audits the books and records of licensees. The Agency subtracts commissions from its royalty payments to publishers.

The Harry Fox Agency handles the following kinds of music uses:

- Use on CDs, tapes, and records distributed to the public for private consumption
- Use in movies, television, home video, and commercial advertising
- Use in background music and syndicated radio
- Use in recordings made outside the U.S. and imported to the U.S. for sale

Note that these uses all involve *fixing* the composition in some playable form. The Harry Fox Agency does not handle licensing for the *performance* of music on radio, television, and in concert (although it does license U.S. theatrical motion picture performing rights). Performance licensing is handled by performing rights societies such as ASCAP and BMI (discussed on page 221).

For more information about the Harry Fox Agency, call 212-370-5330.

SYNCHRONIZATION LICENSING FEES

In the music business, the term *synchronization* means combining recorded music with visual images. Copyright owners have the right to grant synchronization licenses for uses of their compositions in movies, television, and home video.

Movies

A synchronization fee for the use of a song in a movie is negotiable and can total between $10,000 and over $50,000. The amount depends on such variables as the movie production budget, how well known the song is, whether the song is sung onscreen or used as background, the duration of the use (in minutes and seconds), the term of use, the territory of use, and whether the movie company guarantees inclusion of the song on a soundtrack album. (If the song will be used on a soundtrack album there will be separate mechanical royalties for the song owner, which is why owners sometimes agree to reduce the sync licensing fee if a soundtrack album will be issued.)

Television

Synchronization fees for the use of compositions in television series, special programs, or made-for-TV movies can range from several hundred dollars to many thousands of dollars per composition. The amount will depend on many of the same variables cited in the preceding section about movies. Some other variables include whether the program will be released on home video, broadcast in additional media, or released in foreign movie theaters. Typically, the licensee will initially pay for a specified set of conditions and request an option to buy more as needed.

Home Video

A synchronization fee for the use of a composition in a home video is paid in one of the following ways: a per-unit royalty (usually from 6¢ to 12¢ per song); a single buyout fee covering all quantities sold; or a rollover advance covering a set number of copies, with additional amounts payable for additional specified quantities sold.

COMMERCIAL ADVERTISING LICENSING FEES

Licensing fees payable for the use of a composition in commercial advertising can range from a few thousand dollars to upward of half a million dollars. The amount will depend on such variables as how well known the song is; the advertising budget; the kind of media used (free television, basic cable, pay cable, radio, print); the geographic territory of use (local, regional, national, international); the term of use (usually one year, with an option to extend the license); the number of commercials produced in various formats (such one 30-second TV ad and one 60-second radio ad); and whether the advertiser wants exclusivity.

By the way: Television commercial licenses are synchronization licenses. Radio licenses, on the other hand, are not sync licenses, because radio doesn't contain visuals. Radio involves *transcription licenses*, as does background music, discussed next.

BACKGROUND-MUSIC
REVENUE SOURCES

Background music—as supplied by such companies as Muzak and 3M—is music played in stores, malls, restaurants, hotels, offices, airlines, elevators, and other public places. It is meant to accompany activity, to relax people, to override ambient noise, and to create a pleasant atmosphere. For that reason it is sometimes called *functional music*.

The creators of background music normally record their own versions of music for which they have obtained what are called transcription licenses.

The method of remunerating the copyright holder for a transcription use varies depending on the background music company seeking the license. One method is a fixed payment for the use of a song over a set period of time. Another method is a penny-rate royalty on each copy of a transcription tape sold or leased by the background music company to its commercial clients.

PERFORMANCE
LICENSING FEES

In addition to owning the rights to grant mechanical and synchronization licenses for the use of his or her music, the copyright holder owns what are called performing rights. The term *performing right* refers to the right of the copyright holder to grant licenses for public performances of the music, whether the performance is over the airwaves, in concerts, or in various types of public venues.

That means that if a singer's recording of your song is played on the radio, you get money. If the singer sings it in concert, you get money. If the song is played on TV, you get money. If it's played in a disco, you get money. And so on.

Let's make sure we're clear on the difference between *mechanical/synchronization uses* of music and *performances* of music. The former refers to the incorporation of the music into a product such as a compact disc, movie, or TV show, for which the music owner must be paid. The latter refers to the actual playing of music on radio, television, or elsewhere, for which the music owner also gets paid—separately. Got that?

Performance licensing fees are collected from music users and distributed to copyright holders by performing rights organizations, of which ASCAP and Broadcast Music, Inc. (BMI) are the largest. (See the following description.)

ASCAP AND BMI

A vast number of music performances occur in an equally vast number of electronic media outlets and public establishments every day. If every radio station, television station, and concert promoter had to obtain licenses directly from the individual owners of all the songs they wanted to broadcast or perform, the task would be enormous. That's where ASCAP and BMI come in.

The American Society of Composers, Authors, and Publishers (ASCAP) and Broadcast Music, Inc. (BMI) are performing rights societies. They represent many thousands of music creators and publishers, and serve as one-stop clearinghouses for the collection of performance royalties from music users and the distribution of royalties to members whose works are performed.

Instead of granting separate licenses for individual compositions, ASCAP and BMI issue blanket licenses to music users. A *blanket license* allows the licensee to use all the songs in a society's repertoire for a single fee, paid yearly. (This saves users from the hassle of having to obtain licenses directly from many different copyright holders—a process known as *source licensing*.) ASCAP and BMI then use surveys and airplay-logging systems to estimate the total number of times individual compositions are performed in a specific time period. Based on those calculations, and on the type of use, the medium in which the composition was performed, the size and importance of the logged station or outlet, and (in the case of TV) the time of day of the performances, ASCAP and BMI determine royalties and pay them to their members out of the pool of collected license fees.

Both societies pay out royalties seven times a year. (ASCAP pays four times for U.S. performances and three for foreign; BMI pays four times for U.S. performances, twice for foreign, and once for commercials and concerts of "serious" music.)

If writers and publishers want to make sure they are paid for performances, they essentially have to join either ASCAP or BMI (or a third, much smaller performing rights society called SESAC). Once affiliated, the writers and publishers register each of their published songs with the performing rights society.

Both ASCAP and BMI are affiliated with performing rights societies outside the United States, so that they can collect royalties for foreign performances.

To find out more about the societies, contact ASCAP's membership office at 212-621-6240 or BMI's Writer/Publisher Relations department at 212-586-2000.

Music Uses That Generate
Performance Royalties

Because there are so many contexts in which music is performed, and because there are so many different royalty rates depending on the context, we'll simply summarize here the array of possible performance royalty sources.

- Radio—network and local.
- Television—network and local.
- Cable services—pay (like HBO) and basic (like MTV).
- Concert halls. (See page 194 for information about performance licenses as an expense incurred by concert promoters.)
- Background music services like Muzak and 3M.
- Restaurants, nightclubs, discos, bars, hotels, amusement parks, shopping malls, stadiums.
- Circuses, ice shows, Las Vegas–type revues.

In all of these cases, the proprietors pay license fees to one of the performing rights organizations, which in turn pay royalties to affiliated writers and publishers.

Types of Music Uses That Affect
Performance Royalty Rates

Royalty amounts payable to writers and publishers vary depending not only on the context or medium (as listed above) but also on the type of use in the given medium.

Here are types of uses listed in BMI's payment schedule:

- Radio feature performance—"a performance lasting not less than 90 seconds which is the sole sound broadcast at the time of the performance"
- Radio theme—"a work regularly used at the opening and closing of a regularly scheduled program"
- Radio background music or cue music
- Television feature performance—"a performance that constitutes the main focus of audience attention at the time of the performance"
- Television theme—a work that "comprises both the opening and closing musical works performed on the program"
- Television background music—"music used other than as feature or theme"

MARKETING AND PROMOTING IN THE
MUSIC PUBLISHING ENVIRONMENT

It's been said before in this book, and now we'll say it again: marketing and promoting music for use within the industry—that is, for use by record companies, movie and TV producers, performing artists, and others—depends a lot on who you know. That's why established music publishers are well positioned to do this sort of work. They have connections throughout the industry—managers, producers, A&R people, and more, whom they contact periodically to check on their current music needs and to make them aware of songs that might be appropriate for their use.

So the primary guideline for anyone embarking on an attempt to license songs is to build a network and a list of music industry contacts. Remain in touch with these contacts in whatever ways possible—via telephone, through the mail, and by attending trade shows, conventions, and other industry events. Regularly read trade publications in the fields of music, movies, and television to stay abreast of upcoming projects that might require music such as yours. Be proactive in ascertaining and offering to meet the music needs of potential clients. And build a reputation for reliable and knowledgeable service.

Perhaps the most direct way to promote a song is to contact a friend who also happens to be a recording artist and offer your song for his or her use. But don't be offended if they decline. Business is business, after all.

THEATER MUSIC

Occupying a somewhat out-of-the-way sector of the music marketplace is theatrical music. It's out of the way in the sense that money-making opportunities in the theater are fewer than in the standard music market of recording artists, albums, and touring. The most significant amounts of theater music money are earned in the Broadway show sector. Unfortunately, there are relatively few Broadway shows produced—and fewer that are successful. Still, theater music is a potential source of money for songwriters, and for that reason it deserves a mention.

If You Are the Writer
or Co-Writer of a Show

Money can come to writers of musical shows in a number of ways and from a variety of sources. They include option payments from a producer for the right to produce the show; an advance based on capitalization of the show; royalties during the main run of the show (usually

4.5 percent of gross weekly box office receipts until costs have been recouped, and 6 percent thereafter); royalties from the touring version of the show; monies from revivals and amateur versions of the show; mechanical royalties from an original cast album; performance royalties for songs from the album; mechanical and performance royalties for cover versions of songs from the show; synchronization fees from movie versions of the show and from uses of songs in other movies; mechanical royalties from a movie soundtrack album; performance royalties for songs from the movie soundtrack album; and monies for home video, television uses, commercials, and a host of other sources.

For more information about payments to writers of theatrical music, contact the Dramatists Guild, Inc., at 212-398-9366.

If Your Song Is Used in Someone Else's Show

If a producer decides to use your pre-existing song in a show, the payment to you is often a fixed dollar amount, paid weekly. Another way is to pay you a percentage of the weekly gross box office receipts, prorated according to the total number of songs used in the show or according to the duration of the song in relation to the total running time of all music in the show.

PRINTED MUSIC

As previously mentioned, another source of income in the music publishing business is the selling of music in printed form.

The options available for marketing printed music are numerous. Here are a few different ways in which printed music can be presented:

- Sheet music of a single song
- Folios (collections, including record album songbooks)
- Music collections for educational purposes
- Music collections for various vocal and instrumental combinations: choral group, band, keyboard, guitar, brass, strings, and so on

Printed music can be aimed at different markets. Sheet music and collections of popular songs appeal to amateur singers and instrumentalists, who number in the tens of millions in the United States. Certain types of song collections are aimed at the high school and college band market. Miniature scores are widely used for study in college music classes. Instrumental sheet music may be used by serious amateurs or practicing professionals.

If you perceive a market for a certain kind of printed music and you wish to enter that market as a publisher, there are two main ways to go about it: (1) you, the publisher, handle the entire publishing process; or (2) you enter an agreement with a separate company to handle certain aspects of the publishing process.

Handling the Complete Print Publishing Process

In this case, you oversee the complete preparation of the printed music. Here are some of the steps that are involved:

1. Obtain the rights to use the music, if you are not the original publisher or writer. (A copyright notice for each piece of music must be printed in a prominent place on the publication.)

2. Have the music arranged for the intended use (whether solo guitar, piano, vocal plus guitar, string quartet, or some other configuration).

3. Have the music professionally typeset, using either traditional engraving or computer-based (desktop publishing) methods.

4. Arrange for the preparation of an attractive cover design.

5. Estimate the number of copies to be printed, based on your knowledge of the size of the audience.

6. Negotiate an agreement with a distributor, establishing a retail price and a distributor discount (often around 50 percent of the retail price) that will ensure you'll make a profit.

7. Arrange for printing, binding, and delivery to the distributor.

8. Arrange to pay royalties to the composer of the music (if you're not the composer), the amount of which will depend on the type of publication, as follows:

   - For sheet music of a pop-song piano/vocal arrangement, between 6¢ and 10¢ per copy

   - For collections of songs, around 10 percent of the wholesale price, divided among all the participating writers

   - For multi-instrument arrangements, between 10 percent of the wholesale price and $12\frac{1}{2}$ percent of the retail price, depending on the publisher's royalty system.

Bear in mind the following general rule about sales of printed music: Publishing sheet music of current hits can be highly risky; the song's popularity may have dwindled by the time you reach the market. On the other hand, long-established hits—"standards" in music parlance—can continue to sell for many years. And additional money can be made by repackaging such songs for different types of users: school bands, community choirs, guitar students, and so forth.

Having Other Companies Handle Aspects of the Publishing Process

You may have neither the expertise nor the inclination to handle such tasks as music preparation, production, and printing. In such a case, you may opt to have an independent folio publisher-distributor handle these responsibilities. The organization may serve as either a licensee or a selling agent.

Independent Publisher-Distributor as Licensee. In this situation, you license an independent publisher-distributor to handle and pay for production and printing and to handle distribution. It pays you, the publisher, a royalty (a portion of which—generally 50 percent—goes to the writer). The royalty amount depends on the type of publication, as follows:

- For regular (piano-vocal) sheet music of a pop song, a penny rate per copy (of around 60¢) or 20 percent of the retail price. (The writer sheet-music royalty share is as listed in "Handling the Complete Print Publishing Process"—it's a departure from the usual 50 percent.)

- For band arrangements, choral arrangements, and other separately printed copies, 10 to 15 percent of the retail price.

- For folios, 10 to $12\frac{1}{2}$ percent of the retail price. (If the folio is a "personality folio"—with a single artist's songs culled from a single album or several albums—an additional royalty of 5 percent is payable to the artist.)

Joint Venture with an Independent Publisher-Distributor. It's also possible to set up a joint venture with an independent publisher-distributor licensee. In this case, you and the partner split the profits after the costs of production and printing have been recouped, and after a deduction of a 10-to-15-percent administration fee for the partner publisher-distributor.

Independent Publisher-Distributor as Selling Agent. In this case, you commission an independent publisher-distributor to handle distribution and to make available its production facilities. The selling agent handles the production and printing, although you pay for it. You receive all sales receipts minus a 20-to-30-percent commission for the selling agent.

Finding an Independent Publisher-Distributor. For listings of companies that specialize in producing and distributing sheet music, look in *Billboard's International Buyer's Guide* (published annually) in the section on "Sheet Music & Folio Suppliers."

If Your Song Is Used in Someone Else's Publication

You may not be interested in publishing music via any of the above approaches. Still, another publisher or producer may want to include one or several of your songs in some type of published product. Here are a few of the possibilities:

Printed Music Collections. In such a case, you would receive a royalty prorated to reflect the percentage of the total collection represented by your music. That is, if your song is one of 10 compositions used, you get one-tenth of the total available royalty.

Music and Lyrics Printed in Magazines. For the use of your lyrics in a magazine, the payment to you is a lump sum, usually in the range of $100 to $300 (per issue). This amount may be higher if your song is a major hit, or if the magazine has a high circulation.

For the use of both music and lyrics in a magazine, the payment to you is sometimes a pro rata share of a royalty.

Lyric Reprints in Books. Book publishers will sometimes request permission to print song lyrics—in total or in part—in a novel or nonfiction book. The fee is a lump sum, the amount of which depends on a number of factors including the number of lyric lines used, the context in the book, the size of the budget, whether the book is hardcover or paperback, and the territory of publication. A minimum fee would be around $100.

There are innumerable other possible uses for printed lyrics, from greeting cards to calendars to product packages. Don't worry too much about promoting your material to producers of such products. If your composition is famous enough to boost the value of a product, the producers won't hesitate to contact you. Your job is to make your music well known, so that commercial demand for it will be as high as possible.

15

Monitoring and Managing the Marketing Program

Marketing a music product is a complex operation. It encompasses numerous activities, from product development to distribution to promotion—all of which work together to support a sales-generating whole, functioning like a well-oiled machine.

But the machine, once assembled and turned on, can't be left untended. It requires upgrading and occasional modification. Promotional strategies may have to change. New distribution methods may have to be adopted. The musical approach may require adjustment.

In other words, the music marketing program has to be monitored and managed to ensure its ongoing effectiveness.

Before looking at what's involved in fine-tuning the marketing machine after it has been set into motion, let's assemble an overview— a marketing management master list—of the essential marketing tasks discussed in preceding chapters.

THE MARKETING MANAGEMENT MASTER LIST

A "big picture" view of the entire marketing enterprise is essential in working the individual parts so that they fit and support the whole. Use the following checklist as a tool for keeping tabs on where you are in the marketing program and what you still need to do to manage it effectively.

Market Research

- Target your market: identify the audience to which you plan to sell music.
- Estimate the size of the audience.
- Research the interests of the target audience.

- Identify the ways the audience satisfies those interests; identify the stores they frequent, the magazines they read, and so on.
- Plan to sell the music through those stores and media.
- Identify distributors that service those stores.
- Initiate contact with distributors and find out what they need from you in order to establish a business relationship.
- Assemble a media list that includes the information sources— newspapers, magazines, Web, radio, and television—used by the target audience.
- Assemble a customer list, initially culled from personal contacts and supplemented with rented mailing lists, if necessary.
- Identify the qualities of your product that will be most attractive to your targeted audience. Plan on emphasizing those qualities in product packaging, promotional material, and ads.

Business Preliminaries

- Obtain a Fictitious Name Certificate from your local office of the county clerk to establish your business's name as a DBA (doing business as).
- Obtain a Universal Product Code (UPC), which you'll use on all your products, from the Uniform Code Council.
- Obtain a seller's permit (resale license) from your state board of equalization if you're operating in a state that has sales tax.
- Consider registering your business name (trademark) with the U.S. Patent and Trademark Office.

Product Development

- Decide on your basic product format—usually CD and/or cassette.
- Assemble a final list of the music compositions to be included in the product.
- If you are the writer and/or publisher of any of the music, register it for copyright through the U.S. Copyright Office.
- If you are the writer and/or publisher of any of the music, join one of the performing rights societies—ASCAP, BMI, or SESAC— and provide them with clearance forms for each music composition to be included on the album.
- If you are the publisher of any of the music, consider engaging the services of the Harry Fox Agency for help with administering

mechanical, synchronization, and transcription licenses for uses of your music by others.

- For compositions on the album that are not written or published by you, obtain mechanical licenses from the copyright holders. This involves contacting the Harry Fox Agency or going directly to each copyright holder not affiliated with Harry Fox.

- Set a release date for the recording. This will govern the scheduling of your promotion plans.

- Assign the album a unique catalog number.

- Obtain a bar code (in the form of film) from a local supplier.

- Plan and execute the preparation of packaging and promotion materials, emphasizing in their design the qualities of your product that will be most attractive to your targeted audience.

- Anticipate, to the extent possible, all of your near-future print needs (including, for example, direct mail flyers and brochures) and have them designed and produced at the same time as product packaging, to save money.

- Estimate the number of CDs and cassettes you will manufacture, based on your estimate of the size of the audience.

- Get bids from several different disc and cassette manufacturers, and choose the one that offers the combination of price and service that best meets your needs.

- Determine the "suggested retail list price," based on your cost, customer expectations, and competitors' pricings.

Distribution

- Decide on a distribution approach: reaching retail stores through standard distribution channels, using direct marketing (including the Internet), or a combination.

- For direct marketing, create an ordering and fulfillment system: deal with product storage space, postal regulations, toll-free phone numbers, and credit card ordering systems.

- For direct marketing, plan and execute the preparation of mailers, a brochure, direct-response advertising, or other sales tools.

- Look into record clubs and gift catalog companies that might have an interest in selling your product via mail. Provide them with information on your product.

- Prepare a product information sheet (a "one-sheet") to use when trying to interest a distributor in taking on your product.

- Line up a distributor. If necessary, handle distribution yourself on a local basis until you have enough of a success track record to attract distributors' interest.

- Start with local and regional distribution; build up to national (and international) later.

- Make sure your price to the distributor is not too low. You do want to make a profit, after all.

- Use restraint when deciding how many copies to press in the first run. If you press too many, there may be lots of copies returned unsold. Pressing fewer will help ensure sell-though, a distributor reorder, and the distributor's timely payment for the first order as an incentive to get you to press more copies.

SOUNDSCAN

SoundScan, started in 1991, is a system of electronically tracking and counting retail record sales. Each sale is counted when a product bar code is "read" at a store cash register. The aggregate information—which is used by *Billboard* magazine in its music charts and by record companies—provides a highly accurate picture of what's selling at any given time. The statistics can be sorted in numerous ways to indicate sales trends.

As of mid-1997, SoundScan had the participation of 85 to 90 percent of music retailers in the United States.

SoundScan's impact on the music industry has been enormous. Before SoundScan's arrival, information was tallied using methods that left room for inaccuracy. With SoundScan, record companies have a reliable means of determining their success at the retail level. This in turn helps companies to make more-effective business decisions.

Promotion

- Plan and execute Web-based promotion. (See Part 3.)
- Aim to obtain prominent display of your album and promotional materials in retail stores.
- Consider buying co-op advertising through retail stores.
- Prepare press kits.
- Schedule concerts, nightclub dates, and other personal appearances to coincide with the release of the album.
- Mail press kits to the local press and other media several weeks in advance of personal appearances. Follow up to ensure receipt and to (tactfully) urge coverage.

- Place ads for performances and the recording in local and national media, as affordable.
- Arrange special promotional events—such as record store autograph sessions—to coincide with local performance dates.
- Sell the recording at live performances.
- At live performances, provide a mailing list for customers to sign.
- At live performances, provide table cards, postcard questionnaires, and other tools for gathering information about the audience's interests and opinions.
- Perform first at the local level, then build up to regional and national tours booked by major booking agencies and concert promoters.
- Direct publicity efforts at regional and national publications as touring expands.
- Set up cross-promotions with other business entities that cater to the customer group that you're targeting.
- Leave no stone unturned in coming up with imaginative, innovative ways to promote your product.
- Choose songs to promote to radio. Promote them to radio by starting with local and regional college and noncommercial stations. Build up to national radio networks.

BROADCAST DATA SYSTEMS (BDS)

Broadcast Data Systems, owned by *Billboard,* is a computer-based system of tracking radio play of individual songs. It is used by *Billboard* in the compilation of its music charts, and by ASCAP in its survey of radio airplay for purposes of calculating performance royalties payable to its members.

BDS works by monitoring radio station airplay and matching music it "hears" with music that is stored in its database. It can output the music title, date of performance, and time of performance, thus yielding highly accurate information for use by those whose business decisions rely on radio airplay data.

- As popularity increases, prepare a promotional video.
- Promote the act to television by starting with local and regional cable programs. Work up to national programs.
- As the marketing program broadens, consider engaging the services of independent publicity and promotion firms.

Expanding the Marketing Program

- Develop additional formats for the delivery of your music, possibly including DVDs and new-media formats.

- Promote your music to all possible business customers, including producers of television, movies, commercial advertising, and compilation albums.

- License the artist's name and likeness to manufacturers of merchandise to sell at retail and on tour.

Managing the Money Flow

Set up a system for handling on a timely basis the following types of payments:

INCOMING PAYMENTS (ACCOUNTS RECEIVABLE):

- Retail sales revenues for all product formats.
  Payable to product owners (such as record companies) by distributors (for store sales) and by individuals and credit card companies (for direct mail sales).

- Live performance fees.
  Payable to the artist by nightclub owners, booking agencies, and other customers.

- Television appearance fees.
  Payable to the artist by producers, booking agencies, and advertising agencies.

- License fees for uses of the recording on television, in movies, and in other contexts.
  Payable to the owner of the recording by television and film production companies and advertising agencies.

- License fees for use of the artist's name and likeness in non-music merchandise.
  Payable to the record company or to the artist by merchandising companies.

- Royalties for public performances of music compositions (whether on radio and television, in concert, or in other public settings).
  Payable to writers and publishers by ASCAP, BMI, or SESAC.

- Royalties for mechanical uses of music compositions (in records, tapes, and CDs).
  Payable to publishers by record companies (often through the Harry Fox Agency).

- Royalties for synchronization uses of music compositions (in movies, television, and home video).
  Payable to publishers by production companies and advertising agencies (in some cases through the Harry Fox Agency).

- Royalties for transcription uses of music compositions (in background music and syndicated radio programming).
  Payable to publishers by production companies and syndicators (often through the Harry Fox Agency).

- Royalties for printed versions of music compositions.
  Payable to publishers by independent print-music publishing companies.

OUTGOING PAYMENTS (ACCOUNTS PAYABLE):

- Payments for production and manufacturing (of all product formats), including recording, packaging, and duplication costs.

- Artist royalties.

- Mechanical royalties for uses (on records, tapes, and CDs) of compositions owned by others.
  Payable to publishers (often through the Harry Fox Agency).

- Synchronization royalties for uses (in audiovisual products) of compositions owned by others.
  Payable to publishers (in some cases through the Harry Fox Agency).

- Licensing fees for uses (say, on compilation albums, or as sound samples) of pre-existing master recordings.
  Payable to owner(s) of the recording (usually a record company).

- Promotional costs, including materials, postage, advertising, and services of independent publicists and promoters.

- Fees for legal and financial advisors.

- Payments of salaries, rent, telephone, utilities, equipment, and other overhead.

- Taxes.

NAVIGATING THE SHIFTING CURRENTS OF THE MUSIC MARKETPLACE

Managing an in-motion marketing program requires knowledge and decisiveness. To illustrate, let's expand the "marketing machine" metaphor a bit: Picture the machine as powering a forward-moving enterprise.

The marketer is essentially the navigator. Like the captain of a new ship crossing uncharted waters amid changing weather conditions, the marketer constantly monitors the "seaworthiness" of the enterprise amid a changing business climate and then adjusts course as necessary.

Monitoring the progress of the marketing enterprise provides information on (1) the success or failure of marketing efforts to date, and (2) changes in the marketplace. These factors will, in turn, guide decisions about future courses of action.

Monitoring Progress

Obtaining information about the progress of the marketing plan is a relatively straightforward process. It involves paying close attention to the impact of the marketing effort on several fronts, including live appearances, the press, retail sales, and electronic media.

Determine a reasonable amount of time for the marketing and promotion effort to take hold ("reasonable" can mean anything from months to years, depending on your level of patience), and then focus on the following questions (not all of which will apply to all types of performers):

- Do audiences respond positively to the performer in concerts and other live appearances?
- Is the act able to obtain regular and frequent bookings?
- Has attendance increased at live appearances over time?
- Has the act graduated from small venues to larger ones?
- Has the act made progress in expanding from local appearances to regional and national bookings?
- Has the act received press coverage?
- Has press coverage been positive? Negative? Mixed?
- Have distributors shown interest in handling your product?
- If stores have stocked your CDs and tapes, are they selling, and at what rate?
- Has radio shown interest in playing your music?
- If there has been radio play, has there been a corresponding increase in retail sales and concert attendance?
- Has there been progress in expanding from college, local, and noncommercial radio to national programs and networks?
- Has the act been listed in sales and radio-play charts in trade magazines like *Billboard?*

- Has there been interest in the music on the part of movie producers, television producers, printed-music publishers, other artists,
other record companies, and other types of business customers?

and, most importantly,

- Are the checks rolling in?

The answers to these questions should give an accurate indication
of your progress to date.

Now what do you do about it?

MUSIC TRADE MAGAZINES

Information about record sales, radio play, and music industry trends—
sometimes in the form of charts—can be found in such trade magazines
as *Billboard, Cash Box, Radio and Records, Gavin Report,* and *CMJ.*

Billboard, regarded as the leading music trade publication, is best
known for its music popularity charts. These are weekly rankings of songs
and albums based on radio play as monitored by Broadcast Data Systems
(BDS) and retail sales statistics as compiled by SoundScan. Although
Billboard features numerous charts covering different styles and formats
(including video), the best known are the Hot 100® Singles and the
Billboard 200® charts (the latter a ranking of top-selling albums).

The *Billboard* charts have a powerful impact on the industry. Radio
programmers are more likely to add a new song to their playlist if they
see it is already on the charts. Increased radio play, in turn, fuels retail
sales—which helps push the music to even higher chart rankings.

Responding to Successes and Failures

Different outcomes of marketing efforts require different approaches to
moving forward.

But whatever the outcomes may be, it is better to have prepared for
a range of outcomes ahead of time—with a corresponding range of
courses of action—rather than be caught by surprise and have to impro-
vise less-than-ideal changes in strategy on the spur of the moment.

You should have plans in place for dealing with best-case, worst-case,
and most-likely scenarios.

The Best-Case Scenario. In the best-case scenario, marketing efforts have
yielded positive results at each stage of the operation. In such a case,
management decisions should focus on either maintaining the present
level of activity or expanding the marketing program—whichever is
preferred.

Expansion might mean finding new ways to promote the artist or exploit his success—through books, for example, or some other side product line (think of the neckties based on designs by the Grateful Dead's Jerry Garcia). Expansion might also mean spinning off new musical projects, such as collaborations with other artists or explorations of new musical approaches (think of rock artist Elvis Costello's collaboration with the classical group the Brodsky Quartet on the album *The Juliet Letters*). Expansion could also involve moving into new geographical territories.

Whatever the expansion plan, care should be taken not to alienate the core audience. Elvis Costello's *Juliet Letters* worked because it was in keeping with his style-surfer reputation. Middle-of-the-road crooner Pat Boone's 1997 foray into heavy metal did not work: it offended his conservative Christian loyalists.

Maintaining the present level of activity is also an option. But doing so may not be as simple as it sounds. External factors may enter into the picture and require action, as discussed a little later in the chapter.

The Worst-Case Scenario. Some products never even make it to the marketplace. But what if the marketing effort has reached the stage of distributing products to stores, but the sales are minimal, and intensive live performing over an extended period of time seems to be having no beneficial effect on sales?

At some point, the decision may have to be made to end the program and do what is necessary to cut further losses. This may involve a cessation of promotion spending and the establishment of steep price discounts to help sell off the remaining product.

Most people are familiar with "cutout bins" in record stores, where albums sell for a dollar or so. This is where records go that have been deleted from record company catalogs and tagged as "excess inventory"—in other words, left for dead. This is the final option for squeezing any last pennies out of a failed album—except for the final-final option of selling the inventory as scrap.

But it's not over till it's over. There is always the possibility of restarting from scratch with the same artist: reworking the music, rebuilding the image, aiming for a new market, and hoping that customer memories are short.

The Most Likely Scenario. Typically, marketing efforts yield mixed results. An artist may do well in live performances while having difficulty in getting radio play. A record may be successful in one region and have no impact whatsoever in another. Critics may praise the product, yet record sales are not up to par.

Every record release and artist promotion has its own unique set of problems. For that reason it would be pointless to try to address every possible scenario here. The main point to keep in mind is that if an artist is doing well in one sector of the marketplace, it's an encouraging sign: it means that with patience, hard work, and creative thinking, there's a decent chance that in time you'll win over the holdouts. For example, many a performing artist has worked on the road for years before getting the attention of radio programmers and national record buyers.

In such cases, keep adding to the promotion kit: update bios and fact sheets to include the latest successes, add new press clippings, and include samples of new recordings. Use the kit to keep in contact with sectors of the market that you're trying to enter. As the artist's track record lengthens, chances increase that formerly reticent observers will finally see the light and show some enthusiasm.

Responding to Changes in the Marketplace

Success or failure of a marketing effort is affected not only by the pros and cons of the product itself (and the marketing plan) but by factors related to the external environment. Such factors include shifts in public tastes, changes in consumer buying patterns (such as seasonal fluctuations), economic booms and downswings, technological developments, and evolving trends in delivery systems. Any new factor that can potentially influence the short- or long-term success of the marketing program should be analyzed and, if necessary, met with a shift in marketing strategy.

16

Marketing and Promoting Music in Foreign Countries

The burgeoning global market offers music makers tremendous potential for increasing revenues.

In addition to worldwide retail sales, touring income, and licensing fees, the international market can provide certain types of revenue streams that are not available domestically—such as performance royalties for record companies.

Entertainment companies of all kinds have increasingly come to rely on international sales as a major source of income. Performers are groomed for multinational appeal. Artists who don't catch on—or have gone out of fashion—in one territory may still be able to generate revenues in another. Movies are created with international audiences in mind (action films do particularly well, since they use minimal dialogue).

To increase their ability to market such products across international boundaries, large conglomerates establish foreign offices or gain ownership of foreign media companies, and smaller companies build global networks of business partners.

The reward for developing a worldwide marketing program can be very significant, even for an independent label: in the case of Alligator Records, for example, 20 to 30 percent of its business comes from international sales.

Music—the so-called international language—is especially well suited for sale all over the world. It provides enjoyment that can transcend cultural differences. Western pop music, in particular, is in ever-growing demand among worldwide populations.

So thinking globally is a natural way to extend a music marketing program. To begin, however, you need to understand both the means of building a worldwide presence and the kinds of business conventions that govern international music commerce. The following discussion summarizes key aspects of global marketing.

HOW TO ESTABLISH AN
INTERNATIONAL PRESENCE

To establish a commercial presence in a foreign territory so that you can tap the sources of income available there, you will need to affiliate with, or gain representation by, distributors and publishers that handle the territory.

There are different types of organizations that do this. Giant media companies like Sony and BMG have international reach, so that if you are signed with or distributed by one of those companies you generally have access to its worldwide marketing mechanism. Other less large companies may operate on a regional basis, with capabilities extending to several countries. Finally, there are companies that do business only in one country.

If you're not affiliated with one of the media giants, you'll most likely end up working with several different companies. For example, you may want to partner with a multinational company to do business in only those countries in which it has proven effective. In other countries, you would deal with separate companies that have been successful in your targeted region. Many small record labels, such as Alligator (see Bruce Iglauer's interview on page 276), choose to build networks of foreign representatives on a country-by-country basis.

Finding the right companies is of key importance. You'll want to find organizations that have proven track records of success marketing music like yours.

One way to start is to pick up a record you like (of music roughly similar to yours), call the publicity office of the record company that released the disc, and ask for the names of the companies that handle foreign distribution. You can then place exploratory phone calls to those companies and follow up by mailing them promotional materials (the same type that you would use to present your music to a domestic distributor, as described on page 119).

You can check directories for the names of foreign companies and then research their track records and music specialties. *Billboard's International Buyer's Guide,* for example, lists international record labels, music publishers, distributors, performing rights and mechanical rights organizations, professional associations, PR and record promotion firms, and other types of companies.

The Internet is another effective source of international distribution information. Look in the music and entertainment sections of leading search engines, or type in such keywords as *music distributors* and *international music distribution.*

Attending music industry conferences and conventions is a way to speak directly with attending distribution and label personnel and ask them for referrals to reputable foreign business entities. One such conference is MIDEM (International Music and Publishing Market), which is held each January in Cannes, France. The U.S. trade shows and conventions cited on page 182 are also good potential networking opportunities for those seeking to find international partners.

Again, it's essential, before establishing a business relationship with a foreign organization, to thoroughly research its track record and reputation. You'll be entrusting the company with your music, and for that you need nothing less than the best.

FOREIGN DISTRIBUTION AND SALE OF MUSIC PRODUCTS

To get your records into foreign stores, you'll need to work with distributors that can service those stores. As mentioned previously, if you're not affiliated with an international media conglomerate with its own foreign branch affiliates, you may find it necessary to work with a number of independent foreign distributors on a country-by-country basis.

Once you have identified reputable foreign distributors, there are several different types of arrangements that can be entered into. They include the following:

- Licensing the foreign distributor to manufacture and distribute your product
- Exporting your product through a foreign distributor
- Setting up a joint venture with a foreign record label

It's entirely possible that a record company may not only work with several different foreign companies but also have different types of business arrangements with different companies, depending on what makes the most financial sense. For example, in one territory it might be more profitable to license a record company to manufacture and distribute, while in another territory the best arrangement is a simple export deal.

Licensing Foreign Companies to Manufacture and Distribute Products

In this very common arrangement, the record owner (you) grants a foreign record label a license to issue your recording in its local territory. The licensor (again, you) provides the licensee with a master recording, from which the licensee manufactures copies and handles local distribution.

Such licensing often involves distribution using the licensee's—not the licensor's—label. Alternatively, the record may be distributed under a split label—that is, using both the licensor's and the licensee's labels.

The licensee may prepare a new album cover, in some cases using photos and artwork from the original cover, or it may order printed covers from the licensor.

Compensation paid by the licensee to the licensor is generally 8 to 17 percent of the local retail list price, less taxes and packaging costs, for 90 to 100 percent of records sold. (Sometimes payment is based on 100 percent of records sold minus promotional copies and returns.)

More frequently, the royalty is computed not on the retail price but on what is called the *published price to dealer* (PPD), which is roughly equivalent to what in the United States is called the wholesale price. When this is the case, the royalty percentage is set higher so that the amount earned is equivalent to 8 to 17 percent of retail.

In another type of licensing deal, the licensor provides manufactured albums to the licensee, who buys them at the manufacturing cost and then pays a royalty on sales. This arrangement makes sense when estimated sales are not high enough to justify the foreign label bearing the cost of local manufacturing.

Depending on the previous sales track record of the album, you may be able to negotiate a sizable advance against projected royalties. In any event, a record of previous sales is usually necessary to attract the interest of a foreign distributor, just as it is with a domestic distributor.

Exporting Products to International Distributors

In some cases, it makes the most financial sense for the record owner to export its finished recordings to a foreign distribution company, who simply distributes.

In the export scenario, the exporter (you) sets a price that permits a reasonable profit above manufacturing cost. (That price will be roughly the same as the distributor wholesale price you charge domestically. See page 122.) One independent record label set its export price at roughly 50 percent of the domestic suggested retail list price. That same label offered some foreign distributors an additional discount of 15 to 20 percent. In other cases the label provided foreign distributors with an advertising allowance in the form of a discount off the export price.

Typically, the foreign distributor pays for freight and duties.

Also typically, the exporter is responsible for paying mechanical royalties (since it is the manufacturer of the product).

Joint Ventures with International Companies

The owner of a recording may want to exert more control over how a product is manufactured, marketed, and distributed in a foreign territory.

An effective way to do this is to set up a joint venture with an internationally present major or independent label. In such cases, the two business entities share resources, control, costs, and profits. (For more information about joint ventures, see page 128.)

Performance Royalties for Record Companies

In many countries outside the United States, record companies are paid royalties when their recordings are publicly performed—say, broadcast on radio and TV. (In the U.S., only writers and publishers get performance royalties.) Such performance fees are generally shared by licensees and licensors, typically on a 50-50 basis.

Recording Artist Royalties for Foreign Sales of Music Products

Royalties payable to a recording artist on foreign sales of various types of music products are generally lower than domestic royalties. And as with domestic royalties, they vary depending on the type of product.

Artist Royalties for Foreign Record Sales. Artist royalties on foreign sales of records vary depending on the territory. They also vary depending on whether the record company markets through a foreign affiliate or licenses through an independent label in the territory.

In general, the royalty rate on records sold in Canada is 85 percent of the U.S. rate.

For records sold in what are termed major territories (the United Kingdom, France, Germany, Italy, the Netherlands, Australia, and Japan), the rate is generally 60 to 75 percent of the U.S. rate.

For records sold in the rest of the world, the rate is generally 50 to 60 percent of the U.S. rate.

Foreign royalties are negotiable, of course, depending on the recording artist's track record of product sales and his or her popularity in particular territories. (The more popular the artist, the greater the artist's negotiating strength.)

Artist Royalties for Foreign Merchandise Sales. Artist royalties on foreign sales of tour-related merchandise (see page 196) are around 80 percent of the domestic rate (which, in turn, is generally 25 to 40 percent of gross sales).

Artist royalties on foreign sales of retail merchandise (see page 212) are also around 80 percent of the domestic rate. (The domestic rate, in this case, is 10 to 20 percent of the wholesale price for retail store sales.)

FOREIGN EARNINGS FOR WRITERS AND PUBLISHERS

Earnings for music writers and publishers (as differentiated from record companies and recording artists) come from the same types of uses in foreign territories as they do domestically: manufacture and distribution of recordings (mechanical uses), incorporation of music in visual works (synchronization), and public performances. (For basic information about writer and publisher revenue sources, see Chapter 14.)

There are several different ways that domestic publishers can secure representation of their catalogs—and ensure collection of their earnings—in foreign territories: through a multinational publisher, through a network of local subpublishers, through a joint publishing venture, and through a combination of these.

Multinational Publishers

If the foreign representative is a multinational organization, songs are exploited, and foreign earnings are collected, through its foreign affiliated offices. For the writer or publisher dealing with such an organization, this may be the most convenient way to ensure blanket coverage of numerous territories. The risks are twofold: (1) certain local offices of the multinational company may not be particularly effective, and (2) the song or catalog may not get the attention it would in a smaller company.

Foreign Subpublishers

For the smaller domestic publisher, earnings are usually collected on a territory-by-territory basis by foreign *subpublishers*—that is, local foreign publishers with whom the domestic publisher has set up what are called subpublishing agreements. Subpublishers perform the same tasks in their territories that domestic publishers do at home, from exploiting songs for potential new uses to collecting and paying out royalties. Foreign subpublishers generally retain between 10 and 25 percent of money earned (including the writer share), submitting the remainder to the domestic publisher. (Thus, foreign royalties received by domestic writers are generally less than their domestic royalties, because the total amount of foreign royalties—of which writers get 50 percent—is reduced by the amount kept by the subpublisher.)

The subpublisher share may be higher under certain circumstances. This is sometimes true in the case of performance royalties, because the writer share of these royalties is paid directly to writers (through performing rights societies) rather than to the subpublisher, thus justifying an increase in the subpublisher's percentage to compensate for the overall 50 percent reduction in the total amount on which they calculate their share. Subpublishers also tend to take a higher share of earnings for local cover versions the subpublisher procures. The share is generally 40 to 50 percent. The justification is that in such cases they are taking a more active role than when simply collecting foreign earnings for a domestically recorded song.

Subpublishers often pay advances to original publishers, against expected earnings. The amount of an advance usually depends on the perceived value of the catalog.

Subpublishing agreements may cover an entire catalog, a few songs, or even one song.

At-Source Royalty Calculation. In some cases a foreign subpublisher will have a foreign licensee in another country collect earnings for that country and submit them to the subpublisher. The foreign licensee may retain a percentage before submitting monies to the subpublisher, who then deducts its percentage before forwarding monies to the domestic publisher. This, obviously, would reduce the overall amount of money received by the domestic publisher and, ultimately, the writer. For this reason, some subpublishing agreements include an "at-source" provision, stipulating that the domestic publisher's percentage will be based on the total amount earned at-source, before the sublicensee deducts its percentage.

Joint Publishing Ventures

As with foreign record distribution, a foreign publishing operation can be set up as a joint venture, with responsibilities, costs, and profits split between the domestic and the local foreign partners.

Territory-by-Territory Publishing Arrangements

Another option for exploiting songs in foreign territories is using a combination of the previously described options—that is, using a multinational publisher in some territories, and using separate subpublishers in territories where the multinational's offices are not particularly effective.

Mechanical Royalties for Music Distributed Internationally

In most foreign countries, the local mechanical rights collection agency collects mechanical licensing fees from record companies in that territory for all songs used on records, then distributes them to publishers who make claims for those songs. (U.S. publishers can deal directly with these agencies rather than having a foreign subpublisher deal with them; the Harry Fox Agency [see page 218] can also act as a representative for a U.S. publisher, dealing with foreign mechanical rights agencies instead of the U.S. publisher having to go through—and compensate—a foreign subpublisher.)

Foreign mechanical earnings sometimes go unclaimed by original publishers. Accrued money for unclaimed songs is eventually distributed to local publishers in amounts proportionate to individual publishers' percentages of total mechanical earnings.

Mechanical license rates differ in different countries. Typically, the rate is a percentage of the published price to dealer (PPD), which is roughly the same as what the U.S. terms the wholesale price. (Canada, like the U.S., computes mechanical fees on a penny basis.)

Synchronization Fees for Audiovisual Works Distributed Internationally

Licenses of music for use in TV shows, movies, and home videos originating in specific countries are issued by the subpublishers in those countries (if subpublishers are used). Since this is work performed by the subpublisher, the amount it retains before submission of money to the domestic publisher may be higher than the usual 10 to 25 percent— sometimes 50 percent.

License agreements for home videos of movies and TV programs produced in the U.S. tend to be for the entire world. That is, generally the producer will pay the U.S. publisher the established rate (say, 8¢ a video) regardless of the country of sale. This way, producers avoid having to deal with many individual foreign subpublishers.

Payment for Foreign Performances

Foreign territories have their own performing rights societies like ASCAP, BMI, and SESAC. For performances of U.S. works, local performing rights societies collect money from local users and pay publisher shares to local subpublishers (or, for music with no local subpublisher, directly to the original publisher's domestic society—ASCAP, BMI, or SESAC) and writer shares to ASCAP, BMI, or SESAC. ASCAP, BMI, and SESAC then distribute collected foreign royalties to their members.

Royalty-generating performances in foreign countries include movies, unlike in the United States. Fees are based on one of several possible formulas, including a percentage of net box office receipts (usually 1 to 2 percent) or a dollar amount per seat times the total number of seats in the theater.

"Black box" collections—money collected for songs not identified as having ownership—go into general funds that are eventually distributed to local publishers.

Printed Music Sold in Foreign Territories

A domestic publisher may arrange to have a foreign subpublisher manufacture and sell sheet music of its song. In this arrangement, the subpublisher pays the domestic publisher 10 to 15 percent of the suggested retail price. In the case of a folio consisting of multiple works owned by different publishers, this royalty is paid out on a pro rata basis.

Alternatively, a domestic publisher may arrange to license a foreign subpublisher to sell already printed music. In this scenario, the subpublisher keeps 10 to 25 percent of the money earned and submits the remainder to the domestic publisher.

Lyric Translations

Obviously, a song may be easier to exploit in a foreign territory if it is translated into the local language. For this reason, subpublishers retain the right to hire local translators.

Local writers who translate lyrics get a percentage of the subpublisher's share of earnings for local mechanical and synchronization uses and for sales of printed music. For performances, local performing rights societies deduct the translator's percentage from payable writer royalties, submitting the remainder to the domestic performing rights society. Percentages vary depending on local practice and the negotiating strength of the translator.

PROMOTION IN THE INTERNATIONAL MARKET

As in domestic promotion, international promotion involves publicity, radio play, television broadcast, the Internet, personal appearances and touring, and advertising. Most of the tactics described in Chapter 11 apply as much to foreign territories as to the domestic market. For information about promoting on the Internet, see Chapter 19.

When a domestic company works with a foreign company to get music into a foreign market, there is a question of which company foots the bill for local promotion. Typically, it's answered as follows: In export scenarios, the exporter supplies the distributor with a budget for promotion. In licensing situations, the licensee pays for promotion. In joint ventures, costs are shared by the partners.

INTERNATIONAL TOURING AND LIVE PERFORMANCE

As in domestic touring, foreign tours are generally set up to coincide with the release of an album.

While international headliners routinely book world tours, mid-level performers may limit foreign performances to those territories in which they have had success with distribution and sales, and in which they have received some press attention.

An interesting case of selective popularity is that of jazz musicians from the United States, many of whom find more enthusiastic audiences in foreign territories—say, Europe and Asia—than they do in their homeland. There have also been many cases of rock performers who have gone out of fashion in one part of the world and yet are able to mount hugely successful tours in other regions.

Bookings for foreign performances may be handled by foreign agents, foreign subagents of domestic booking agencies, or large domestic agencies—like William Morris, ICM, and CAA—that have foreign offices. Tours can also be booked by artists or their managers dealing directly with foreign concert promoters.

PART

3

Music Marketing
and Promotion
on the Internet

CHAPTER

17

An Alternative Worldwide Information and Distribution Network

There was a time when getting your music heard by masses of people—especially if you were an independent artist—was a pipe dream, the stuff of fantasy, a one-in-a-million long shot.

The problem began with the fact that expanding your audience, even a little beyond your immediate region, required acceptance of your music by a chain of middlemen—record company executives—who seemed to remain ever out of your reach.

If you're an artist, the dream was quite specific. It often involved getting discovered in some club, getting signed to a lucrative deal with a major label, and releasing an album that established you as both commercially successful and critically acclaimed.

The reality, however, may be quite different.

By now, the various pitfalls that lie within the music industry are well documented. A record company or music publisher may simply ignore your demos. Or they may decide your fan base is too limited or not developed enough. The traditional avenues may feign interest in your act but never follow through because of corporate red tape. Also, corporate politics at the top can adversely affect your act: often, when a record company president leaves, that means the end of many projects currently in development. Even finished CDs may end up shelved for one reason or another.

The era of high technology, however, has ushered in new marketing possibilities for music makers.

AUTHORS' NOTE: It should be pointed out that, at press time, Internet technology is changing very, very rapidly. The authors have done their best to compile information that is accurate and up to date. But, given the mercurial nature of the computer industry and the Internet, it is entirely possible that some dramatic new technology may be emerging by the time this book is on the shelves. So, in our opinion, it's in your best interest to keep up with events in high technology by regularly checking commercial Web sites and reading Internet trade publications and news reports.

CONVENTIONAL WISDOM

Standard music marketing avenues are really the only way to sell music.

ALTERNATE REALITY

By early 1998, The Artist (formerly known as Prince) was using the Internet to promote and sell his music and communicate with his audience. In mid-1998, Twin Tone Records announced that it would begin distributing music exclusively over the Internet.

A DO-IT-YOURSELF ALTERNATIVE

In the short time since its phenomenal growth in popularity that began in the early 1990s, the Internet has had a widely noticed impact on the music industry.

At the time of this writing, opinions differ on where this global network of interconnected computer systems is taking us and how the music industry will evolve with it. But regardless of the ongoing Internet-music business debate, certain facts are undeniable:

The Internet, along with the digital technology that's arisen with it, has enabled music entrepreneurs to make and market their own products. Do-it-yourself is now a reality.

The Internet has opened new doors for musicians and marketers. By turning on a computer and hooking up to the Net, you are only a couple of keystrokes or clicks away from millions of potential customers "surfing" cyberspace. These are people you can get your music to directly, without the say-so, the approval, the backing, and the direction of the old-world record company-conglomerate. You're manning the controls. All you have to do is get the music you create (whether in your home studio or at a professional facility) onto the Internet and then draw attention to it through a variety of means. The rest is up to the people who hear your stuff. They either like it or they don't—a refreshingly simple equation compared to the complex series of approval procedures you had to go through in the past.

Use of the Net and the World Wide Web can add entire new vistas to an emerging or established act's career plan. This can include direct communication with fans, realizing additional sales, and reaching more foreign markets—all vital to an act's overall business picture.

The purpose of this section of the book is to introduce you to the Internet as a potential boon to your music marketing and promotion. It's designed to get you versed in the basics of the Internet as a business resource so you can start making the most of its vast possibilities.

A BRIEF HISTORY OF THE INTERNET

During the 1960s the framework for the Internet was developed by European and North American scientists as a Cold War technology. The idea was to establish a worldwide network of interconnected computer communications systems. This way, in the event of nuclear war, if one country's system was knocked out, the various allies' governments and military would still have high-speed communications via computers and phone lines.

Over the next two decades, the Internet—a text-only system then—was gradually opened up to educational institutions around the world. By the dawn of the 1990s, the Internet had evolved into a mammoth network, shared and supported by government, military, educational, and corporate entities.

Soon after it was opened up to the general public in the early 1990s, the Internet's popularity skyrocketed. That happened largely due to the development of the World Wide Web, a sector of the Internet capable of displaying data in multimedia form, offering a galaxy of graphics, animation, and audiovisual possibilities. Quickly, music of all kinds became one of the most popular topics on the Web.

The middle and late 1990s also saw phenomenal growth in the personal computer industry, with cheaper and more powerful systems and software made available to mass audiences. By the close of the decade, millions of music fans around the world were using this technology to enjoy tens of thousands of music-related Web sites. These offered a plethora of services to the fan, including chat sessions, music news, downloadable music clips, and videos and animation, to name just a few.

At the time of this writing, the end of the Internet explosion is nowhere in sight. The arrival of the new century promises even more advances in Net and Web technology—which will, of course, affect how music is distributed, promoted, and sold.

Many music pioneers of the Internet are fueled by a vision, and it's looking more and more like reality. The vision is this: You, the music maker, are turning away from the middlemen, record contracts, and music business strategies of the past. Now you're the boss, standing before a vastly changed field of commercial operations.

That field, as this book is being written, is completely wide open.

CHAPTER

18

Distributing Your Musical Product via the Internet

Today, the idea of seeking out music on the Internet, previewing it, and then downloading the music straight into your computer is no longer theory or science fiction. It's reality.

Now, with the increasing availability of powerful personal computers, easy-to-use software, and fast transmission speeds over the Internet, it's becoming quite a lot easier to give your music a presence in cyberspace. Established performers have already begun to take advantage of this: In early 1998, artists as diverse as Herbie Hancock and Joan Jett and the Blackhearts were offering single releases on the Net for free downloading.

You may be ready to start distributing your own music over the Internet. You've got your music recorded, and you've got it stored as a digital file ready for uploading.

But there's just one problem: Where's the distribution outlet? Where's the storefront?

As a marketer-distributor, you've got a couple of options. One is to place your product with an established "store"—a Web site that is a collection or archive of different types of music by a variety of artists. The other option is to set up your own "storefront"—that is, build your own Web site and take care of business yourself.

AFFILIATING WITH A MULTI-ARTIST WEB SITE

At press time, there were already several shopping centers on the Web devoted to music. They included the Internet Underground Music Archive (a large, multi-service Web site popularly known as IUMA); CDnow; Tower Records; and N2K's Music Boulevard. In addition, book retailers like Amazon.com are beginning to sell music online.

Depending on your act's status, aligning with one of these multi-artist sites could add a vital marketing and promotion boost to your overall career picture. The key word here is *exposure*—that is, communicating with existing fans, making new ones, and giving them not only a chance to preview your product but also an easy, safe way to purchase it.

Here are some items you'll need in order to sign with a multi-artist Web site:

- Access to a personal computer and the software needed for uploading music and other information to the Internet
- Finished copies of your CD
- A copy of your act's logo in a digital file (optional)
- Bio information on your act
- Any tour news or other information that you wish to post

Depending on your choice, one of the multi-artist sites can take care of the whole banana for you. This includes warehousing the CDs, order taking, accounting, and shipping via standard (as opposed to electronic) mail.

But before doing anything, carefully consider your act's positioning on a multi-artist site. You don't want your product to simply be lost in a cyber-maze of hundreds of other bands. You can solve this problem by linking your own separate Web site (as discussed in the next section) to the multi-artist site, thus increasing the opportunities for fans to find you on the Web and then get more information by following the link to the other site.

What's involved in affiliating with a multi-artist site? In the case of IUMA, you pay a yearly fee of around $250, send in your CD, and supply them with a bio and other information. IUMA also permits you to sell CDs, cassettes, videos, and T-shirts through the site on consignment. Check with individual sites to find out their particular affiliation procedures.

SETTING UP YOUR OWN WEB SITE

Some people prefer the control and flexibility of setting up their own Web site dedicated to their music. Having such a dedicated Web site may help you stand out from the crowd more than if you're just one of many on a group site.

Having your own Web site requires special attention to advertising and promotion, since without it no one will know the site exists. More on this topic in the next chapter.

These days a key question, according to Internet analyst and writer Russell Shaw, "is not whether to put up a site or not, or how to do it, but what should be on it."

The Basic Structure of a Web Site

The typical music site opens with a "home page"—the first visual the fan sees upon visiting. The home page may feature the act's logo as a centerpiece. Somewhere on the page, the fan will find several hyperlinks, "hot buttons," or active graphics. The fan can easily click on these to go to various areas beyond the home page.

The kinds of features typically included in effective Web sites include the following:

- Extended text about the background of the artist, the music, and related topics of interest
- Current news about the artist
- A tour schedule, or a list of upcoming club performances
- A "bulletin board," where fans can post mail to the artist or to other fans
- Information about recordings available for purchase, along with ordering instructions
- A list of all song recordings, which could include the singer(s), the people who played the instruments, the producer and engineer, and the date and location of the recording
- Song lyrics
- Audio clips of old songs and sneak previews of works in progress
- Interesting graphics, although not too complex, since some users will be viewing the site using an Internet browser that won't display the graphic in quite the form intended, or they'll be using slow equipment that may take too much time to display anything fancier than plain text, testing the user's patience
- Video clips of the artist
- Audio interviews with the artist
- Links to other sites of interest, such as online stores, other artists' sites—anything the proprietor of the main site thinks will be of interest to a fan

When developing the content of your site, think in terms of accessibility and promoting your act as intelligently and creatively as possible. You may want to add an 800 phone number to the site, to make it easy for fans to order your product. Other methods of permitting customer contact include adding a "MailTo" feature that enables the customer to e-mail you directly from the site, or setting up a more complex on-site ordering and preferences form using CGI scripts. (To create these, you'll need to consult a Web development manual, such as Laura Lemay's excellent book *Teach Yourself Web Publishing in a Week with HTML*.)

As pointed out earlier, you may wish to have both an alliance with a multi-artist site and your own site, with both linked together. This could help you maximize visibility and hence sales.

Constructed creatively and intelligently, a Web site can serve as a near-ideal promotional-marketing-informational-archival-purchasing one-stop.

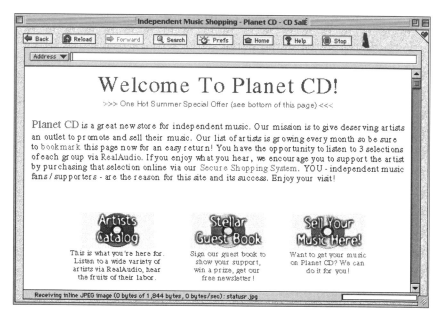

The home page of PlanetCD, a Web site that promotes independent bands.

Doing It Yourself

The following suggestions for building your own page on the World Wide Web come from Katie Garcia, a Portland, Oregon, freelance writer and heavy Internet user:

> "With the potential audience for Internet Web pages numbering in the millions, it is easy for Web page developers to justify charging small fortunes for Web page development. What they don't tell you is that building your own Web page is a relatively easy endeavor and can be completed over a weekend.

Whether you are an up-and-coming band or a well-established name in the music business, you can save money by constructing your own Web page to market your act. The plus of it is that you do not need to know any higher math or a computer language. You can also be sure that your Web page reflects who your band really is.

You just need a basic computer hardware setup, an account with a local Internet service provider (ISP), some spare hours, and the tips that follow.

Required Hardware

A basic computer hardware setup consists of a monitor, keyboard, hard drive, processor, memory, sound card, CD-ROM drive, printer, and a modem. There are various minimum requirements for speed, RAM, hard drive space, and other factors. The values provided below have a built-in hedge of protection from becoming hopelessly outdated in the near term. They may not be the fastest or the best of the best, but they will do the job quite nicely with minimal fuss.

Here are some of the specifics of what you'll need:

- **A 15-to-17-inch color monitor.**

- **A keyboard.**

- **A hard drive with plenty of memory**—enough to enable you to store any graphics and music files you might want to include on your Web page. If you are planning on having a lot of pictures or music, a four-gigabyte hard drive will keep you happy for quite a while before you will have to upgrade. It will also allow plenty of room for the other jobs your computer may have.

- **For working on the PC platform, a 200 MHz or better Pentium processor with MMX capability** (multimedia, sound, and video are handled better with MMX). You can also go with the Pentium II. If you prefer the Macintosh platform, aim for a 200 MHz or better computer with a 604e or a G3 processor.

- **At least 32 megabytes of RAM** (random access memory).

- **A sound card.** This is what enables your computer to play high-quality sound.

- **A CD-ROM drive.** This will not only allow you to install and use software that comes stored on a CD-ROM but also enable you to record your music files straight from your band's CDs. (It also enables you to listen to music while you work on the computer.) A minimum speed would be 12x to 24x.

- **A modem, with a minimum speed of 28.8 Kbps** (though it's much better to have at least 33.6 Kbps). The numbers represent how fast your computer communicates with the computer "serving" the Web site you're visiting. If you have ever surfed the Web with an old, slow modem and tried to view a graphic-intensive site, you will understand why the Web has earned the nickname the World Wide Wait. Lots of graphics mean lots of data, which require fast modems. Also, the faster your modem, the less time it will take you to upload your Web page and files to the Internet.

- **A printer,** which enables you to edit the text of your Web page in "hard copy." (For some people, it is easier to spot their mistakes when they have a piece of paper to view.) You don't have to spring thousands for a good laser or photographic printer. High-quality printers can be purchased for under $300.

You can, of course, use higher-speed modems and CD-ROM drives, larger monitors, and more expensive printers, but the above list will suit your needs nicely if you don't feel the need to have all the latest technological bells and whistles.

Additional Hardware Options

Those were the basics. Now let's talk about the optional but great-to-have hardware.

- **A scanner**. This hardware allows you to scan your own graphics and pictures—anything from your band's logo to the latest publicity shot—for use in your Web page. Scanners have come down in price to the point where they are very affordable.

- **A digital camera.** This is a great tool for capturing your own images of your act and bringing them directly into your computer for use. Like the scanned images, you can manipulate the images on the computer to suit your needs. Depending on your software, you can crop the shot, enhance or tone down colors, and perform a variety of other alterations.

Web Authoring Options

When constructing a Web site, you have the option of working with raw HTML—the language or code (spelled out as *hypertext markup language*) that is at the heart of Web page creation—or using commercial Web page authoring software. What method you use is entirely up to you. The result will be pretty much the same.

Commercial software, available at computer stores, takes most of the guesswork out of building your page. You tell it what you want and it does the HTML "writing" for you. Most come with clip art and background patterns that you can use. Not all programs are created equal, and I recommend asking friends what they like and use, checking with computer stores, and reading reviews in computer magazines. You can also call your Internet provider to get their recommendation. Currently popular programs include Adobe PageMill, NetObjects Fusion, and Claris Home Page.

It's possible to get free software from the Internet itself. Many "shareware" and "freeware" programs are out there for the general Net public to download and use.

Many of the latest versions of Internet browsers (such as Netscape Communicator 4.0) come with Web authoring tools built in. Also, most new office and word-processing programs, such as Word 97, have built-in tools for building your Web page.

There's always the option of building your Web page from scratch, using plain HTML and a simple word processor such as Notepad.

Adding Graphics, Sound, and E-Mail Links

As part of your Web page design, you will want to add graphics, sounds, and links that allow your viewers to e-mail you. Again, the tool that you use to construct your Web page will influence the way you handle these.

There are several methods of adding graphics and sounds. The most satisfying way is to create your own. (For artist sites, of course, you'll almost invariably want the sound to be clips of original music.) Here are ways to go about it:

- Scan an existing illustration or photograph into your computer. The computer stores it as a .GIF file or a .JPEG file (GIF and JPEG are graphic image designations, as opposed to HTML, which refers to text) and you can insert it into your page.

- Draw or paint an image using a graphic design program, then place it in your Web page.

- Create simple animation using GifBuilder, an easy program downloadable (with instructions) from the Web for free.

- Create a music or sound clip using music production software and "import" the clip into your Web page.

- Set up a simple e-mail link by creating an instruction on the page and linking it to your regular e-mail address.

Another fun option is to borrow from the endless supply of public domain images and sounds on the Web. Conduct a search on one of the search engines using the keywords *graphics, backgrounds, wav files*. (Wav, or WAVE, files are music or audio files.) When you find one or several you would like to use, right-click on the image (if you're working in Windows 95), select the Save As instruction, and choose where you want to save your images.

Just a word of caution: Be aware that there are copyrighted images and music files on the Web. Avoid them and stick with the public domain images available for use on your site.

Uploading the Site to the Internet

You have spent many dry-eyed hours in front of your computer, building your Web page. You have double-checked it for grammar and spelling. It projects your band's image exactly the way you envisioned it. You're happy, you're tired, and you are confused. How do you get the page "out there" in cyberspace?

First, you'll need space on the Web for storing your Web page. Ask your ISP if your account includes it. Many service providers offer at least 2 to 10 megabytes of such space. If yours does not, then shop around for one that does.

You will need an FTP (File Transfer Protocol) client. This refers to the software that moves a file from your computer to the "space" on your server (your Internet provider's computers). If you are using Web authoring software, it might include an FTP client. If not, or if you are using the raw HTML method, you will need to download an FTP client from the Internet. The first place to check would be your ISP's home page, or call them and ask how you might get an FTP client. If, by some small chance, the ISP can't help, perform a search on one of the major search engines (yahoo.com or Webcrawler.com) for *FTP client*. Usually you can obtain one as freeware.

Step-by-step information on how to upload your Web page files via your FTP client is obtainable from a variety of sources, including the manual that came with your Web authoring software, books on Web page creation, numerous Web sites (search the keywords *file transfer protocol*), and your ISP.

If you want to make it easy for people to find your page, you can register a domain name. Domain names tend to be simpler and more memorable (for example, www.rollingstones.com) than the long strings of characters that ISPs often assign their customers. Anyone can register a domain name with the InterNIC by filling out an online registration form or contacting them by phone or mail.

Some ISPs will do the registration for you (for an added fee), or you can register the name yourself and notify your ISP.

Registration for domain names costs $100, and that covers your first two years. After that, you are charged $50 per year, charged on the anniversary of your initial registration.

You can contact InterNIC at http://www.internic.net or by phone at 703-742-4777. **"**

THE INTERNET DISTRIBUTION PROCESS

Distributing music to customers, once you've established a "store front" or set up "shelf space" on the Web, can be done in one of two ways: (1) via standard mail, or (2) via direct download.

Standard Mail

Today, fancier Web sites allow fans to order right on the spot.

After the potential customer has had a chance to check out sound clips on the Internet, the order is placed right on the Web site, and the CD is sent to the customer via standard mail ("snail mail," that is).

Simpler sites feature a toll-free number for ordering CDs.

Direct Download

At the time of this writing, direct downloading of music is a somewhat controversial topic: it remains unclear just how the traditional music retail industry is going to coexist with direct-download technology.

Here, in a simplified example, is how it works: The act or label prepares the musical product. The CD single, for example, is then uploaded to an affiliated site (such as muzic.com) using audio "streaming" software such as RealAudio. The customer can log on to the site and preview the music using a free downloadable version of the streaming software. If the customer chooses, he or she can download the entire single straight to a computer hard drive—in a matter of seconds.

At press time, the technology already has sophisticated encoding for secured credit card purchases, anti-piracy features, and tracking for licensing and accounting. (See Scott Burnett's interview on page 286 for more about these capabilities.) In addition, affordable hardware enabling consumers to download entire albums and then "burn" them on their own CDs, right at home, is appearing on the market.

CHAPTER

19

Promoting Music on the Internet

The Web site is set up, the key information is on it, and you know that as soon as someone hits it they'll love the thing and want to order or download your music.

But what if no one comes?

It's not such a farfetched possibility. Your site is but one of scores of thousands erected by large companies, small companies, educational institutions, special-interest groups, and individuals. Sure, somebody could wander into yours by accident, but just sitting back and waiting for that to happen is no way to ensure success.

To get the maximum promotional benefit from your site, you've got to do two things: (1) attract attention to your Web site, so people actually want to check it out, and (2) use effective promotion techniques on the site itself to make sure it helps to market your music.

ATTRACTING ATTENTION TO YOUR SITE

What can you do to get potential customers to visit your Web site? There are a number of options. Internet writer Katie Garcia suggests the following:

- Register your page with the numerous search engines— the companies like Yahoo, Excite, and InfoSeek that help surfers find what they're looking for on the Web. By registering, you'll ensure that the search engines will display a link to your Web site when someone types in its title or name. You can go to each of the search engines' home pages and select "submit or add URL" (URL being your Web page address, known in Netspeak as a Uniform Resource Locator).

- Make sure you list your page address on all other publicity and sales materials (even your demo tapes).

- Get press coverage and reviews of your page. Let your publicity people (if you have them) get the word out—via e-mail, snail mail, or press release—that you are on the Internet. Magazines, newspapers, and television shows—especially Internet and computer "infotainment" publications and programs—review pages for their audiences, and they are always in need of new sites to report on.

Here are some more visitor-attracting ideas:

- Advertise on larger and more established sites. This depends on your budget. But if you can swing it, it's one way to make sure a large number of music fans become aware that your site exists. However, make sure your site is running smoothly and your system of links is fully in place before buying advertising. A dissatisfied visitor will mean your money will have been wasted.

- Have other sites set up links with yours. If wisely chosen, this can greatly enhance your site's presence, increasing the number of ways people can find out about you. This is an area in which to be cooperative—not competitive. Consider offering a trade deal, where you'll set up a link to a partner's site and they'll link to yours (and maybe provide an enthusiastic endorsement).

- Be sure your site is integrated into your act's overall publicity and promotion plan. Promote your site at live shows with posters and flyers. Make sure your site address is everywhere your act's logo appears—from press kit jackets to the equipment truck.

USING YOUR SITE AS AN EFFECTIVE PROMOTIONAL TOOL

Just like an advertisement, your site has only a couple of seconds to grab the visitor's attention and interest. If the visitor is not someone who was directed to your site or who heard good things about it, the likelihood is that they hit on it by accident. That means their finger is on the mouse and ready to click elsewhere at the first sign of boredom. Don't let them click! Give them pause. Provide them with an instant reason for sticking around.

Be Creative, Different, and Eye-Catching

This is an area to really put some thought into. Study other established music sites—from the lavish to the simple—to see how they're done. Also, study existing sites for errors or bad design, so you won't repeat the mistake.

A key element here is updating the site frequently. Nothing drives a visitor away faster than a site that's obviously out of date. The Internet has proven to be a time-sensitive medium.

Make the Interface Intuitive

Don't frustrate customers by setting up a site that is confusing to navigate. Instead, befriend them by offering clear subject headings, common-sense hot buttons, an easy way to get back to the home page, and logical links to other related sites.

Make the Site Design Match the Personality of the Music

This is similar to packaging a product to appeal to the targeted customer. An inappropriate design may send the wrong message: for instance, that the band is a sugary pop group instead of a bone-crushing bunch of heavy-metal heads; that the artist has no sense of humor, where the fans expect humor, and so on. Communicate the artist's true personality in the design you choose for your site.

This is not a difficult concept. You can use a funky roadhouse design for a blues band, high-tech imagery for an electronic group, floral patterns for a plaintive poet-singer, a colorful fifties diner setting for a pop group. But whatever you do, see that the design complements the approach you have taken in designing other promotional materials, from CD covers to posters. Consistency is the key to establishing a readily recognizable *brand*.

Provide Clear Methods of Ordering Products

Make it easy for the customer to either order products directly from the site or go elsewhere to get them. Numerous acts now use an 800 number for easy, quick phone orders. You can also set up your site so that fans can securely key in credit card numbers for instant ordering. Or you can align your site with one of the online stores, and they'll take care of the rest.

Respond to Customer Preferences

Give the fans what they want, whether it's information about band members' hobbies and charity work, anecdotes from the studio, or complete song lyrics and recording credits. Your knowledge of fan preferences is the force that should guide many of your "content" choices.

MEASURING THE SUCCESS OF YOUR SITE

After your site has been online for a while, you'll need to get a sense of how well it's doing—of whether it's been successful in attracting visitors. Writer Katie Garcia offers the following suggestions for measuring the effect of your presence.

- Use onsite counters that keep track of how many hits or visitors your page gets. (Keep in mind, however, that a "hit" represents only a stop-off at your site that may be no more than a one-second glance on the way to another site.) Although the counter won't provide an exact measure of "interested" visits, it will give you a general idea of how many times your server was queried for your page. (Ask your ISP whether it provides counters; some do and some don't.)

- Provide a "guest book" for your visitors to sign. A guest book is basically an e-mail form on your page asking the name, e-mail address, and other general questions of the visitor.

- Offer your latest CDs and other band paraphernalia to your fans through online ordering. For the do-it-yourselfer, keep this simple by listing a telephone number for receiving your orders. (While you have the customers on the telephone, you might conduct a simple survey by asking such questions as "How did you hear about our page?") If you choose this method, you should contact your ISP to check on whether you should sign up for a business account, which means paying them extra.

When considering the use of the Web, keep this simple psychological point in mind: the typical music fan likes to feel close to the act and its music. The more personal the relationship, the more loyal the fan will be. (Remember the one-to-one marketing relationship discussed in Chapter 5? If not, take another look at page 50.) Establishing a Web presence is an excellent way to build this close seller-customer relationship.

CHAPTER

20

Making Money on the Internet

There are conflicting views, to put it mildly, of the Internet as a commercial medium. On one hand, there are the Net devotees who've been with it from the beginning, adamant that it remain the free communication network that gave it its rowdy, grassroots, antiestablishment character. On the other hand, multitudes of companies and individuals are struggling to find ways to turn it into the new-medium goldmine they envision.

What this means is that any effort to market and make money over the Internet must be done very carefully. The masses of people who surf the Net regularly are used to it as a free medium and may get turned off by obvious efforts to exploit it—and them—for money.

Consequently, ways must be found to retain the Internet's "free" character while also setting up some means of making it viable for profit-making enterprises.

In the meantime, the path to profitability is littered with the remains of companies who tried to make it, and failed. In the summer of 1996 a spate of Net companies made initial public offerings, and Wall Street went into overdrive selling high-priced stock in these companies amid a gold rush–style buying frenzy. It's not much of a stretch to say that at that time, if you had a company with the word Internet in its name, you could have made a killing going public.

What happened after that is a matter of public record. For most of these companies, once the infusion of stockholder cash drained away, there was nothing left. All but a handful failed to find a steady revenue stream from sales to customers of their "product." Before long, Internet became a bad word, or at least a risky one, to venture capitalists.

Yet in the wake of this high-tech wipeout, some workable methods have emerged of generating income from Internet activity. Perhaps you'll be able to adapt them to your own needs as a music marketer.

Better still, maybe you'll come up with a method that no one has considered yet—and that will be viewed as ethical, non-exploitative, and even convenient by veteran Net surfers. Remember, this is a field that is still wide open.

ONLINE SALES

The aim of many enterprises is to set up a system for direct online ordering of product.

The process works as follows: The customer browses through an online "catalog" of products, whether recordings or some other kind of merchandise (T-shirts, for example). In the case of recordings, the customer is given the option of listening to snippets of various pieces of music. Having chosen to order one, the customer clicks on a button labeled "Order" and is then transferred to a screen containing a form for submitting credit card information. The product is then shipped to the customer.

As discussed in the interview with Scott Burnett on page 286, a major focus of attention for most Internet-oriented marketers is direct downloading of music. In this case, after the customer places an order, the music is transferred (that is, downloaded, via streaming audio technology such as that provided by Liquid Audio) from the Internet server to the customer's computer hard drive. The customer then transfers the music file from the hard drive to a recordable CD.

Direct download to a hard drive and then "burning" to CD is a process that, as of this writing, is still off in the future—at least for most consumers. (See "Facts and Figures About Online Music Commerce" later in this chapter.) But most music professionals agree that it has the potential of transforming the music industry, perhaps rendering retail stores—and even traditional record companies—obsolete.

SUBSCRIPTION

Many Web sites now operate the equivalent of toll gates. The initial part of a given site is free to anyone who enters it. Beyond a certain point, to get more information or to see more of the site, the surfer must become a "member." This is done by subscribing to the site.

While this technique is used primarily by informational and entertainment sites, such as online magazines, there are other potential applications. In a 1997 issue of *Music and Computers* magazine, the artist and producer Todd Rundgren offered an innovative suggestion: He raised the notion of using the subscription technique to directly connect the artist with the customer (which would have the effect of putting the record company out of the loop). An artist would have a dedicated Web site, through which customers could subscribe to the artist for a specified period—say, a year. During that time, the artist would upload music to the site as it is created. A subscriber could then download the music. At the end of the period, the artist would send the customer a collection of all that music, like an album.

As of this writing, Rundgren's idea hasn't been widely embraced. But perhaps it is the kind of radical, potentially revolutionary idea you should be looking for as part of a guerrilla Internet marketing effort.

ONLINE ADVERTISING

One of the more commonplace methods of making money on Web sites is through advertising.

It works much the same way magazine advertising does. A Web site, because of its content, attracts a given number of viewers, or "hits." Based on the number of hits (calculated via the use of on-site counters), the Web site develops an appropriate rate to charge advertisers. The advertisers pay to have an ad on the Web site, which is seen by the site's customers.

The way to go about getting advertisers is this: First, identify potential advertisers. Look for them in magazines, on other Web sites, and at trade shows that deal with customers like the ones you target with your music. Determine from the size of their magazine ads which ones spend the most money. Then send them information about your site, including the size of the audience and your ad rates. Follow up with their marketing departments and sell them on the idea of taking out an ad.

By now, most potential advertisers, from beer companies to guitar makers, have their own Web sites. E-mail them to check out your site. Also, don't overlook your local community and surrounding region. Think in terms of how local and regional businesses might tie in to your music—and then let them know about it.

FACTS AND FIGURES ABOUT ONLINE MUSIC COMMERCE

Over the past several years, the growth of music commerce on the Internet has been nothing short of phenomenal, and forecasts indicate that the expansion shows no sign of abating. The following marketing-pertinent information was compiled by author and Internet consultant Russell Shaw:

"New York marketing research firm Jupiter Communications has predicted that sales of prerecorded music through the World Wide Web will reach a total of $1.6 billion, revenue-wise, by 2002. It is also projected that by 2002, this mode will represent 7.5 percent of total global unit sales.

The Jupiter report, which was issued in July 1997, surveyed top music industry executives at major and independent labels, online and traditional retail, and various media Web sites.

The study also reports that international music sales through the Internet have already reached an estimated $18.2 million in revenues from the sales of 1.4 million units in 1996, the latest year for which figures are available. Jupiter expected this market to grow to $47 million in 1997.

Additional revenue is being gained through ancillary Internet music businesses, such as content licensing deals for artist biographies and reviews, music-related merchandising, and ticket sales. Total worldwide online revenue for music and its affiliated businesses is expected to rise from $71 million in 1997 to more than $2.8 billion in 2002. Ad revenue on music sites is predicted to grow from $12.1 million worldwide in 1997 to more than $200 million in 2000.

Internet-specific retailer CDnow leads all other electronic retailers of music, with a 33 percent market share of 1996 worldwide online sales, according to the report.

Tower Records' independent Web site combined with its America Online site netted about 14 percent of the online music market, while N2K's Music Boulevard generated about 12 percent of all Internet music purchases in 1996.

A major driving force in online music retail is international sales, which already account for 30 to 40 percent of online music sales. Non-U.S. music distributors are affected most by this development, since consumers outside the U.S. are often able to purchase CDs at a lower cost on the Internet than in their local record stores. As online orders increase, the report concludes that there may be a consolidation of international distributors and a slow realignment of some international revenue toward the domestic side.

The Internet Consumer

Internet consumer buying patterns are significantly different from traditional retail sales, says Jupiter. Specifically, back-catalog releases and specialty titles, rather than newer releases, are selling well on the Web. This is partially due to the demographic differences between computer users and traditional retail consumers. Mainstream music is less likely to flourish online until the Internet itself becomes more mainstream. Online retail efforts targeting the mainstream consumer, such as MCI's ill-fated 1-800-MusicNow (which failed), are languishing, while retailers that emphasize specialty genres, such as classical and jazz, are doing well.

About 20 percent of all online households worldwide shopped via the Web in 1996, according to Jupiter. However, increasing consumer confidence in online security and the development of new payment mechanisms could boost interest in online shopping to 70 percent of connected computer owners by 2002.

The average online music consumer purchased about three music units in 1996, which accounted for about 15 percent of his or her total music purchases for the year. By 2002, it is estimated that online music consumers will purchase five units annually, or 25 percent of their total music purchases for the year.

Digital Delivery of Music

Digital distribution of music, which has already taken hold on the Internet, is expected to emerge slowly as a business over the next few years. Though some complete albums are expected to be available for sale via digital download this year [1998], digitally delivered music will represent less than 1 percent of the market by 2002, according to the study. The sales growth of digitally delivered music is restricted by limited hard-drive space, ongoing copyright controversies, and the preponderance of slow modems.

At the same time, you have to think about the hoops that die-hard fans will jump through to obtain this music. The musical styles whose core demographics most closely match the techno-aware, "early adopter" technology users will do the best in the digital download market. ”

IN CLOSING

Internet commerce is a highly speculative and volatile area, as is the entire realm of music marketing and promotion. But you just might be among the visionaries and determined marketers who find ways to make it work, who manage to open up whole new panoramas of profit possibilities by using their imagination and wits. On your way to that point, be professional, do your homework, keep on top of the Internet, and keep your marketing gears in motion.

And finally, good luck with your career—and selling your music.

In the Words of the Professionals: Interviews

Roy Gattinella

VICE PRESIDENT, MARKETING AND SALES
EMI-Capitol Entertainment Properties
Los Angeles, California

Let's get a little background on you.

RG: My professional background includes time spent as a working musician with an MBA. So I've been fortunate to have combined both in my career. I founded a couple of retail music stores on the East Coast while I was in college. After college, I worked for a company called Monster Cable for a few years. Then I went to Windham Hill Records, a small boutique label based in Northern California. I joined it when it was a very, very small company and I left after 10 years when the company was sold to BMG. It's now a big little company. And I've been at Capitol for a little over two years—running the catalog group at Capitol Records and then on to this division of EMI-Capitol.

I oversee what the company calls "entertainment properties." They are, in essence, the musical assets, the intellectual property of EMI-Capitol, which means that we manage the ancillary marketing for all of the catalogs that we own, including worldwide rights to the Beatles, the Beach Boys, Pink Floyd, Nat King Cole, Frank Sinatra, and new and young baby bands as well. But we really have a stable of world-class artists whose music will definitely have a long life if we care for it correctly and market it strategically.

In a very general sense, talk about the challenges facing music marketers today.

RG: I think today, marketing music is probably more difficult than it ever was. Marketing any consumer product today is very, very difficult compared to how it was years ago.

The choices for consumers are unlike they've ever been in the history of modern marketing. No matter what you're buying, whether it's breakfast cereal, toothpaste, or music, the choices and the options available at the retail store are unbelievable. They're confusing to consumers, and they're overwhelming to retailers.

The fight for shelf space at retail is a battle. The fight for the ear of the music consumer is even more difficult.

One of the problems in music these days—it's also a challenge and an opportunity—is that while the debut album of a band or an artist can do very, very well, unlike in the past there is absolutely no guarantee that the second record is going to come even close to that kind of success. Because by the time the second album comes out by that band or artist, their loyal—or what is perceived to be their loyal—fan base is now on to the next new thing.

It didn't used to be that way, I know. Not to date myself, but, as you remember, when the Beatles were ready to put out a new album, I mean, we lined up. We couldn't wait for it. Well, it's not that way anymore. I mean, it's just amazing to watch bands come and go so quickly because of the ephemeral nature of this industry. So, that's the state of it.

The options for reaching consumers are probably more narrow than they used to be, but they're also very much the same as they used to be. Things haven't really progressed that much. You can turn on the radio and hear music, and that, primarily, would drive most people to buy new music. It was that way 30 years ago and it's that way today. That doesn't mean that there are no other options or opportunities available to reach consumers, but it still reigns as number one.

There's a segmented marketplace out there, which I think allows opportunity for companies like Windham Hill, whom I used to work for, or companies like Blue Note Records or companies like Sub Pop and small rap labels. There are opportunities for those companies to reach consumers [in ways] that bypass the traditional methods like radio. And that's one good thing that's out there today. There are lots of small players that have reached consumers in ways that never used to exist.

So it's really opened up the field a little bit. Of course you have the Big Six that are leading the charge, and all the indies, but you've also got a fairly strong stable of young, up-and-coming guerrilla labels that can go out and really score hits. If you pick up the *Billboard* charts these days, you're liable to see some unknown labels at the top. And that's very promising for the whole industry.

You've got artists who have their own labels. You've got Madonna, who started Maverick Records. And they've had a number one hit in the past couple of weeks with the Prodigy and, of course, Alanis Morissette, who was riding in the top 10 of *Billboard* forever. So there are all kinds of interesting trends to be followed that are outside the mainstream, which I find very, very heartening and exciting from an artist and marketing perspective.

The advent of the compact disc in the 1980s led many consumers to replace their vinyl LP collections. Is that trend still going on? And how is it affecting the music industry?

RG: Actually, the early nineties, more than the eighties, saw the record business shoot up hugely—great big percentage increases every year. A lot of it [was] due to replacement purchasing—people buying CDs to replace vinyl. And that went on for lots and lots of years. The more CD players that were sold, the more people went out and bought CDs. And lots of those were to replace favorite albums that they had. Now it's slowed down quite a bit. With CD hardware penetration being in the 90-some percent range, you're not seeing as many CD players being sold. So the CDs that people are buying now are new releases. So new releases are more important to fuel the market, instead of catalog sales.

Catalog sales overall are down 30 percent over the last year or two. And that's a big drop. Typically, catalog has fueled marketing spending of labels. By selling your back catalog you generate revenue that you can use to develop your emerging acts. Without that, it's real hard to spend money to develop acts.

But, hey, it's still a big business, you know. The record business itself will do probably eleven or twelve billion this year.

In the broadest sense, what is the task of the music marketer?

RG: The reason that I got into this business, and the main reason that I stay in it, is this: For me it's very, very gratifying to take the work of an artist, who in many cases you've never heard of before, and grow [their careers] to the point where their music is being heard and shared by a huge number of people throughout the world—to reach critical mass.

So the ultimate task is to take great music and get it out there so that people can hear it, enjoy it, and hopefully enrich their lives from it.

How do you go about doing that, specifically?

RG: The first thing we do as music marketers—depending on the level you might be working with in the organization—is interpret the artist's music. Then we have to somehow convey and communicate the essence of their art to consumers—faithfully, and as compellingly as possible.

So the first thing that you do is sit with the artist, get to know them, get to know their music and where it comes from, and work with them to develop their careers in a way that you can best present them to their potential audience. That's the real key. And that [involves] lots of components.

There's visual marketing—how to present them visually. Everything from the graphic design and packaging of the product to the advertising and marketing message. If there are music videos, it extends to the production of the visuals of the music video itself.

Then singles need to be chosen for appropriate formats of radio.

Also, retail stores will be targeted to service the record to. If you've got an adult-oriented artist, you want to make sure Borders Books and Music, Barnes & Noble, and those kinds of accounts are covered. If you've got a rap artist, you want to make sure that your indies and your mom-and-pop record stores in urban centers are covered. These are only a few of the distribution challenges.

How about a word or two about publicity?

RG: Publicity is a major ingredient for success. What media are going to be targeted to reach the audience? Say you've got a jazz artist. If you want to reach that buyer, you have to do that through the right media. And get media excited about it.

The opinion leaders become extremely important—the *New York Times, Down Beat* magazine, *JazzIz,* "The Tonight Show," the large jazz festivals, the jazz literati.

Early on in a project you want to make sure to identify what we call "champions." If you have an artist that has a particular sound or vibe, a real shrewd marketer of music will know who in the media—and who in the retail community as well—would really turn on to that music. And you want to identify them and get them involved early. So you want to go to a Robert Christgau with the *New York Times,* let's say, with the kind of music he would like. Or, for a key writer for the *L.A. Times,* you want to make sure that you present to him or her early on the kind of music they would be responsive to so they're champions of the project from the very first day. And that goes a long, long way.

What skills will professional music marketers need in order to gain a competitive edge in the near future?

RG: I think that the successful music marketer is one who can not only adapt to change but also spot trends before they happen. So a real successful music marketer, especially now in the late 1990s, is going to be somebody who has a really broad knowledge of consumer behavior, who understands music and the art form. Also, it's somebody who understands things like online marketing, electronic delivery, the changing retail environment, target marketing, segment marketing—all of those concepts.

So the successful marketer should be aware, as quickly as possible, of new trends.

RG: Yes. And they should be on it before anybody is. Because those who push the competitive edge will be the ones who successfully rise above the clutter and drive this business in the future.

Bruce Iglauer

PRESIDENT
Alligator Records
Chicago, Illinois

You're president of Alligator Records.

BI: Yes. And founder. Usually a distinction, because it lets people know you didn't buy the damn thing.

When did you actually open the label?

BI: 1971, when I released my first record. And there was one a year for about five years until I could afford to do two. And now we're up to about 12, and we kind of stay there. In fact, sometimes we have less than that because we find that if we—because we're very genre-specific—that if we do too many, that they compete with each other for the same media, same airplay, same print, and the attention of my staff. So we try to keep it at kind of a manageable number.

Tell us a little about the Alligator success story.

BI: I believe there's some question as to whether it is a success story. I guess surviving makes you a success. But, like I said, we were always genre-specific. I always wanted to do a label that represented my particular tastes in music, which are, of course, blues.

Blues was the only kind of music that I really felt I had a correct aesthetic sense for. I can't tell a good rock band from a bad rock band. I certainly can't tell a good classical artist from a bad classical artist. Blues is the only thing I pretend to know. And I knew also that there was a whole market—a potential market—of blues fans very much like myself: baby-boomers. People who got interested in blues through either the folk music revival, like I did, or through bluesy rock and roll—especially the English bands, the Butterfield Band, John Mayall, Clapton, Cream to some extent, Led Zeppelin, Charlie Musselwhite.

Also, fans who weren't being reached by labels that were very, very specialist oriented, like Delmark and Arhoolie, which were models for me. And, of course, when I first got involved, Chess Records had been sold and was doing very little active production.

So there was this sort of gap, and I recognized that there was a market and knew what my potential customers were like—because they were like me.

At the same time, radio was changing. The genre of radio that we now think of as progressive rock was growing. And with that came an opportunity for artists who hadn't been able to be on rock and roll radio to be heard.

It was a very, very small window of opportunity that I happened to be able to crawl through starting in 1971. If I had started in, say, '73—by the time progressive rock radio became album-oriented rock and consultants were saying black music is the kiss of death for rock and roll radio—I probably would have failed. So it was a combination of a certain amount of vision and great luck and timing.

Can you talk a little about the scope of marketing today for a small label?

BI: Well, the term marketing is often used these days just to describe plain old advertising or the combination of advertising and what we usually call "retail grease." This is the practice that's grown up in the last few years of having to buy your way into stores—buying end caps, buying featured rack space or front racks, buying listening posts, so that you have multiple copies of your records in the stores. Those—buying that and buying advertising—have come to be the most specific definition of marketing. When somebody at a distributor is in charge of marketing, they're in charge of disbursing the label's money to retail and to media.

How has the field changed?

BI: Well, it's harder and harder, for example, to get in-store displays. Many stores, for example, now don't have display space at all. Like Best Buy or Blockbuster stores. Or like Tower: they produce their own displays, which are bought and paid for. So getting somebody to slap up a poster is harder and harder. Getting somebody to feature your record in the store unless you're paying for it, or play your record in the store unless you're paying for it, is harder than it ever was.

The stores' margins have gone down because of the price wars. They've compensated by basically charging the labels for doing more than bringing a single copy in. And now, with most of the major chains buying centrally, so that the situation is that it's often two and three and four weeks after a record is sold before it's replaced, if you don't have multiple copies in those stores you'll never see significant sales. Because they'll always be out of stock if the record is at all popular.

How does a small label like Alligator compensate for changes like that in the retail arena?

BI: Well, there are a number of things that we do. First of all, we do play this game. We spend anywhere from ten to twenty thousand dollars on a new release for price positioning, listening posts, end caps, and anything else related to retail placement.

Beyond that, one of the key things that we do is we have artists, at least for the most part with our current catalog artists, who tour just constantly.

So a great deal of the advertising and the promotion is around live performance dates. Typically, when an album is in its first four to six months, we'll support a number of the live performances with advertising, especially in weekly-type print media, à la *Creative Loafing*, for example, the *Reader,* and the *Village Voice,* or if we can find the right day of the week and the right show, sometimes we'll do radio advertising. Radio is very expensive.

For the most part, our radio play is now on AAA format stations—Adult Album Alternative—which are sort of the latest version of the old progressive rock format minus the hardest-edge stuff. And a lot of those stations either play some blues in their regular format or have a specialty show. And from time to time we'll support those stations by advertising, if we can afford it.

And we also do some sponsorships, around gigs, of Public Radio shows. You can't buy a real ad on a public station; you buy an announcement, or, you know, "Brought to you by a gift from Alligator Records, who wants you to know that Tinsley Ellis is performing at the Variety Playhouse."

So those are the kinds of markets or the kinds of media in which we might advertise. And beyond that, we feel that in order to play the majors' game we have to do a lot of things that a lot of other labels think their distributors are doing.

For example, I have two people who do nothing all day but call retail stores. And the irony of that is that we don't sell to retail stores. We sell through distributors. We're a real independent company. We don't sell around our distributors at all. But we call up stores and just talk to them about our new releases, about artists coming into town, about numbers on SoundScan reports. We talk about radio play in their market or other media in their market. We invite them to gigs, basically greasing them. Shmoozing them. Getting them to remember our product; talking to them about bringing titles in. I don't think that there's anybody else at our level of the independent industry who works so closely with retail.

We also think that we're in the business of career building, and we stick with our artists for a very long time. And because our artists are genre-specific, what we learn from one artist helps us with another artist. And the artists often work in the same venues or for the same promoters, so that we know that when one of our artists comes to Atlanta, for example, they're going to work at either Blind Willie's or the Variety Playhouse.

There may be three venues in town where they're likely to work. And those venues know us. They also know that when a record is new, we'll provide them with posters, we'll provide them with photos, we'll provide them with in-club play copies, and we may well do some advertising.

Plus we set up the artist's interviews and do our own press and radio. We're very, very media-oriented. And a lot of labels just simply don't do as much as we do in that regard.

What about market research? Do you gather fan profiles or demographic information?

BI: A little bit. Now we have business reply cards in our CDs, partly because we have mail-order business. And every once in a while we'll do a little study of our market. But what we discover is, first of all, we can tell a lot just by going to the gigs, and second, the market information very rarely changes.

What we see is: we sell over 90 percent to men, with the exception of a few of our female artists; we tend to sell to adult men, late twenties and up into the early fifties; we tend to sell to well-educated men. It's very much an AAA radio demographic, exactly the market AAA radio wants, as we keep trying to tell them over and over. They don't always believe us. Our fans are well read; they aren't all hard-core blues fans at all. A lot of them like blues in a music mix.

Perhaps you could also talk about your experience with the Internet thus far.

BI: You know, we have rather a fancy Web site. It's fun. It's visually kind of interesting and it has a little sense of humor to it. And it also shows our entire mail-order catalog as well as all of our promo items—our clothing and our key chains and our shot glasses and our coffee mugs. Also, our artists' posters and photos and T-shirts. And it has constantly updated tour itineraries, which I think are a very important part of it. Artists' bios. The story of the label. I know that, for example, promoters have downloaded artists' bios to send to press rather than wait for us to give them a hard copy. We also have sound bites.

But our actual sales from the Internet are miniscule. They come through our mail-order company and they might amount to two or three orders a week.

I don't believe yet that the Internet is an effective entity. I'm just not convinced yet that this is the wave of the future. I'm not convinced that it's not, but I feel as though for the Internet to be more interesting, it's got to be more like what it reminds you of, which is TV. It needs to be more immediately interactive; it needs to be quicker; it needs to be more thought out. It's too static.

I'm not at all sure that it's the ideal way for people to buy music. Now the technology, of course, exists for full CDs to be downloaded. It just takes too long, and then there's the question of what you're going to download them on to. But it is doable.

What role does international marketing play in your marketing mix?

BI: International amounts to between 20 and 30 percent of our overall business. We do a number of different things. We have some license deals. We used to license everywhere, and sometimes we would actually have the companies in foreign countries physically producing the albums. Sometimes we would act as their supplier, but they would buy from us at a pressing cost and then pay us a royalty after they made the sale.

More and more now, as the dollar has become a little bit stronger, we've moved to exclusive exportation deals. So, for example, right now we license in France, and everywhere else in Europe—and I want to make sure it's true if I say "every"—we're exporting.

And we export at sometimes some attractive prices. But we're still making our money rather quickly, rather than waiting for licensing deals and royalty statements. The disadvantage is that we don't get any advance, which you normally get on a licensing deal. We also have to provide them with a budget for advertising. You know, if you have a licensee you expect them to do advertising, radio, and press promotion at their expense. You've got an importer, you're going to expect that you can do it at your expense, which would be just like a U.S. distributor.

In Japan we license, but they don't release everything, and in Australia we license. In South America, in Brazil, and in Argentina we license.

Are there any other points you'd like to make about the current state of the small-label music market?

BI: I've watched the changes from the days when there were a dozen independent distributors in every market to the days when there may be 15 viable independent distributors in the whole country. Distributors are going berserk and going away. It's changing all the time. There's definitely an implosion. There are going to be less people recorded. It'll be harder to get a deal.

Eva Dickenson-Post
Luann Sullivan Myers
EvaLuTion Entertainment Marketing, Inc.
Hollywood, Florida

Tell us a little about your company.

EDP: We've got what I consider a vast amount of experience and a varied amount of experience. My background is promotion and radio; Luann's is sales and distribution and marketing.

Basically, we're [an independent] creative marketing firm. We step into a project at the invitation of a label or by approaching them and soliciting the services we can offer. Sometimes they say, "Here's what we're doing. What else could we be doing for this project?" And we'll come up with a 10- or 15- or 20-point-suggestion marketing plan from which they'll pick—who knows?—1, 3, 19 ideas.

Or they will come to us and say, "We are doing X, Y, and Z for a project, but we need you to cover A and B." That's because they need records distributed to restaurants in 15 tour markets, that *aren't* coffeehouses, that *will* play CDs. They know what problems we can solve very readily, and they come to us to solve them.

LSM: When I was preparing for this interview, I looked in the dictionary for the definition of *marketing*. Number one, it is buying or selling in a market. Number two, it is all activities involved in the moving of goods from the producer to the consumer, including selling, advertising, etcetera. And I think that where we fit in is at the "etcetera" point.

What we do is not always tangible. The results are not always quantifiable. What we try to do is look at the targeted demographic consumer that that particular label has in mind for a release, see what else they're interested in, and aim at exposing the music through those other areas of their lifestyle.

EDP: Basically, we're in the idea business, whether it's evaluating a project or being told by a label, "We need to accomplish this. How would EvaLuTion do it?"

We create ideas. And what we try to do as a specialty is to create means of exposing music without necessarily having to get it on the radio—and sometimes even bypassing the traditional music retailer. That's not to say that there's no value in getting music on the radio, because obviously it's the number-one way to expose it. That's not to say that having your record on an end cap (a preferred display) at Blockbuster is not an effective way to get it to the public.

Over the years those two areas, for very good reasons, have been emphasized very greatly. But today there's more to consider.

We have so much information available to us these days—whether it's through the Internet or through 200 TV channels. There are a lot of other ways to sort of sneak into somebody's lifestyle. And that's what we try to do. What we do is a supplement to a label's standard efforts of getting a record on the radio and making sure the distribution channel is ready to take it into the system.

What are some other examples of how the business is changing?

EDP: Now, you have a population of people who buy music for all different kinds of reasons and in all different kinds of places. It's affecting the music business because it affects every business, whether it's the Internet that distracts people from the radio or television, or cable distracting people from [network] broadcasts. People are distracted. I think you just have to hit them from all sides—or as many sides as you can possibly identify. The key is identifying what those sides are. There's a lot of data available that can tell you how people live and how to get their attention. But in its raw form it could apply as much to tissues and candy bars as it can to music. And I think the real skill of a savvy marketer is recognizing useful raw data and refining it into a useful resource for marketing music.

You have worked closely with the Coalition of Independent Music Stores. Please tell us a little about them.

LSM: Okay. They came to us a year ago and wanted to institute a new program where they would have listening booths in the majority of their stores. They needed somebody to organize selling those slots each month. So they wanted a program that would be like buying a listening booth in a chain store.

They wanted this to be a uniform thing, where they could put one artist in this particular listening program and it would be in all these cool independent stores around the country. There are 52 right now in the listening booth program. There are actually 67 stores in the Coalition. But they're about to add a few more.

We've heard a lot of talk about how bitter the competition is just among the mega-stores. How in the world can smaller stores compete against a mammoth chain, like Borders or Tower?

LSM: When all of these big chains started selling CDs below cost, it was putting a lot of the independent stores in those same markets out of business. But the Coalition came along, and they've banded together and can offer [promotion] programs to labels and distributors, where it's just not the same as doing it with the chains. Because these [indies] are still the core stores that labels target to break artists.

EDP: And they know their customers. There are certain stores in the Coalition that have an amazing jazz catalog or an amazing blues catalog or an amazing techno department, which is obviously not nearly as traditional and doesn't have nearly the amount of catalog or the history. They really know their customers.

LSM: [No single] genre is going to work in every store. They all have their niches, as Eva's saying. But the majority of independent retailers are still the places where the labels will go to break a new artist, no matter what the genre is.

Has it become more difficult to break an artist via the traditional routes?

EDP: I think in some respects, yes. It's difficult to break an artist with even a 500-store chain like Blockbuster because there's so much else out there and there's not really the [program] cohesiveness there needs to be. And if something gets put in their ad program, then, yeah, it's going to be on sale and they're supposed to sell it, but it's not like the people in that store are actually working to sell that record.

LSM: You can micro-market with the Coalition. Their goal is to be as flexible as possible. Let's say you can't afford the listening booths because your band is only touring in the Southeast and they're only doing 16 dates. You can probably find seven, eight Coalition markets where there's a store and just do what you need to do with those stores. I know you can do that with most of the chains, too, but I just don't think it's going to stand out as much.

It's not as easy, either, because the chains need a lot more lead time to set something like that up. Because they are booked into so many of these other big national programs they only have so much time and energy to do other micro-marketing-type things. Which is a shame. It's led to their own demise, in a way.

Don VanCleave

PRESIDENT, COALITION OF INDEPENDENT MUSIC STORES

OWNER, MAGIC PLATTER COMPACT DISCS

Birmingham, Alabama

Tell us about the Coalition of Independent Music Stores. What makes the Coalition tick in this age of megastores?

DV: Well, we're the guys that are out there breaking new bands, unlike the megastores who don't bring in product and support it early unless there's money and a story behind it. Our stores are famous for culling out new releases that we think are very, very good. We provide a lot of support in the stores very early for new bands and new records that maybe would get by the chain stores' ears.

We have 67 stores in the group now and are growing very slowly. We've ranged between 55 and 65 since we got started. We're pretty settled in at this size until we figure out how to get compliance out of more stores.

You're represented in medium-sized markets as well as some major metro areas.

DV: Few major metros. Mainly medium-sized markets. But we are all over the country.

Do you handle any particular types of music?

DV: No. Across the genres. We're working three titles right now and two of them are by deejays—you know, dance-oriented, like DJ Shadow and Goldie. And one of them's a Cuban record with Ry Cooder, *The Buena Vista Social Club*. That's another record we're really all over right now. It's a stunning record—we've got 67 stores around the country really pumping that record.

How are you approachable by, say, independents or bands who've done their own CD?

DV: As individual stores, we're very approachable by anyone. As a Coalition, you pretty much have to have national distribution for us to mess with you. There's just basically no way for us to coordinate anything unless we have a distributor out there that's handling the shipping and the bill collecting and things like that.

Any advice to younger acts, emerging acts, and regional bands?

DV: Yeah. Just know who your local retailer is. Most of these local retailers will give these guys a lot of support and advice on how to navigate the industry. In my store, I can't tell you how many little bands have come in and we've just sat them down and said, "Here's how you do it. Here's what you don't do."

And there's a lot of etiquette in dealing with record stores. Bands need to be cognizant that they're running a business and treat the relationship that way. I can't remotely tell you how many bands have come in and left us product on consignment and never come back. You know, be serious about your business. Or, they'll come back three years later. That's even worse. I mean, we kick them out of the store.

Understandably.

DV: Well now, they don't understand it. You know, it's just common business things: being professional, understanding that you're leaving your product with a business who has to run a business and pay rent on the space that your record's taking up. And, you know, if you consign your product into one of these retail stores, make sure you tell people, "You know, you can go to this store or that store to get our record." Don't expect the store to be your sales agent. You've got to drive the sales yourself.

So that's the basic advice. Get to know your local retailer. We've got kids working at our store who are working with bands all over the South right now, on their own without me telling them to. It's just what they dig doing, and they know a lot—they can hook them up with people at record labels. You know, it doesn't have to be the owner. You've just got to get a relationship going with your local retailer.

Scott Burnett

VICE PRESIDENT, MARKETING
Liquid Audio
Redwood City, California

Tell us about Liquid Audio.

SB: Liquid Audio is a start-up company, funded by venture capital. It's based in Redwood City, which is pretty much the northern part of Silicon Valley, right between San Jose and San Francisco.

Liquid Audio is dedicated to enabling the next wave of distribution of content—digital content of audio, ultimately of video—starting first and foremost with the music industry. [We provide] the tools and the software and the systems to allow the industry to distribute content digitally in a secure, safe manner over the Internet and over other digital networks.

There are three components of the software, so let's start on the left-hand side, which would be the content [provided by] the artist or the label. The music is recorded in a studio, then you've got a mixed master that now is going to be replicated for CD distribution. We have a suite of tools called the Liquifier, which is the encoding tool used to extract bits from the master and put them into our compression algorithm in our file format for distribution over the Internet for streaming (which is just listening at low bit rates and with modems at 28.8 or 56 Kbps or ISDN lines or better) and then also for download.

We're able to compress the files [in a] 10-to-1 ratio to the original file size and still have CD-quality audio come out the other end. So a typical three-minute song would take about 15 minutes to download on the Internet on 28.8 Kbps speed. With cable modems, which are starting to hit the market, you're looking at anywhere between 30 seconds to a minute to download that.

So to recap: on the left side there, we're getting content in our file format for both preview and for download with those encoding tools.

And then on the right side of the coin is the consumer, who has the *decoding* device, which [we call] the Liquid Music Player. It is about a meg-and-a-half-size file that you can download from your Web site or that might be bundled or prepacked with software or a CDR [CD recorder] for a computer. And you install it in the Helper application to Netscape or to Internet Explorer (Microsoft), and that becomes the device you use to navigate on the Web and click on sound files and stream the audio and listen to sound files and make decisions as to what you'd like to purchase. And it's also the mechanism with which to download the music.

Along the way, when we're publishing music, when an artist or a label or a recording studio is "liquifying" that track, there's a "watermark" that is put into the file, embedded into the audio wave form. [This is] information on which Liquifier device, if you will, was used to encode the music, and who the content owner is. And when that file is published to the server to be distributed on the Net, the Liquid Music server then puts another watermark in the file, which identifies which server it's coming from, which is who's selling the music. And then when the consumer buys the music for $1.49 or $1.99 or 99¢, when it's downloaded to the Liquid Music Player, there's [yet] another watermark put in the file, which is the "Certificate of Music Passport."

So in essence, when the file is done, so to speak, and it's sitting in the hard disk drive of the consumer, there are three layers of watermark that are inside the file that identify who owns the music, who distributed the music on the Net, and who bought the music. That allows for traceability in case somebody were to take a copy off of the PC, for instance—you know, just plug into a headphone jack and record onto cassette or some other analog device and then knock off a number of cassettes. We can redigitize those analog tapes and identify who bought it, who sold it, and where the music came from.

The security aspect is really at the heart and soul of this. There is essential administration that takes place in the system, which is called the Liquid Operations Center, called the LOC, and that Liquid Operations Center is keeping track of the activity of downloads from these Liquid Music servers and keeping track of the activity of the Liquid Music Players in order to ensure that security is not broken.

It's also an essential administration tool for rights and royalty reporting and flows of money due to the music publisher and to the content owners who have rights attached to the piece of music. So whether it be performance rights that are due to ASCAP or BMI in the U.S., whether it be mechanical rights due to Harry Fox on the sale or license of the music, all that is kept track of inside the LOC. And then those rights, those tamper-proof logs that we keep, are accessible to the industry to properly account for the royalties due.

What are some other Internet distribution capabilities?

SB: [Imagine you're] looking for jazz on the Internet—you can find it on an individual site—and [you're] able to then insert your credit card information and download the track. And once the track is downloaded to the PC, it doesn't end there. You know, a lot of us have nice-sounding PCs, with the new monitors and speakers that are available, enough to enjoy a high-fidelity multimedia presentation. But it isn't our stereo, and we can't take it in the car. You want to get the music out into the portable device, the portable medium that we all use, which is the CD. So then, connected to the PC is the CDR, the CD recorder. Costs are coming down below $300 now for CD recorders. And the medium costs somewhere around $2.00 per blank optical CD. It's becoming more like an audiocassette type of scenario as far as making a copy. So you download to the PC and in the output is a CDR. [You] put together your playlist that you would like to "burn" to CD, make your own custom compilation at home, [and] plug it into the stereo.

And then it goes where you go—you know, to the Walkman or car or whatever.

SB: Right. In essence, the track that's on that CD is the same track that you could buy at Tower Records from a master disc that was then stamped out in manufacturing. Except it's got the three layers of watermarking. So it's actually even more secure than if you bought it off the shelf at a traditional retail store, because that information's in there as to who bought it, who sold it, who owns it.

I don't know if you have had a chance to do this, what I've just described in buying music this way. But the first time I did this myself, when I actually sat down and said, "Okay, I'm going to register my own music player, and I'm going to insert my own credit card information, and I'm going to download this track, then I'm going to burn it to the CDR that's connected to my PC and I'm going to take that thing out and put it into my stereo," it's like a religious experience. All of sudden you say, "Oh, my God. It works! Hey, wait a minute. This is pretty cool."

Has Liquid Audio worked with any of the major record labels?

SB: The first experience we had with mainstream, with any of the majors, was with Capitol Records with Duran Duran.

Capitol has a huge catalog of materials dating back to the thirties.

SB: Well, I can tell you this: this is a perfect vehicle for marketing and promoting back-catalog content. And the reason is, once [you've taken care of] the encoding process, getting [the music] liquified, as we call it, getting the file format—once you've done that one time, that's your virtual inventory. You don't have to worry about cranking out 50,000 CDs and sending them out to stores and getting the returns. It's just up there for sale.

I wouldn't really forecast that with the majors. They will probably look at this as a continuing marketing promotional vehicle for mainstream artists. Because they don't want to cannibalize their retail brethren. They've got that relationship going.

It's still a sensitive issue. The first thing that happened with Duran Duran with Capitol Records was Capitol's selling the tracks direct, and the tracks are out there [on the Internet] before they're available on a CD single to the retailers. Well, that's the death knell to the retailers.

That's not the purpose here. The purpose is to drive awareness and to provide a new experience for the consumers that there is an album out by Duran Duran, who hasn't produced something in a couple of years, and to then connect into the loop and draw them back to retail to go [get] the album. [Given] bandwidth today, with a 28.8 modem it's going to take hours to download an album. Plus not everybody has a CDR. It's going to take some time. And so it's toeing into the water, so to speak, with the majors on the use of this technology for promotion.

One thing we're very interested in is the impact of music technology on international marketing. Do you have any thoughts on that subject?

SB: [What if I want to] get at Brazilian music, get at Japanese music, get at the German rock scene? How do I do that in the traditional world? I'm very limited. What I see happening here is that the Internet provides that global aspect of being able to serve up content for anybody, anywhere. There were 27,000 records released in the U.S. this year—which is a massive product glut—thrown onto traditional retailers, who are kind of in a lose-lose situation, because how do you promote and market all of those things? You're only going to get so many end caps. Only the cream of the crop or the ones that have the most money with the promotional dollars behind them get marketed and get retail space. And all this other content is kind of behind the scenes or not available to the consumer. So the Internet becomes the enabling vehicle to allow for promotion and marketing of content that you wouldn't traditionally find front and center on the shelf at Tower.

For instance, I was flying back from Rio a couple of years ago and listening to the headsets and thinking there's some great music here. And thinking, well, how do I get hold of this music? Who is this? And now you're on a search-and-find mission. Who is this artist and where do I find it and how can I get it? If I can just get at something that I hear that I like immediately, that's what I want as a consumer. And I think the Internet provides that opportunity: instantaneous access to hundreds of thousands of pieces of music organized in ways that we would like to get at it. And then allowing us the opportunity to evaluate and make an immediate purchase.

Any thoughts on opportunities for making money on the Internet, now or in the future?

SB: Yeah. Right now I look at all of this as incremental opportunities for the industry. If you look at the repurposing of content over the years, first we started with 45-rpm singles, which were incremental to an LP. Then the LPs were repurposed on CDs. [It was] an opportunity for the [entire] catalog to move to that medium. And now we look at the Internet as another incremental revenue opportunity for those who have content who are looking to repurpose it now that they've already done the CD, they've ridden that wave. Now there's a new opportunity unfolding: take all that content on a track-by-track basis, put it into the Internet pipeline, and allow consumers to get at it however they want to get at it and repurpose it by putting together their own compilations at home, where those compilations reside on your hard disk and you have your virtual jukebox, or where those compilations end up being assigned to burn to CDR, which would then be custom compilation CDs in the car or anywhere else.

We're in the middle of this whole—I hate to use the term *paradigm shift,* because it's overused, but this really is one in the record industry.

[It's also] a vehicle to get the artists excited. For instance, The Artist Formerly Known As Prince has a project where he's looking to get 100,000 orders in advance of his next album release. Because he's breaking away from Warner Brothers; he's got his own thing going on right now. He's got a large following. And in doing so, for $50 in advance, if you look at 100,000 and getting that money in advance of the production, getting $5 million in advance—now you know how successful you're going to be in advance of even releasing it. I mean, that's to take it to the ridiculous.

There's also advertising revenue that can be generated.

There's a lot of economic opportunity, I think, on the back end if you start to look at it—even as a precursor to when the bandwidth opens up and the spigot is opened and then the consumer can get at the music in 30 seconds for a download, which is where it really needs to go. That'll happen, I think, sooner than anybody's forecast.

Jeff Patterson

CO-FOUNDER
Internet Underground Music Archive (IUMA)
Santa Cruz, California

Tell us about your background.

JP: When I was going to U.C. Berkeley, I took a joint major of music and computer science, and it just seemed natural to blend those things together. When we were trying to look for a way to distribute my band's music, we didn't have enough money to produce a bunch of tapes or press a bunch of CDs, so we turned to the Internet and said maybe we'll just put it out on the Net and see what happens. That was in '93. What we did was record a couple of our songs and compress them using a format called MPEG, put those up on the Net along with various images on a J-card, and told [Net surfers] to record the music onto a tape and print out the J-card and they'd have a demo tape and it wouldn't cost them a thing. That's how it all started.

What was the name of the band?

JP: The name of the band is the Ugly Mugs. We're still going. We're actually finally pressing our CDs. They'll be ready in a couple of weeks.

What genre would you classify it in?

JP: Probably experimental. It's kind of a mix of carnival music, soundtrack-type music, and electronica.

Did you feel that that kind of music didn't really have a place in mainstream music?

JP: Yeah. With our music we knew that it would never be something you would hear on the charts or be selling thousands of copies of, and it's probably not the kind of thing that would be ever be picked up by a label. But we knew there were people like us out there that hopefully would like it. So by putting it on the Net, we were actually able to reach the couple of handfuls of people who might enjoy us. And by having feedback on the stuff we're working on…it's a great feeling.

How did you start IUMA?

JP: After we put my band up there, we started getting responses from mostly people in other countries who really liked being able to download music from the U.S. We started getting requests for more music and more bands, and so we started putting a couple of our friends' bands up there and told people on the Net that if they wanted to put their music on there we'd put it up. And that turned into IUMA.

It was a hobby for us the first year or so. We were still in college. It got to the point where we had so many bands sending their stuff in that it would take a couple of months for us to get a band up there because our backlog was so huge. So we started asking for donations. We said we're poor and struggling college students.

And you've certainly grown much larger. How many bands do you have on the site now?

JP: Right now we have just over 1,000 bands. More and more each week.

Let's say I'm in a band and I've got some songs and I'm playing some small gigs, but I really want to get the word out. How would you advise me to use the Internet to do that?

JP: I think the Internet is a great promotional tool. There are a lot of bands who are starting to build their own Web sites, and they can really keep control of their music, which is important for bands.

The only problem is getting the traffic to come to your site. We tell bands, go ahead and create your own site and maintain it, but then come up with a plan that will really direct traffic your way. I think what they need to start doing, once they create a presence on the Web, is include the address in everything they're doing—on CDs, tapes, flyers—so if they see a flyer for your show they can check out your Web site beforehand and see if they would be interested in going or not.

But how can a band make their Web site stand out?

JP: Find sites where music lovers are going. The UBL—the Ultimate Band List—is a great place to go. Make sure you're registered in there. A site like IUMA. If you're a punk band, don't go posting to alt.celtic whatever.

What are the success stories so far?

JP: I think the whole world is still waiting for the Internet success story, and it's probably not too far away from happening.

For those bands doing well that started out on IUMA, do you know how that happened for them?

JP: I think it was a combination of off-the-Net promotion and Internet promotion working in conjunction with each other. The bands who think they're going to put their stuff up on the Net and that's their ticket,

I think they're definitely mistaken. Bands have to go out there and play gigs and grow a fan base off the Net as well. I think the Internet really enhances the interest that they're out there getting by creating a place where fans can come and gather and collect information about what the band's like.

Can people directly buy music from your site?

JP: How we have it right now is a user can go and sample the music, they can download whole songs from the band, and if they like it they can purchase their CDs.

And they can do that right there on the site?

JP: Right. Through a secure form they can punch in their credit card number and we ship the CD in a couple of days. We've definitely grown exponentially in the past year as far as how many CDs we've sold. The next thing: We're going to be launching with Liquid Audio [see Scott Burnett's interview, page 286] a way that people will be able to purchase the music digitally so that they won't have to purchase the CD. And they can purchase, you know, five songs that they like by an artist.

Electronic distribution, that's really where our goals are. To enable artists to not only use [the Internet] as a promotional vehicle. They'll be able to record a master and digitize it and sell it to people who can record it onto tapes.

What about the future of the Internet?

JP: It's going to change the music industry as we know it.

Russell Shaw

INTERNET ANALYST, AUTHOR, AND CONSULTANT

Portland, Oregon

Give us a comparative view of selling through traditional stores as opposed to using the Internet.

RS: The charm about the Internet for content, even digitized content such as music, especially digitized on CD, is the very low distribution cost. You have an incremental cost of maybe several hundred or a couple of thousand dollars to actually purchase or get access to a server that can beam your CD [to] a Web site and enable people to download it. Whereas if you press your own CD it's not only the pressing cost that can easily exceed that per unit but it's the distribution cost. It's putting the CDs in the back of a trunk and making appointments with independent retailers. If you do it yourself and set it up through a post office box without the Internet, there's obviously mailing and postage, which is only going to go up. As the cost of technology goes down, the cost of analog technology goes up, so you have a disconnect there. And there have been a number of consolidations in the retail marketplace… so that the retailers are under incredible profit pressure. They'll tend to offer more Mariah Carey records and less of your act. There'll be fewer chances even than in the past.

So the typical emerging act is getting frozen out of the—

RS: Of the traditional retail channels. [They] may have some access to independent channels, but then at the same time they are frozen out of airplay except in noncommercial stations.

     [You may be] a local act in Des Moines that has two clubs that you can play at and maybe sell your CDs there and in the local independent record store or college bookstore. You're going to have to get a lot of critical mass to even make your money back from your CD. Whereas the Internet is worldwide distribution.

[Those are the two benefits of] Internet-related distribution: the saving on the cost of distribution and then widening your distribution arc to cover not necessarily your neighborhood, your town, your city, your club circuit, but the world.

It's important to distinguish the types of music merchandising that are done online. And there are [a couple of] basic models.

The first model is the promotional model of presenting information about an act and putting out press materials, like maybe transcripts of interviews with the folks in the band.

The second model is online ordering. There are three options. One, you can just write down the name of the band [after listening to a sound clip online] and hope your store carries it. Another is you can physically place an order for the music through a broker like CDnow or Tower Records (which now has an online store), and use either an 800 number or a secured credit card to order it, and then a week or two later you'll get the product in the mail or through UPS. And then the newest form is—and this is pretty new and as of this writing it's fairly rare—but if rewritable CDs take off (which so far they have not but they might if there are enough killer applications), to download an album off the Internet and then capture it on your CD drive or DVD drive, if that indeed takes off.

There's been a lot of talk about the need for the Internet to become more "invisible," like your TV—easier to access, friendlier. What are some of the technical challenges still facing Web developers?

RS: It's a bandwidth issue. You know, is this information—whether it's art on a Web site or the online ordering—intelligently constructed? Are there a lot of thick graphics that will take several minutes to transfer, or is it [set up so] that if you click onto a Sheryl Crow site—or just the site of a group that you're interested in—you can (a) find the site and (b) find the information that you need intelligently constructed without [your having to wait] a minute or two?

So, clearly, in the near future we'll see more bandwidth and faster delivery.

RS: Uh-huh. And that's important because, if you think about music, ever since I can recall, recorded music merchandising has been visually oriented. Why do they spend thousands of dollars, many thousands of dollars, on first LP covers and now CD covers? Then spend thousands of dollars on their image, hundreds of thousands of dollars on their staging, probably several hundreds of dollars apiece to get their hair styled. So it's largely a visual medium. Even if you look grunge, that's a visual aspect, too.

The Internet's been around in visual form only a few years now. Sometimes there's [still] a disconnect between the speed at which visuals load on your machine and the hyperkinetic desire of some Web site designers that work for some of these acts and labels to put as much graphic [information] on them as they want. It's an obstacle to the Internet to have pages that take two and three minutes to load. Things like Java help, but more Web site designers have to realize that maybe you put in a low-bandwidth version of your site as well. It's more than a technical thing. It cuts to the heart of the marketing. There's research that shows that the average user, if the page is not loaded within 20 to 30 seconds, will click off.

What's important is not only having a Web site but knowing how to present it.

Any closing thoughts about the present or the near future as related to music or marketing?

RS: Just because there's a lot of new technology, it won't mean that the old technology will go away. There'll still be promotion men knocking on doors of radio consultants and syndicators, pleading for airplay.

And there'll still be traditional stores. The big stores and even the independent music sellers are not going to go away.

RS: Yeah. Just like videos did not kill movies, and TV did not kill radio, and modems did not kill print. We're writing even better than ever.

So there will be some kind of coexistence.

RS: Yeah, the coexistence of point marketing and promotional campaigns.

Someone recently said, "Well, there's some psychology involved here. It's that people like the physical feel of a CD jacket in their hands. They like going away with it. They like putting it in their car."

RS: Right now you see in online commerce (and this has been the case for the last couple of years and I don't see it changing) that a lot of people will go to online commerce sites, whether it's an Amazon.com for books or a CDnow for music, and do their window shopping there but will physically go to the actual retailer—not to the [Web] site, but to the actual retailer—to do it. I do that when I plan a business trip. Sometimes I will call the 800 number for the hotel but I'll do the research as to what fares are best and what hotel might be located near where my meeting is. I'll do that online. So there is a hybrid application of the Web. It's not necessarily the turnkey solution for marketing music, but [it can provide part of] the window-shopping aspect.

Appendix:
Sources of Information

Audience Characteristics and Research

Arbitron Company. 140 W. 57 St., New York, NY 10019, (212) 887-1300, www.arbitron.com. Provides business subscribers with reports on radio and television audience sizes, demographics, and viewing patterns.

Census of Population. U.S. Department of Commerce, Bureau of the Census, www.census.gov. Statistics on makeup of U.S. population by sex, race, age, education, occupation, income, and other factors.

Marketing to Generation X. Karen Ritchie. New York: Lexington Books, 1995.

MediaFinder.
See Marketing.

Nielsen Media Research. www.nielsenmedia.com. Provides business subscribers with reports on television audience sizes, demographics, and viewing patterns.

SRDS Advertising Source Books. See Movies, Television, and Video; Print Media; Radio.

Government Agencies

Federal Trade Commission (FTC). Room 130, FTC, Washington, D.C. 20580, (202) 326-2222, www.ftc.gov. Trade regulation agency. Publishes a variety of brochures on FTC rules.

United States Copyright Office, Register of Copyrights, Library of Congress. 101 Independence Ave., SE, Washington, D.C. 20559, (202) 707-6850, www.loc.gov/copyright. The place to go to register music copyrights.

United States Patent and Trademark Office (USPTO). (703) 308-HELP, www.uspto.gov. The place to go to register a trademark.

United States Postal Service. www.usps.gov. Publishes the booklets *Designing Letter Mail*, *Designing Reply Mail*, and others of interest to businesses engaging in mail-order commerce.

Internet and Web Development

Electronic Musician. Magazine on electronic music techniques and equipment.

Music and Computers. Magazine for music computing enthusiasts.

Network Solutions, Inc. ATTN: InterNIC Registration Services, 505 Huntmar Drive, Herdon, VA 20170, (703) 742-4777, www.internic.net. The place to go to register your Internet domain name.

Teach Yourself Web Publishing with HTML in a Week. Laura Lemay. Indianapolis: Sams.net. Excellent, frequently updated book on creating Web sites.

Manufacturing (Disc and Cassette)

Billboard International Tape/Disc Directory. New York: BPI Communications. Lists of services and suppliers.

Marketing

Catalog Age. Trade magazine for catalog marketers.

Direct Marketing. Monthly magazine.

Direct Marketing Association. 1120 Ave. of the Americas, New York, NY 10036, (212) 768-7277.

The Do-It-Yourself Direct Mail Handbook. Murray Raphel and Ken Erdman. Philadelphia: The Marketer's Bookshelf, 1986.

Do-It-Yourself Direct Marketing. Mark S. Bacon. New York: Wiley, 1994.

The Fast Forward MBA in Marketing. Dallas Murphy. New York: Wiley, 1997.

Marketing. Robert D. Hisrich. Hauppauge, N.Y.: Barron's, 1990.

MediaFinder. www.mediafinder.com. Web site with links to a range of marketing resources.

Media (General)

All-in-One Media Directory. New Paltz, N.Y.: Gebbie Press. List of U.S. media, including radio and TV stations, newspapers, and magazines.

Gale Directory of Publications and Broadcast Media. Detroit, Mich.: Gale Research. Lists contacts for radio and television stations, cable companies, and print media.

MediaFinder. See Marketing.

SRDS Advertising Source Books. See Movies, Television, and Video; Print Media; Radio.

Movies, Television, and Video

All-in-One Media Directory. See Media (General).

Broadcasting and Cable Yearbook. New Providence, N.J.: R.R. Bowker. Directory covering the television and radio industries.

Gale Directory of Publications and Broadcast Media. See Media (General).

Hollywood Reporter. Daily publication focusing on the film and entertainment industry. Also on the Web at www.hollywoodreporter.com.

Hollywood Reporter Blu-Book. New York: BPI Communications. Annual directory to Hollywood entertainment industry.

SRDS TV & Cable Source. Des Plaines, Ill.: SRDS (Standard Rate and Data). Directory listing TV stations and networks, providing names of personnel, coverage data, market demographics, and other information.

This Business of Television, Rev. Ed. Howard Blumenthal and Oliver Goodenough. New York: Billboard Books, 1998.

TV on the Web. www.gebbieinc.com/tvintro.htm. Links to Web sites of TV stations.

Variety. Daily and weekly publication covering the entertainment industry. Also on the Web at www.variety.com.

Video Business. Weekly publication.

VideoLog. New York: Muze. Lists all videos available to consumers.

Music Distribution

Association for Independent Music (AFIM). See Organizations and Trade Associations. Publishes a directory of members, including distributors.

Billboard's International Buyer's Guide. New York: BPI Communications. Yearly directory that lists distributors by state.

The Internet Music Pages. See Music Industry (General).

National Association of Recording Merchandisers (NARM). See Organizations and Trade Associations.

Music Industry (General)

All You Need to Know About the Music Business, Rev. Ed. Donald S. Passman. New York: Simon & Schuster, 1997.

ASCAP Web Site. www.ascap.com. Provides a range of information for music professionals.

Billboard. Weekly trade magazine of music and home entertainment; includes pop music charts, plus articles on retailing, radio programming, and more. Also on the Web at www.billboard.com.

CMJ New Music Report. Weekly trade publication focusing on new music, including current radio airplay data. Hosts yearly music convention. Also on the Web at www.cmj.com.

The Gavin Radio & Record Industry A to Z. San Francisco: Gavin. Yearly music business phone directory of people, companies, radio consultants and networks, record labels, independent promoters and marketers, trade magazines, music publishers, artists, and artist managers.

The Gavin Report. Weekly publication providing up-to-date information on what radio stations are playing. Includes airplay charts and news. Also on the Web at www.gavin.com.

How to Make and Sell Your Own Recording, 4th Ed. Diane Rapaport. Englewood Cliffs, N.J.: Prentice-Hall, 1992.

The Internet Music Pages. www.musicpages.com. Web site providing links to music industry resources, including distributors.

Music, Money, and Success. Jeffrey Brabec and Todd Brabec. New York: Schirmer Books, 1994.

The Musician's Guide to Touring and Promotion. New York: BPI Communications. Contains city-by-city listings of nightclubs, radio stations, record stores, and local media; listings of music industry Web sites and online services; and much more.

Radio and Records. Weekly news magazine serving the radio and record industries with radio airplay data and other information. Also on the Web at www.rronline.com.

Recording Industry Sourcebook. Emeryville, Calif.: Cardinal Business Media. Annual directory of record companies, publishers, managers, attorneys, and other music-related businesses.

This Business of Artist Management, 3rd Ed. Xavier M. Frascogna, Jr., and H. Lee Hetherington. New York: Billboard Books, 1997. Overview of the music business from the perspective of artist management.

This Business of Music, 7th Ed. Sidney Shemel and J. William Krasilovsky. New York: Billboard Books, 1996. Overview of the music business with an emphasis on legal issues.

The Ultimate Band List. www.ubl.com. Web site containing mass of links to record companies, radio stations, magazines, record stores, and more.

Worldwide Internet Music Resources. www.music.indiana.edu/music_resources. Provides access to vast amount of information on all aspects of music industry.

Music Industry Conferences and Seminars

Association for Independent Music (AFIM). See Organizations and Trade Associations.

CMJ New Music Convention. See Music Industry (General).

South by Southwest (SXSW) Music and Media Conference and Festival. P.O. Box 4999, Austin, TX 78765, (512) 467-7979, www.sxsw.com. Annual conference providing networking opportunities for artists, the media, and the music industry.

National Association of Music Merchants (NAMM). See Organizations and Trade Associations.

National Association of Recording Merchandisers (NARM). See Organizations and Trade Associations.

Music Retailing

Billboard Record Retailing Directory. New York: BPI Communications.

National Association of Recording Merchandisers (NARM). See Organizations and Trade Associations.

The Ultimate Band List. See Music Industry (General).

Organizations and Trade Associations (Music and Entertainment)

American Federation of Musicians (AFM). 1501 Broadway, Ste. 600, New York, NY 10036, (212) 869-1330, www.afm.org. The musicians' union. Sets pay rates and work standards.

American Federation of Television and Radio Artists (AFTRA). 260 Madison Ave., 7th Fl., New York, NY 10016, (212) 532-0800, www.aftra.com. Union representing performers.

American Society of Composers, Authors, and Publishers (ASCAP). One Lincoln Plaza, New York, NY 10023, (212) 621-6000, www.ascap.com.

Music rights clearinghouse. Licenses members' music for public performances.

Association for Independent Music (AFIM). P.O. Box 988, 147 E. Main St., Whitesburg, KY 41858, (606) 633-0946, www.afim.org. Organization promoting the independent recording industry. Publishes directory of members and holds an annual convention.

Broadcast Music, Inc. (BMI). 320 W. 57 St., New York, NY 10019, (212) 586-2000, www.bmi.com. Music rights clearinghouse. Licenses members' music for public performances.

The Harry Fox Agency, Inc. 711 Third Ave., New York, NY 10017, (212) 370-5330, www.nmpa.org. Music licensing agency. Licenses affiliated publishers' music for a variety of commercial uses.

National Association of Music Merchants (NAMM). 5790 Armada Dr., Carlsbad, CA 92008, (760) 438-8001, www.namm.com. Organization promoting music products industry. Presents two yearly trade shows.

National Association of Recording Merchandisers (NARM). 9 Eves Dr., Ste. 120, Marlton, NJ 08053, (609) 596-2221, www.narm.com. Organization promoting the interests of its music industry members, who include retailers, distributors, and software (that is, music) suppliers.

National Music Publishers' Association (NMPA). 711 Third Ave., New York, NY 10017, (212) 370-5330, www.nmpa.org.

Promotes the interests of music publishers. Parent organization of the Harry Fox Agency.

Recording Industry Association of America (RIAA). 1330 Connecticut Ave., NW, Ste. 300, Washington, D.C. 20036, (202) 775-0101, www.riaa.com. Trade association promoting the interests of record companies. Certifies gold and platinum record awards.

Screen Actors Guild (SAG). 7065 Hollywood Blvd., Hollywood, CA 90028, (213) 465-4600, www.sag.com. Performers' union.

SESAC, Inc., 156 W. 56th St., New York, NY 10019, (212) 586-3450, www.sesac.com. Music rights clearinghouse. Licenses members' music for public performances.

Print Media

All-in-One Media Directory. See Media (General).

Gale Directory of Publications and Broadcast Media. See Media (General).

Magazines on the Internet. www.gebbieinc.com/magurl.htm. Links to Web sites of magazines, including 'zines about music.

MediaFinder. See Marketing. Links to magazines and directories in a range of fields, including music.

SRDS Community Publication Advertising Source. Des Plaines, Ill.: SRDS (Standard Rate and Data). Includes information on circulation and ad rates.

SRDS Consumer Magazine Advertising Source. Lists magazines by category and includes information on circulation and ad rates.

SRDS Newspaper Advertising Source.
Includes information on
circulation and ad rates.

Standard Periodical Directory. Detroit,
Mich.: Gale Research.

The Ultimate Band List.
See Music Industry (General).

Worldwide Internet Music Resources.
See Music Industry (General).

Publicity

The Billboard Guide to Music Publicity,
Rev. Ed. Jim Pettigrew Jr. New
York: Billboard Books, 1997.

Radio

All-in-One Media Directory.
See Media (General).

Billboard.
See Music Industry (General).

Broadcasting and Cable Yearbook.
See Movies, Television, and Video.

BRS Radio Directory.
www.radio-directory.com. Web
site listing radio stations by call
letters, by state, and by programming format.

CMJ New Music Report.
See Music Industry (General).

*Gale Directory of Publications
and Broadcast Media.*
See Media (General).

*The Gavin Radio & Record Industry
A to Z.*
See Music Industry (General).

The Gavin Report.
See Music Industry (General).

Getting Radio Airplay. Gary Hustwit.
San Diego: Rockpress, 1992.

MIT List of Radio Stations on the
Internet. wmbr.mit.edu/stations/
list.html.

*The Musician's Guide to
Touring and Promotion.*
See Music Industry (General).

Radio and Records.
See Music Industry (General).

Radio on the Web.
www.gebbieinc.com/radintro.htm.
Provides links to Web sites of
U.S. radio stations.

*Radio Power Book of Music Radio and
Record Promotion.* New York:
BPI Communications.

SRDS Radio Advertising Source. Des
Plaines, Ill.: SRDS (Standard Rate
and Data). Directory listing AM/
FM commercial radio stations,
networks, and syndicators. Includes information on stations'
formats and audiences.

The Ultimate Band List.
See Music Industry (General).

Recording Catalogs

PhonoLog. New York: Muze. Regularly
updated listings of currently
available recorded pop and
classical music releases.

Schwann Record and Tape Guide.
Woodland, Calif.: Schwann
Publications.

Touring and Live Performance

*Billboard's International Talent and
Touring Directory.* New York:
BPI Communications. Lists
booking agents, among others.

*Gigging: The Musician's Underground
Touring Directory.* Michael Dorf
and Robert Appel. Cincinnati:
Writer's Digest, 1989.

*The Musician's Guide to
Touring and Promotion.*
See Music Industry (General).

Index

The Authors

Tad Lathrop, a producer of books and music and a former senior editor of Billboard Books, has been associated in writing and editing capacities with the Web music news service SonicNet; the publishing companies Holt, Rinehart and Winston and Cherry Lane Music; and a number of advertising and marketing communications companies. He is a co-author of the book *Cult Rockers* and co-producer of its accompanying compact disc. Mr. Lathrop has lectured on music and music industry topics at New York City Technical College and San Francisco State University's Music Recording Industry Program.

Jim Pettigrew Jr. is the author of *The Billboard Guide to Music Publicity* and a former music publicist who has worked on the campaigns of a number of platinum-selling acts, including the Allman Brothers Band, ZZ Top, and the Atlanta Rhythm Section. He has also served as director of public relations for the Atlanta Symphony Orchestra. Currently a freelance writer, Mr. Pettigrew is a contributor to numerous magazines and co-author of the syndicated radio documentary "The Southern Rock Special." In the 1980s he taught at Georgia State University's School of Commercial Music/Recording.

Picture Credits

Courtesy of Alligator Records: p. 69 (Shemekia Copeland). Courtesy of Astralwerks/Caroline Records: p. 69 (Fluke). Courtesy of EvaLuTion Entertainment Marketing: pp. 157, 174. Courtesy of Imaginary Road Records: p. 69 (Will Ackerman). Courtesy of Mark Pucci Media: pp. 153, 154. Courtesy of Morton Beebe & Associates: p. 137 (Windham Hill catalog cover). Courtesy of PlanetCD: p. 256. Courtesy of Ralph America: p. 137 (bottom). Courtesy of Shanachie Entertainment Corp.: p. 69 (R. Crumb and His Cheap Suit Serenaders). Courtesy of Smithsonian Masterworks Orchestra: p. 67. Courtesy of Windham Hill/BMG Entertainment: pp. 69 (Will Ackerman), 137 (top), 139.